Learning Modern Linux
A Handbook for the Cloud Native Practitioner

Michael Hausenblas

Beijing · Boston · Farnham · Sebastopol · Tokyo

Learning Modern Linux

by Michael Hausenblas

Copyright © 2022 Michael Hausenblas. All rights reserved.

Published by O'Reilly Media, Inc., 1005 Gravenstein Highway North, Sebastopol, CA 95472.

O'Reilly books may be purchased for educational, business, or sales promotional use. Online editions are also available for most titles (*http://oreilly.com*). For more information, contact our corporate/institutional sales department: 800-998-9938 or *corporate@oreilly.com*.

Acquisitions Editor: John Devins	**Indexer:** WordCo Indexing Services, Inc.
Development Editor: Jeff Bleiel	**Interior Designer:** David Futato
Production Editor: Gregory Hyman	**Cover Designer:** Karen Montgomery
Copyeditor: Piper Editorial Consulting, LLC	**Illustrator:** Kate Dullea
Proofreader: Amnet Systems, LLC	

May 2022:   First Edition

Revision History for the First Edition

2022-04-15:   First Release

See *http://oreilly.com/catalog/errata.csp?isbn=9781098108946* for release details.

978-1-098-10894-6

[LSI]

Table of Contents

Preface

A warm welcome to *Learning Modern Linux*! I'm glad that we will walk this journey together for a bit. This book is for you if you've already been using Linux and are looking for a structured, hands-on approach to dive in deeper, or if you already have experience and want to get some tips and tricks to improve your flow when working with Linux—for example, in a professional setup, such as development or operations.

We'll focus on using Linux for your everyday needs, from development to office-related tasks, rather than on the system administration side of things. Also, we'll focus on the command line, not visual UIs. So, while 2022 might be the year of Linux on the desktop after all, we'll use the terminal as the main way to interact with Linux. This has the additional advantage that you can equally apply your knowledge in many different setups, from a Raspberry Pi to the virtual machine of your cloud provider of choice.

Before we start, I'd like to provide some context by sharing my own journey: my first hands-on experience with an operating system was not with Linux. The first operating system I used was AmigaOS (in the late 80s), and after that, in technical high school, I mainly used Microsoft DOS and the then-new Microsoft Windows, specifically around the event system and user interface–related development. Then, in the mid- to late 1990s, during my studies at university, I mainly used Unix-based Solaris and Silicon Graphics machines in the university labs. I really only got into Linux in the mid-2000s in the context of big data and then when I started working with containers, first in 2015 in the context of Apache Mesos (working at Mesosphere), and then with Kubernetes (initially at Red Hat on the OpenShift team and then at AWS on the container service team). That's where I realized that one needs to master Linux to be effective in this space. Linux is different. Its background, worldwide community of users, and versatility and flexibility make it unique.

Linux is an interesting, ever-growing ecosystem of open source individuals and vendors. It runs on pretty much anything under the sun, from the $50 Raspberry Pi to the virtual machines of your favorite cloud provider to a Mars vehicle. After 30 years in the making, Linux will likely stick around for some time, so now is a good time to get into Linux a bit deeper.

Let's first set some ground rules and expectations. In the preface, I'll share how you can get the most out of this book as well as some administrative things, like where and how you can try out the topics we'll work through together.

About You

This book is for those who want or need to use Linux in a professional setup, such as software developers, software architects, QA testing engineers, DevOps and SRE roles, and similar roles. I'll assume that if you're a hobbyist encountering Linux when pursuing an activity such as 3D printing or home improvement, you have very little to no knowledge about operating systems in general or Linux/UNIX in particular. You will get the most out of the book if you work through it from beginning to end, as the chapters tend to build on one another; however, you can also use it as a reference if you're already familiar with Linux.

How to Use the Book

The focus of this book is enabling you to use Linux, not administer it. There are plenty of great books about Linux administration out there.

By the end of this book, you will understand what Linux is (Chapter 1) and what its critical components are (Chapters 2 and 3). You'll be able to enumerate and use essential access control mechanisms (Chapter 4). You'll also understand the role of filesystems (Chapter 5) as a fundamental building block in Linux as well as know what apps (Chapter 6) are.

Then, you'll get some hands-on experience with the Linux networking stack and tooling (Chapter 7). Further, you'll learn about modern operating system observability (Chapter 8) and how to apply it to manage your workloads.

You'll understand how to run Linux applications in modern ways by using containers as well as immutable distros such as Bottlerocket and also how to securely communicate (download files, etc.) and share data using Secure Shell (SSH) and advanced tooling like peer-to-peer and cloud sync mechanisms (Chapter 9).

Following are suggestions for ways you can try things out and follow along (and I strongly recommend you do; learning Linux is like learning a language—you want to practice a lot):

- Get a Linux desktop or laptop. For example, I have a very nice machine called StarBook from Star Labs (*https://oreil.ly/1MbY2*). Alternatively, you could use a desktop or laptop that no longer runs a recent Windows version and install Linux on it.

- If you want to experiment on a different (host) operating system—say, your Mac-Book or iMac—you could use a virtual machine (VM). For example, on macOS you could use the excellent Linux-on-Mac (*https://oreil.ly/bqVYG*).

- Use your cloud provider of choice to spin up a Linux-based VM.

- If you're into tinkering and want to try out a non-Intel processor architecture such as ARM, you could buy a single-board computer such as the wonderful Raspberry Pi (*https://www.raspberrypi.org*).

In any case, you should have an environment at hand and practice a lot. Don't just read: try out commands and experiment. Try to "break" things, for example, by providing nonsensical or deliberately strange inputs. Before you execute the command, form a hypothesis about the outcome.

Another tip: always ask *why*. When you see a command or a certain output, try to figure out where it came from and what the underlying component responsible for it is.

Conventions

The following typographical conventions are used in this book:

Italic
Indicates new terms, URLs, email addresses, filenames, and file extensions.

`Constant width`
Used for program listings, as well as within paragraphs to refer to program elements such as variable or function names, databases, data types, environment variables, statements, and keywords.

`Constant width italic`
Shows text that should be replaced with user-supplied values or by values determined by context.

This element signifies a tip or suggestion.

 This element signifies a general note.

 This element indicates a warning or caution.

Using Code Examples

Supplemental material (code examples, exercises, etc.) is available for download at *https://oreil.ly/learning-modern-linux-code*.

If you have a technical question or a problem using the code examples, please send an email to *bookquestions@oreilly.com*.

This book is here to help you get your job done. In general, if example code is offered with this book, you may use it in your programs and documentation. You do not need to contact us for permission unless you're reproducing a significant portion of the code. For example, writing a program that uses several chunks of code from this book does not require permission. Selling or distributing examples from O'Reilly books does require permission. Answering a question by citing this book and quoting example code does not require permission. Incorporating a significant amount of example code from this book into your product's documentation does require permission.

We appreciate, but generally do not require, attribution. An attribution usually includes the title, author, publisher, and ISBN. For example: "*Learning Modern Linux* by Michael Hausenblas (O'Reilly). Copyright 2022 Michael Hausenblas, 978-1-098-10894-6."

If you feel your use of code examples falls outside fair use or the permission given above, feel free to contact us at *permissions@oreilly.com*.

O'Reilly Online Learning

 For more than 40 years, *O'Reilly Media* has provided technology and business training, knowledge, and insight to help companies succeed.

Our unique network of experts and innovators share their knowledge and expertise through books, articles, and our online learning platform. O'Reilly's online learning platform gives you on-demand access to live training courses, in-depth learning paths, interactive coding environments, and a vast collection of text and video from O'Reilly and 200+ other publishers. For more information, visit *http://oreilly.com*.

How to Contact Us

Please address comments and questions concerning this book to the publisher:

O'Reilly Media, Inc.
1005 Gravenstein Highway North
Sebastopol, CA 95472
800-998-9938 (in the United States or Canada)
707-829-0515 (international or local)
707-829-0104 (fax)

We have a web page for this book, where we list errata, examples, and any additional information. You can access this page at *https://oreil.ly/learning-modern-linux*.

Email *bookquestions@oreilly.com* to comment or ask technical questions about this book.

For news and information about our books and courses, visit *http://oreilly.com*.

Find us on LinkedIn: *https://linkedin.com/company/oreilly-media*

Follow us on Twitter: *http://twitter.com/oreillymedia*

Watch us on YouTube: *http://youtube.com/oreillymedia*

Acknowledgments

First off, I'd like to thank the fabulous reviewers of the book: Chris Negus, John Bonesio, and Pawel Krupa. Without their feedback, this book wouldn't be half as good or useful.

I want to thank my parents, who enabled my education and laid the foundations for who I am and what I do today. Big kudos to my big sister, Monika, who was my inspiration to get into tech in the first place.

I would like to express my deepest gratitude to my very awesome and supportive family: my kids, Saphira, Ranya, and Iannis; my wicked smart and fun wife, Anneliese; our bestest of all dogs, Snoopy; and our newest family member, Charlie the tomcat.

In the context of my Unix and Linux journey, there are way too many people who influenced my thinking and from whom I learned a lot. I had the pleasure and privilege of working with or interacting with many of them, including but not limited to Jérôme Petazzoni, Jessie Frazelle, Brendan Gregg, Justin Garrison, Michael Kerrisk, and Douglas McIlroy.

Last, but most certainly not least, I'd like to thank the O'Reilly team, especially my development editor, Jeff Bleiel, for shepherding me through the process of writing this book.

## CHAPTER 1

Introduction to Linux

Linux is the most widely used operating system, used in everything from mobile devices to the cloud.

You might not be familiar with the concept of an operating system. Or you might be using an operating system such as Microsoft Windows without giving it too much thought. Or maybe you are new to Linux. To set the scene and get you in the right mindset, we'll take a bird's-eye view of operating systems and Linux in this chapter.

We'll first discuss what *modern* means in the context of the book. Then we'll review a high-level Linux backstory, looking at important events and phases over the past 30 years. Further, in this chapter you'll learn what the role of an operating system is in general and how Linux fills this role. We also take a quick look at what Linux distributions are and what resource visibility means.

If you're new to operating systems and Linux, you'll want to read the entire chapter. If you're already experienced with Linux, you might want to jump to "A Ten-Thousand-Foot View of Linux" on page 8, which provides a visual overview as well as mapping to the book's chapters.

But before we get into the technicalities, let's first step back a bit and focus on what we mean when we say "modern Linux." This is, surprisingly, a nontrivial matter.

What Are Modern Environments?

The book title specifies *modern*, but what does that really mean? Well, in the context of this book, it can mean anything from cloud computing to a Raspberry Pi. In addition, the recent rise of Docker and related innovations in infrastructure has dramatically changed the landscape for developers and infrastructure operators alike.

Let's take a closer look at some of these modern environments and the prominent role Linux plays in them:

Mobile devices

When I say "mobile phone" to our kids, they say, "In contrast to what?" In all fairness and seriousness, these days many phones—depending on who you ask, up to 80% or more—as well as tablets run Android, which is a Linux variant (*https://oreil.ly/bQ6yJ*). These environments have aggressive requirements around power consumption and robustness, as we depend on them on a daily basis. If you're interested in developing Android apps, consider visiting the Android developer site (*https://oreil.ly/xf5kC*) for more information.

Cloud computing

With the cloud, we see at scale a similar pattern as in the mobile and micro space. There are new, powerful, secure, and energy-saving CPU architectures such as the successful ARM-based AWS Graviton (*https://oreil.ly/JzHzm*) offerings, as well as the established heavy-lifting outsourcing to cloud providers, especially in the context of open source software.

Internet of (Smart) Things

I'm sure you've seen a lot of Internet of Things (IoT)–related projects and products, from sensors to drones. Many of us have already been exposed to smart appliances and smart cars. These environments have even more challenging requirements around power consumption than mobile devices. In addition, they might not even be running all the time but, for example, only wake up once a day to transmit some data. Another important aspect of these environments is real-time capabilities (*https://oreil.ly/zBsRy*). If you're interested in getting started with Linux in the IoT context, consider the AWS IoT EduKit (*https://oreil.ly/3x0uf*).

Diversity of processor architectures

For the past 30 years or so, Intel has been the leading CPU manufacturer, dominating the microcomputer and personal computer space. Intel's x86 architecture was considered the gold standard. The open approach that IBM took (publishing the specifications and enabling others to offer compatible devices) was promising, resulting in x86 clones that also used Intel chips, at least initially.

While Intel is still widely used in desktop and laptop systems, with the rise of mobile devices we've seen the increasing uptake of the ARM architecture (*https://oreil.ly/sioDd*) and recently RISC-V (*https://oreil.ly/Tf0bb*). At the same time, multi-arch programming languages and tooling, such as Go or Rust, are becoming more and more widespread, creating a perfect storm.

All of these environments are examples of what I consider modern environments. And most, if not all of them, run on or use Linux in one form or another.

Now that we know about the modern (hardware) systems, you might wonder how we got here and how Linux came into being.

The Linux Story (So Far)

Linux celebrated its 30th birthday (*https://oreil.ly/fkMyT*) in 2021. With billions of users and thousands of developers, the Linux project is, without doubt, a worldwide (open source) success story. But how did it all this start, and how did we get here?

1990s
> We can consider Linus Torvalds's email on August 25, 1991, to the `comp.os.minix` newsgroup as the birth of the Linux project, at least in terms of the public record. This hobby project soon took off, both in terms of lines of code (LOC) and in terms of adoption. For example, after less than three years, Linux 1.0.0 was released with over 176,000 LOCs. By that time, the original goal of being able to run most Unix/GNU software was already well reached. Also, the first commercial offering appeared in the 1990s: Red Hat Linux.

2000 to 2010
> As a "teenager," Linux was not only maturing in terms of features and supported hardware but was also growing beyond what UNIX could do. In this time period, we also witnessed a huge and ever-increasing buy-in of Linux by the big players, that is, adoption by Google, Amazon, IBM, and so on. It was also the peak of the distro wars (*https://oreil.ly/l6X4Q*), resulting in businesses changing their directions.

2010s to now
> Linux established itself as the workhorse in data centers and the cloud, as well as for any types of IoT devices and phones. In a sense, one can consider the distro wars as being over (nowadays, most commercial systems are either Red Hat or Debian based), and in a sense, the rise of containers (from 2014/15 on) is responsible for this development.

With this super-quick historic review, necessary to set the context and understand the motivation for the scope of this book, we move on to a seemingly innocent question: Why does anyone need Linux, or an operating system at all?

Why an Operating System at All?

Let's say you do not have an operating system (OS) available or cannot use one for whatever reason. You would then end up doing pretty much everything yourself: memory management, interrupt handling, talking with I/O devices, managing files, configuring and managing the network stack—the list goes on.

Technically speaking, an OS is not strictly needed. There are systems out there that do not have an OS. These are usually embedded systems with a tiny footprint: think of an IoT beacon. They simply do not have the resources available to keep anything else around other than one application. For example, with Rust you can use its Core and Standard Library to run any app on bare metal (*https:// oreil.ly/zW4j7*).

An operating system takes on all this undifferentiated heavy lifting, abstracting away the different hardware components and providing you with a (usually) clean and nicely designed Application Programming Interface (API), such as is the case with the Linux kernel that we will have a closer look at in Chapter 2. We usually call these APIs that an OS exposes *system calls*, or *syscalls* for short. Higher-level programming languages such as Go, Rust, Python, or Java build on top of those syscalls, potentially wrapping them in libraries.

All of this allows you to focus on the business logic rather than having to manage the resources yourself, and also takes care of the different hardware you want to run your app on.

Let's have a look at a concrete example of a syscall. Let's say we want to identify (and print) the ID of the current user.

First, we look at the Linux syscall `getuid(2)` (*https://oreil.ly/md15Z*):

```
...
getuid() returns the real user ID of the calling process.
...
```

OK, so this `getuid` syscall is what we could use programmatically, from a library. We will discuss Linux syscalls in greater detail in "syscalls" on page 22.

You might be wondering what the (2) means in `getuid(2)`. It's a terminology that the `man` utility (think built-in help pages) uses to indicate the section of the command assigned in `man`, akin to a postal or country code. This is one example where the Unix legacy is apparent; you can find its origin in the *Unix Programmer's Manual*, seventh edition, volume 1 (*https://oreil.ly/DgDrF*) from 1979.

On the command line (shell), we would be using the equivalent `id` command that in turn uses the `getuid` syscall:

```
$ id --user
638114
```

Now that you have a basic idea of why using an operating system, in most cases, makes sense, let's move on to the topic of Linux distributions.

Linux Distributions

When we say "Linux," it might not be immediately clear what we mean. In this book, we will say "Linux kernel," or just "kernel," when we mean the set of syscalls and device drivers. Further, when we refer to Linux distributions (*https://oreil.ly/U9luq*) (or *distros*, for short), we mean a concrete bundling of kernel and related components, including package management, file system layout, init system, and a shell, preselected for you.

Of course, you could do all of this yourself: you could download and compile the kernel, choose a package manager, and so on, and create (or *roll*) your own distro. And that's what many folks did in the beginning. Over the years, people figured out that it is a better use of their time to leave this packaging (and also security patching) to experts, private or commercial, and simply use the resulting Linux distro.

If you are inclined to build your own distribution, maybe because you are a tinkerer or because you have to due to certain business restrictions, I recommend you take a closer look at Arch Linux (*https://oreil.ly/UBSHM*), which puts you in control and, with a little effort, allows you to create a very customized Linux distro.

To get a feeling for the vastness of the distro space, including traditional distros (Ubuntu, Red Hat Enterprise Linux [RHEL], CentOS, etc., as discussed in Chapter 6) and modern distros (such as Bottlerocket and Flatcar; see Chapter 9), take a look at DistroWatch (*https://oreil.ly/DWmrr*).

With the distro topic out of the way, let's move on to a totally different topic: resources and their visibility and isolation.

Resource Visibility

Linux has had, in good UNIX tradition, a by-default global view on resources. This leads us to the question: what does *global view* mean (in contrast to what?), and what are said resources?

Why are we talking about resource visibility here in the first place? The main reason is to raise awareness about this topic and to get you in the right state of mind for one of the important themes in the context of modern Linux: containers. Don't worry if you don't get all of the details now; we will come back to this topic throughout the book and specifically in Chapter 6, in which we discuss containers and their building blocks in greater detail.

You might have heard the saying that in Unix, and by extension Linux, everything is a file. In the context of this book, we consider resources to be anything that can be used to aid the execution of software. This includes hardware and its abstractions (such as CPU and RAM, files), filesystems, hard disk drives, solid-state drives (SSDs), processes, networking-related stuff like devices or routing tables, and credentials representing users.

 Not all resources in Linux are files or represented through a file interface. However, there are systems out there, such as Plan 9 (*https://oreil.ly/5DkY8*), that take this much further.

Let's have a look at a concrete example of some Linux resources. First, we want to query a global property (the Linux version) and then specific hardware information about the CPUs in use (output edited to fit space):

```
$ cat /proc/version ❶
Linux version 5.4.0-81-generic (buildd@lgw01-amd64-051)
(gcc version 7.5.0 (Ubuntu 7.5.0-3ubuntu1~18.04))
#91~18.04.1-Ubuntu SMP Fri Jul 23 13:36:29 UTC 2021

$ cat /proc/cpuinfo | grep "model name" ❷
model name      : Intel Core Processor (Haswell, no TSX, IBRS)
model name      : Intel Core Processor (Haswell, no TSX, IBRS)
model name      : Intel Core Processor (Haswell, no TSX, IBRS)
model name      : Intel Core Processor (Haswell, no TSX, IBRS)
```

❶ Print the Linux version.

❷ Print CPU-related information, filtering for model.

With the preceding commands, we learned that this system has four Intel i7 cores at its disposal. When you log in with a different user, would you expect to see the same number of CPUs?

Let's consider a different type of resource: files. For example, if the user troy creates a file under /tmp/myfile with permission to do so ("Permissions" on page 80), would another user, worf, see the file or even be able to write to it?

Or, take the case of a process, that is, a program in memory that has all the necessary resources available to run, such as CPU and memory. Linux identifies a process using its *process ID*, or PID for short ("Process Management" on page 17):

```
$ cat /proc/$$/status | head -n6 ❶
Name:   bash
Umask:  0002
State:  S (sleeping)
```

```
Tgid:    2056
Ngid:    0
Pid:     2056
```

❶ Print process status—that is, details about the current process—and limit output to show only the first six lines.

What Is $$?

You might have noticed the $$ and wondered what this means. This is a special variable that is referring to the current process (see "Variables" on page 37 for details). Note that in the context of a shell, $$ is the process ID of the shell (such as bash) in which you typed the command.

Can there be multiple processes with the same PID in Linux? What may sound like a silly or useless question turns out to be the basis for containers (see "Containers" on page 131). The answer is yes, there can be multiple processes with the same PID, in different contexts called *namespaces* (see "Linux Namespaces" on page 133). This happens, for example, in a containerized setup, such as when you're running your app in Docker or Kubernetes.

Every single process might think that it is special, having PID 1, which in a more traditional setup is reserved for the root of the user space process tree (see "The Linux Startup Process" on page 117 for more details).

What we can learn from these observations is that there can be a global view on a given resource (two users see a file at the exact same location) as well as a local or virtualized view, such as the process example. This raises the question: is everything in Linux by default global? Spoiler: it's not. Let's have a closer look.

Part of the illusion of having multiple users or processes running in parallel is the (restricted) visibility onto resources. The way to provide a local view on (certain supported) resources in Linux is via namespaces (see "Linux Namespaces" on page 133).

A second, independent dimension is that of isolation. When I use the term *isolation* here, I don't necessarily qualify it—that is, I make no assumptions about how well things are isolated. For example, one way to think about process isolation is to restrict the memory consumption so that one process cannot starve other processes. For example, I give your app 1 GB of RAM to use. If it uses more, it gets out-of-memory (*https://oreil.ly/kvk1u*) killed. This provides a certain level of protection. In Linux we use a kernel feature called cgroups to provide this kind of isolation, and in "Linux cgroups" on page 135 you will learn more about it.

On the other hand, a fully isolated environment gives the appearance that the app is entirely on its own. For example, a virtual machine (VM; see also "Virtual Machines" on page 217) can be used to provide you with full isolation.

A Ten-Thousand-Foot View of Linux

Whoa, we went quite deep into the weeds already. Time to take a deep breath and refocus. In Figure 1-1, I've tried to provide you with a high-level overview of the Linux operating system, mapping it to the book chapters.

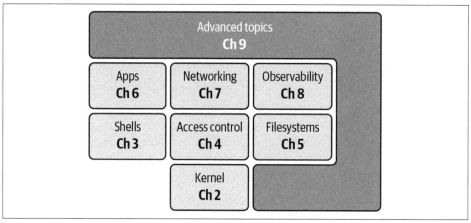

Figure 1-1. Mapping the Linux operating system to book chapters

At its core, any Linux distro has the kernel, providing the API that everything else builds on. The three core topics of files, networking, and observability follow you everywhere, and you can consider them the most basic building blocks above the kernel. From a pure usage perspective, you will soon learn that you will most often be dealing with the shell (Where is the output file for this app?) and things related to access control (Why does this app crash? Ah, the directory is read-only, doh!).

As an aside: I've collected some interesting topics, from virtual machines to modern distros, in Chapter 9. I call these topics "advanced" mainly because I consider them optional. That is, you could get away without learning them. But if you really, really, really want to benefit from the full power that modern Linux can provide you, I strongly recommend that you read Chapter 9. I suppose it goes without saying that, by design, the rest of the book—that is Chapter 2 to Chapter 8—are essential chapters you should most definitely study and apply the content as you go.

Portable Operating System Interface

We will come across the term *POSIX*, short for *Portable Operating System Interface*, every now and then in this book. Formally, POSIX is an IEEE standard to define service interfaces for UNIX operating systems. The motivation was to provide portability between different implementations. So, if you read things like "POSIX-compliant," think of a set of formal specifications that are especially relevant in official procurement context and less so in everyday usage.

Linux was built to be POSIX-compliant as well as to be compliant with the UNIX System V Interface Definition (SVID), which gave it the flavor of old-time AT&T UNIX systems, as opposed to Berkeley Software Distribution (BSD)-style systems.

If you want to learn more about POSIX, check out "POSIX Abstractions in Modern Operating Systems: The Old, the New, and the Missing" (*https://oreil.ly/DO04h*), which provides a great introduction and comments on uptake and challenges around this topic.

Conclusion

When we call something "modern" in the context of this book, we mean using Linux in modern environments, including phones, data centers (of public cloud providers), and embedded systems such as a Raspberry Pi.

In this chapter, I shared a high-level version of the Linux backstory. We discussed the role of an operating system in general—to abstract the underlying hardware and provide a set of basic functions such as process, memory, file, and network management to applications—and how Linux goes about this task, specifically regarding visibility of resources.

The following resources will help you continue getting up to speed as well as dive deeper into concepts discussed in this chapter:

O'Reilly titles
- *Linux Cookbook* by Carla Schroder
- *Understanding the Linux Kernel* by Daniel P. Bovet and Marco Cesati
- *Efficient Linux at the Command Line* by Daniel J. Barrett
- *Linux System Programming* by Robert Love

Other resources

- Advanced Programming in the UNIX Environment (*https://oreil.ly/hS0G0*) is a complete course that offers introductory material and hands-on exercises.

- "The Birth of UNIX" (*https://oreil.ly/MlQ0J*) with Brian Kernighan is a great resource for learning about Linux's legacy and provides context for a lot of the original UNIX concepts.

And now, without further ado: let's start our journey into modern Linux with the core, erm, kernel, of the matter!

## CHAPTER 2

The Linux Kernel

In "Why an Operating System at All?" on page 3, we learned that the main function of an operating system is to abstract over different hardware and provide us with an API. Programming against this API allows us to write applications without having to worry about where and how they are executed. In a nutshell, the kernel provides such an API to programs.

In this chapter, we discuss what the Linux kernel is and how you should be thinking about it as a whole as well as about its components. You will learn about the overall Linux architecture and the essential role the Linux kernel plays. One main takeaway of this chapter is that while the kernel provides all the core functionality, on its own it is not the operating system but only a very central part of it.

First, we take a bird's-eye view, looking at how the kernel fits in and interacts with the underlying hardware. Then, we review the computational core, discussing different CPU architectures and how they relate to the kernel. Next, we zoom in on the individual kernel components and discuss the API the kernel provides to programs you can run. Finally, we look at how to customize and extend the Linux kernel.

The purpose of this chapter is to equip you with the necessary terminology, make you aware of the interfacing between programs and the kernel, and give you a basic idea what the functionality is. The chapter does not aim to turn you into a kernel developer or even a sysadmin configuring and compiling kernels. If, however, you want to dive into that, I've put together some pointers at the end of the chapter.

Now, let's jump into the deep end: the Linux architecture and the central role the kernel plays in this context.

Linux Architecture

At a high level, the Linux architecture looks as depicted in Figure 2-1. There are three distinct layers you can group things into:

Hardware

> From CPUs and main memory to disk drives, network interfaces, and peripheral devices such as keyboards and monitors.

The kernel

> The focus of the rest of this chapter. Note that there are a number of components that sit between the kernel and user land, such as the init system and system services (networking, etc.), but that are, strictly speaking, not part of the kernel.

User land

> Where the majority of apps are running, including operating system components such as shells (discussed in Chapter 3), utilities like `ps` or `ssh`, and graphical user interfaces such as X Window System–based desktops.

We focus in this book on the upper two layers of Figure 2-1, that is, the kernel and user land. We only touch on the hardware layer in this and a few other chapters, where relevant.

The interfaces between the different layers are well defined and part of the Linux operating system package. Between the kernel and user land is the interface called *system calls* (*syscalls* for short). We will explore this in detail in "syscalls" on page 22.

The interface between the hardware and the kernel is, unlike the syscalls, not a single one. It consists of a collection of individual interfaces, usually grouped by hardware:

1. The CPU interface (see "CPU Architectures" on page 14)
2. The interface with the main memory, covered in "Memory Management" on page 19
3. Network interfaces and drivers (wired and wireless; see "Networking" on page 20)
4. Filesystem and block devices driver interfaces (see "Filesystems" on page 21)
5. Character devices, hardware interrupts, and device drivers, for input devices like keyboards, terminals, and other I/O (see "Device Drivers" on page 21)

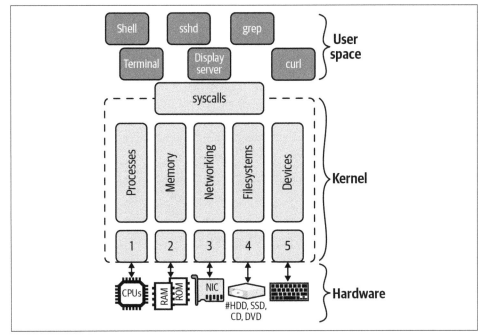

Figure 2-1. A high-level view of the Linux architecture

As you can see, many of the things we usually consider part of the Linux operating system, such as shell or utilities such as `grep`, `find`, and `ping`, are in fact not part of the kernel but, very much like an app you download, part of user land.

On the topic of user land, you will often read or hear about user versus kernel mode. This effectively refers to how privileged the access to hardware is and how restricted the abstractions available are.

In general, *kernel mode* means fast execution with limited abstraction, whereas *user mode* means comparatively slower but safer and more convenient abstractions. Unless you are a kernel developer (*https://oreil.ly/AhAm6*), you can almost always ignore kernel mode, since all your apps will run in user land. Knowing how to interact with the kernel ("syscalls" on page 22), on the other hand, is vital and part of our considerations.

With this Linux architecture overview out of the way, let's work our way up from the hardware.

CPU Architectures

Before we discuss the kernel components, let's review a basic concept: computer architectures or CPU families, which we will use interchangeably. The fact that Linux runs on a large number of different CPU architectures is arguably one of the reasons it is so popular.

Next to generic code and drivers, the Linux kernel contains architecture-specific code. This separation allows it to port Linux and make it available on new hardware quickly.

There are a number of ways to figure out what CPU your Linux is running. Let's have a look at a few in turn.

The BIOS and UEFI

Traditionally, UNIX and Linux used the Basic I/O System (BIOS) for bootstrapping itself. When you power on your Linux laptop, it is entirely hardware-controlled. First off, the hardware is wired to run the Power On Self Test (POST), part of the BIOS. POST makes sure that the hardware (RAM, etc.) function as specified. We will get into the details of the mechanics in "The Linux Startup Process" on page 117.

In modern environments, the BIOS functions have been effectively replaced by the Unified Extensible Firmware Interface (UEFI) (*https://oreil.ly/JBwSm*), a public specification that defines a software interface between an operating system and platform firmware. You will still come across the term *BIOS* in documentation and articles, so I suggest you simply replace it with *UEFI* in your head and move on.

One way is a dedicated tool called dmidecode that interacts with the BIOS. If this doesn't yield results, you could try the following (output shortened):

```
$ lscpu
Architecture:            x86_64 ❶
CPU op-mode(s):          32-bit, 64-bit
Byte Order:              Little Endian
Address sizes:           40 bits physical, 48 bits virtual
CPU(s):                  4 ❷
On-line CPU(s) list:     0-3
Thread(s) per core:      1
Core(s) per socket:      4
Socket(s):               1
NUMA node(s):            1
Vendor ID:               GenuineIntel
CPU family:              6
Model:                   60
Model name:              Intel Core Processor (Haswell, no TSX, IBRS) ❸
Stepping:                1
```

```
CPU MHz:                     2592.094
...
```

❶ The architecture we're looking at here is x86_64.

❷ It looks like there are four CPUs available.

❸ The CPU model name is Intel Core Processor (Haswell).

In the previous command, we saw that the CPU architecture was reported to be x86_64, and the model was reported as "Intel Core Processor (Haswell)." We will learn more about how to decode this in a moment.

Another way to glean similar architecture information is by using `cat /proc/cpuinfo`, or, if you're only interested in the architecture, by simply calling `uname -m`.

Now that we have a handle on querying the architecture information on Linux, let's see how to decode it.

x86 Architecture

x86 (*https://oreil.ly/PoQOT*) is an instruction set family originally developed by Intel and later licensed to Advanced Micro Devices (AMD). Within the kernel, x64 refers to the Intel 64-bit processors, and x86 stands for Intel 32-bit. Further, amd64 refers to AMD 64-bit processors.

Today, you'll mostly find the x86 CPU family in desktops and laptops, but it's also widely used in servers. Specifically, x86 forms the basis of the public cloud. It is a powerful and widely available architecture but isn't very energy efficient. Partially due to its heavy reliance on out-of-order execution, it recently received a lot of attention around security issues such as Meltdown (*https://oreil.ly/nkEVB*).

For further details, for example the Linux/x86 boot protocol or Intel and AMD specific background, see the x86-specific kernel documentation (*https://oreil.ly/CBvRQ*).

ARM Architecture

More than 30 years old, ARM (*https://oreil.ly/E9HIN*) is a family of Reduced Instruction Set Computing (RISC) architectures. RISC usually consists of many generic CPU registers along with a small set of instructions that can be executed faster.

Because the designers at Acorn—the original company behind ARM—focused from the get-go on minimal power consumption, you find ARM-based chips in a number of portable devices such as iPhones. They are also in most Android-based phones and in embedded systems found in IoT, such as in the Raspberry Pi.

Given that they are fast, cheap, and produce less heat than x86 chips, you shouldn't be surprised to increasingly find ARM-based CPUs—such as AWS Graviton (*https://oreil.ly/JpgdQ*)—in the data center. While simpler than x86, ARM is not immune to vulnerabilities, such as Spectre (*https://oreil.ly/M79Yu*). For further details, see the ARM-specific kernel documentation (*https://oreil.ly/i7kj4*).

RISC-V Architecture

An up-and-coming player, RISC-V (pronounced *risk five*) (*https://oreil.ly/wwnIA*) is an open RISC standard that was originally developed by the University of California, Berkeley. As of 2021, a number of implementations exist, ranging from Alibaba Group and Nvidia to start-ups such as SiFive. While exciting, this is a relatively new and not widely used (yet) CPU family, and to get an idea how it look and feels, you may want to research it a little—a good start is Shae Erisson's article "Linux on RISC-V" (*https://oreil.ly/6senY*).

For further details, see the RISC-V kernel documentation (*https://oreil.ly/LA1Oq*).

Kernel Components

Now that you know the basics of CPU architectures, it's time to dive into the kernel. While the Linux kernel is a monolithic one—that is, all the components discussed are part of a single binary—there are functional areas in the code base that we can identify and ascribe dedicated responsibilities.

As we've discussed in "Linux Architecture" on page 12, the kernel sits between the hardware and the apps you want to run. The main functional blocks you find in the kernel code base are as follows:

- Process management, such as starting a process based on an executable file
- Memory management, such as allocating memory for a process or map a file into memory
- Networking, like managing network interfaces or providing the network stack
- Filesystems providing file management and supporting the creation and deletion of files
- Management of character devices and device drivers

These functional components often come with interdependencies, and it's a truly challenging task to make sure that the kernel developer motto (*https://oreil.ly/6YDeF*) "Kernel never breaks user land" holds true.

With that, let's have a closer look at the kernel components.

Process Management

There are a number of process management–related parts in the kernel. Some of them deal with CPU architecture–specific things, such as interrupts, and others focus on the launching and scheduling of programs.

Before we get to Linux specifics, let's note that commonly, a process is the user-facing unit, based on an executable program (or binary). A thread, on the other hand, is a unit of execution in the context of a process. You might have come across the term *multithreading*, which means that a process has a number of parallel executions going on, potentially running on different CPUs.

With this general view out of the way, let's see how Linux goes about it. From most granular to smallest unit, Linux has the following:

Sessions

Contain one or more process groups and represent a high-level user-facing unit with optional `tty` attached. The kernel identifies a session via a number called *session ID* (SID).

Process groups

Contain one or more processes, with at most one process group in a session as the foreground process group. The kernel identifies a process group via a number called *process group ID* (PGID).

Processes

Abstractions that group multiple resources (address space, one or more threads, sockets, etc.), which the kernel exposes to you via */proc/self* for the current process. The kernel identifies a process via a number called *process ID* (PID).

Threads

Implemented by the kernel as processes. That is, there are no dedicated data structures representing threads. Rather, a thread is a process that shares certain resources (such as memory or signal handlers) with other processes. The kernel identifies a thread via *thread IDs* (TID) and *thread group IDs* (TGID), with the semantics that a shared TGID value means a multithreaded process (in user land; there are also kernel threads, but that's beyond our scope).

Tasks

In the kernel there is a data structure called `task_struct`—defined in *sched.h* (*https://oreil.ly/nIgz8*)—that forms the basis of implementing processes and threads alike. This data structure captures scheduling-related information, identifiers (such as PID and TGID), and signal handlers, as well as other information, such as that related to performance and security. In a nutshell, all of the aforementioned units are derived and/or anchored in tasks; however, tasks are not exposed as such outside of the kernel.

We will see sessions, process groups, and processes in action and learn how to manage them in Chapter 6, and they'll appear again in the context of containers in Chapter 9.

Let's see some of these concepts in action:

```
$ ps -j
PID    PGID   SID   TTY    TIME CMD
6756   6756   6756  pts/0  00:00:00 bash ❶
6790   6790   6756  pts/0  00:00:00 ps ❷
```

❶ The bash shell process has PID, PGID, and SID of 6756. From `ls -al /proc/6756/task/6756/`, we can glean the task-level information.

❷ The ps process has PID/PGID 6790 and the same SID as the shell.

We mentioned earlier on that in Linux the task data structure has some scheduling-related information at the ready. This means that at any given time a process is in a certain state, as shown in Figure 2-2.

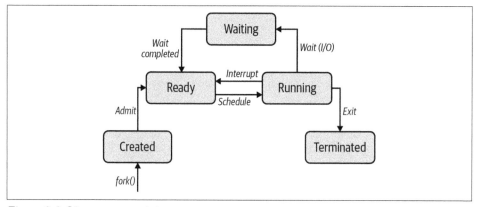

Figure 2-2. Linux process states

 Strictly speaking, the process states are a little more complicated; for example, Linux distinguishes between interruptible and uninterruptible sleep, and there is also the zombie state (in which it has lost its parent process). If you're interested in the details, check out the article "Process States in Linux" (*https://oreil.ly/XBXbU*).

Different events cause state transitions. For example, a running process might transition to the waiting state when it carries out some I/O operation (such as reading from a file) and can't proceed with execution (off CPU).

Having taken a quick look at process management, let's examine a related topic: memory.

Memory Management

Virtual memory makes your system appear as if it has more memory than it physically has. In fact, every process gets a lot of (virtual) memory. This is how it works: both physical memory and virtual memory are divided into fixed-length chunks we call *pages*.

Figure 2-3 shows the virtual address spaces of two processes, each with its own page table. These page tables map virtual pages of the process into physical pages in main memory (aka RAM).

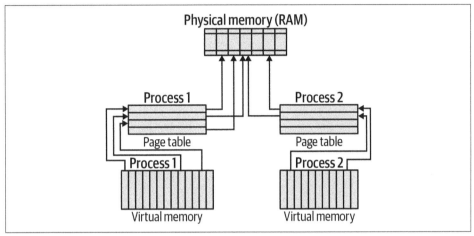

Figure 2-3. Virtual memory management overview

Multiple virtual pages can point to the same physical page via their respective process-level page tables. This is, in a sense, the core of memory management: how to effectively provide each process with the illusion that its page actually exists in RAM while using the existing space optimally.

Every time the CPU accesses a process's virtual page, the CPU would in principle have to translate the virtual address a process uses to the corresponding physical address. To speed up this process—which can be multilevel and hence slow—modern CPU architectures support a lookup on-chip called translation lookaside buffer (TLB) (*https://oreil.ly/y3xy0*). The TLB is effectively a small cache that, in case of a miss, causes the CPU to go via the process page table(s) to calculate the physical address of a page and update the TLB with it.

Traditionally, Linux had a default page size of 4 KB, but since kernel v2.6.3, it supports huge pages (*https://oreil.ly/7rqLO*), to better support modern architectures and workloads. For example, 64-bit Linux allows you to use up to 128 TB of virtual address space (with virtual being the theoretical addressable number of memory addresses) per process, with an approximate 64 TB of physical memory (with physical being the amount of RAM you have in your machine) in total.

OK, that was a lot of theoretical information. Let's have a look at it from a more practical point of view. A very useful tool to figure out memory-related information such as how much RAM is available to you is the */proc/meminfo* interface:

```
$ grep MemTotal /proc/meminfo ❶
MemTotal:        4014636 kB

$ grep VmallocTotal /proc/meminfo ❷
VmallocTotal:   34359738367 kB

$ grep Huge /proc/meminfo ❸
AnonHugePages:         0 kB
ShmemHugePages:        0 kB
FileHugePages:         0 kB
HugePages_Total:       0
HugePages_Free:        0
HugePages_Rsvd:        0
HugePages_Surp:        0
Hugepagesize:       2048 kB
Hugetlb:               0 kB
```

❶ List details on physical memory (RAM); that's 4 GB there.

❷ List details on virtual memory; that's a bit more than 34 TB there.

❸ List huge pages information; apparently here the page size is 2 MB.

With that, we move on to the next kernel function: networking.

Networking

One important function of the kernel is to provide networking functionality. Whether you want to browse the web or copy data to a remote system, you depend on the network.

The Linux network stack follows a layered architecture:

Sockets
For abstracting communication

Transmission Control Protocol (TCP) and User Datagram Protocol (UDP)
For connection-oriented communication and connectionless communication, respectively

Internet Protocol (IP)
For addressing machines

These three actions are all that the kernel takes care of. The application layer protocols such as HTTP or SSH are, usually, implemented in user land.

You can get an overview of your network interfaces using (output edited):

```
$ ip link
1: lo: <LOOPBACK,UP,LOWER_UP> mtu 65536 qdisc noqueue state UNKNOWN mode
   DEFAULT group default qlen 1000 link/loopback 00:00:00:00:00:00
   brd 00:00:00:00:00:00
2: enp0s1: <BROADCAST,MULTICAST,UP,LOWER_UP> mtu 1500 qdisc fq_codel state
   UP mode DEFAULT group default qlen 1000 link/ether 52:54:00:12:34:56
   brd ff:ff:ff:ff:ff:ff
```

Further, `ip route` provides you with routing information. Since we have a dedicated networking chapter (Chapter 7) where we will dive deep into the networking stack, the supported protocols, and typical operations, we keep it at this and move on to the next kernel component, block devices and filesystems.

Filesystems

Linux uses filesystems to organize files and directories on storage devices such as hard disk drives (HDDs) and solid-state drives (SSDs) or flash memory. There are many types of filesystems, such as `ext4` and `btrfs` or NTFS, and you can have multiple instances of the same filesystem in use.

Virtual File System (VFS) was originally introduced to support multiple filesystem types and instances. The highest layer in VFS provides a common API abstraction of functions such as open, close, read, and write. At the bottom of VFS are filesystem abstractions called *plug-ins* for the given filesystem.

We will go into greater detail on filesystems and file operations in Chapter 5.

Device Drivers

A *driver* is a bit of code that runs in the kernel. Its job is to manage a device, which can be actual hardware—like a keyboard, a mouse, or hard disk drives—or it can be a pseudo-device such as a pseudo-terminal under */dev/pts/* (which is not a physical device but can be treated like one).

Another interesting class of hardware are *graphics processing units* (GPUs) (*https://oreil.ly/os7pu*), which traditionally were used to accelerate graphics output and ease the load on the CPU. In recent years, GPUs have found a new use case in the context of machine learning (*https://oreil.ly/qrVcY*), and hence they are not exclusively relevant in desktop environments.

The driver may be built statically into the kernel, or it can be built as a kernel module (see "Modules" on page 26) so that it can be dynamically loaded when needed.

If you're interested in an interactive way to explore device drivers and how kernel components interact, check out the Linux kernel map (*https://oreil.ly/voBtR*).

The kernel driver model (*https://oreil.ly/Cb6mw*) is complicated and out of scope for this book. However, following are a few hints for interacting with it, just enough so that you know where to find what.

To get an overview of the devices on your Linux system, you can use the following:

```
$ ls -al /sys/devices/
total 0
drwxr-xr-x 15 root root 0 Aug 17 15:53 .
dr-xr-xr-x 13 root root 0 Aug 17 15:53 ..
drwxr-xr-x  6 root root 0 Aug 17 15:53 LNXSYSTM:00
drwxr-xr-x  3 root root 0 Aug 17 15:53 breakpoint
drwxr-xr-x  3 root root 0 Aug 17 17:41 isa
drwxr-xr-x  4 root root 0 Aug 17 15:53 kprobe
drwxr-xr-x  5 root root 0 Aug 17 15:53 msr
drwxr-xr-x 15 root root 0 Aug 17 15:53 pci0000:00
drwxr-xr-x 14 root root 0 Aug 17 15:53 platform
drwxr-xr-x  8 root root 0 Aug 17 15:53 pnp0
drwxr-xr-x  3 root root 0 Aug 17 15:53 software
drwxr-xr-x 10 root root 0 Aug 17 15:53 system
drwxr-xr-x  3 root root 0 Aug 17 15:53 tracepoint
drwxr-xr-x  4 root root 0 Aug 17 15:53 uprobe
drwxr-xr-x 18 root root 0 Aug 17 15:53 virtual
```

Further, you can use the following to list mounted devices:

```
$ mount
sysfs on /sys type sysfs (rw,nosuid,nodev,noexec,relatime)
proc on /proc type proc (rw,nosuid,nodev,noexec,relatime)
devpts on /dev/pts type devpts (rw,nosuid,noexec,relatime,gid=5,mode=620, \
ptmxmode=000)
...
tmpfs on /run/snapd/ns type tmpfs (rw,nosuid,nodev,noexec,relatime,\
size=401464k,mode=755,inode64)
nsfs on /run/snapd/ns/lxd.mnt type nsfs (rw)
```

With this, we have covered the Linux kernel components and move to the interface between the kernel and user land.

syscalls

Whether you sit in front of a terminal and type touch test.txt or whether one of your apps wants to download the content of a file from a remote system, at the end of the day you ask Linux to turn the high-level instruction, such as "create a file" or "read all bytes from address so and so," into a set of concrete, architecture-dependent steps. In other words, the service interface the kernel exposes and that user land entities call is the set of system calls, or syscalls (*https://oreil.ly/UF09U*) for short.

Linux has hundreds of syscalls: around three hundred or more, depending on the CPU family. However, you and your programs don't usually invoke these syscalls directly but via what we call the *C standard library*. The standard library provides wrapper functions and is available in various implementations, such as glibc (*https:// oreil.ly/mZPRy*) or musl (*https://oreil.ly/jnTCA*).

These wrapper libraries perform an important task. They take care of the repetitive low-level handling of the execution of a syscall. System calls are implemented as software interrupts, causing an exception that transfers the control to an exception handler. There are a number of steps to take care of every time a syscall is invoked, as depicted in Figure 2-4:

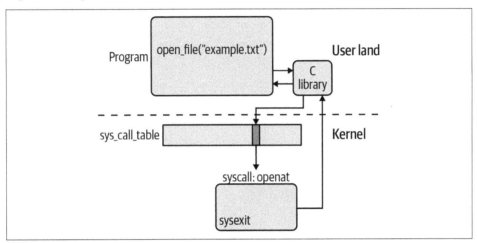

Figure 2-4. syscall execution steps in Linux

1. Defined in *syscall.h* and architecture-dependent files, the kernel uses a so-called *syscall table*, effectively an array of function pointers in memory (stored in a variable called `sys_call_table`) to keep track of syscalls and their corresponding handlers.

2. With the `system_call()` function acting like a syscall multiplexer, it first saves the hardware context on the stack, then performs checks (like if tracing is performed), and then jumps to the function pointed to by the respective syscall number index in the `sys_call_table`.

3. After the syscall is completed with `sysexit`, the wrapper library restores the hardware context, and the program execution resumes in user land.

Notable in the previous steps is the switching between kernel mode and user land mode, an operation that costs time.

OK, that was a little dry and theoretical, so to better appreciate how syscalls look and feel in practice, let's have a look at a concrete example. We will use strace (*https://oreil.ly/ksV9B*) to look behind the curtain, a tool useful for troubleshooting, for example, if you don't have the source code of an app but want to learn what it does.

Let's assume you wonder what syscalls are involved when you execute the innocent-looking ls command. Here's how you can find it out using strace:

```
$ strace ls ❶
execve("/usr/bin/ls", ["ls"], 0x7ffe29254910 /* 24 vars */) = 0 ❷
brk(NULL)                        = 0x5596e5a3c000 ❸
...
access("/etc/ld.so.preload", R_OK)  = -1 ENOENT (No such file or directory) ❹
openat(AT_FDCWD, "/etc/ld.so.cache", O_RDONLY|O_CLOEXEC) = 3 ❺
...
read(3, "\177ELF\2\1\1\0\0\0\0\0\0\0\0\0\3\0>\0\1\0\0\0 p\0\0\0\0\0\0\0"..., \
832) = 832 ❻
...
```

❶ With strace ls, we ask strace to capture the syscall that ls uses. Note that I edited the output since strace generates some 162 lines on my system (this number varies between different distros, architectures, and other factors). Further, the output you see there comes via stderr, so if you want to redirect it, you have to use 2> here. You'll learn more about this in Chapter 3.

❷ The syscall execve (*https://oreil.ly/iasHW*) executes */usr/bin/ls*, causing the shell process to be replaced.

❸ The brk (*https://oreil.ly/HRuNj*) syscall is an outdated way to allocate memory; it's safer and more portable to use malloc. Note that malloc is not a syscall but a function that in turn uses mallocopt to decide if it needs to use the brk syscall or the mmap syscall based on the amount of memory accessed.

❹ The access syscall checks if the process is allowed to access a certain file.

❺ Syscall openat opens the file */etc/ld.so.cache* relative to a directory file descriptor (here the first argument, AT_FDCWD, which stands for the current directory) and using flags O_RDONLY|O_CLOEXEC (last argument).

❻ The read syscall reads from a file descriptor (first argument, 3) 832 bytes (last argument) into a buffer (second argument).

`strace` is useful to see exactly what syscalls have been called—in which order and with which arguments—effectively hooking into the live stream of events between user land and kernel. It's also good for performance diagnostics. Let's see where a `curl` command spends most of its time (output shortened):

```
$ strace -c \ ❶
        curl -s https://mhausenblas.info > /dev/null ❷
% time     seconds  usecs/call     calls    errors syscall
------ ----------- ----------- --------- --------- ----------------
 26.75    0.031965         148       215           mmap
 17.52    0.020935         136       153         3 read
 10.15    0.012124         175        69           rt_sigaction
  8.00    0.009561         147        65         1 openat
  7.61    0.009098         126        72           close
  ...
  0.00    0.000000           0         1           prlimit64
------ ----------- ----------- --------- --------- ----------------
100.00    0.119476         141       843        11 total
```

❶   Use the `-c` option to generate overview stats of the syscalls used.

❷   Discard all output of `curl`.

Interestingly, the `curl` command here spends almost half of its time with `mmap` and `read` syscalls, and the `connect` syscall takes 0.3 ms—not bad.

To help you get a feeling for the coverage, I've put together Table 2-1, which lists examples of widely used syscalls across kernel components as well as system-wide ones. You can look up details of syscalls, including their parameters and return values, via section 2 of the man pages (*https://oreil.ly/qLOA3*).

Table 2-1. Example syscalls

Category	Example syscalls
Process management	clone, fork, execve, wait, exit, getpid, setuid, setns, getrusage, capset, ptrace
Memory management	brk, mmap, munmap, mremap, mlock, mincore
Networking	socket, setsockopt, getsockopt, bind, listen, accept, connect, shutdown, recvfrom, recvmsg, sendto, sethostname, bpf
Filesystems	open, openat, close, mknod, rename, truncate, mkdir, rmdir, getcwd, chdir, chroot, getdents, link, symlink, unlink, umask, stat, chmod, utime, access, ioctl, flock, read, write, lseek, sync, select, poll, mount,
Time	time, clock_settime, timer_create, alarm, nanosleep
Signals	kill, pause, signalfd, eventfd,
Global	uname, sysinfo, syslog, acct, _sysctl, iopl, reboot

There is a nice interactive syscall table (*https://oreil.ly/HKu6Y*) available online with source code references.

Now that you have a basic idea of the Linux kernel, its main components, and interface, let's move on to the question of how to extend it.

Kernel Extensions

In this section, we will focus on how to extend the kernel. In a sense, the content here is advanced and optional. You won't need it for your day-to-day work, in general.

Configuring and compiling your own Linux kernel is out of scope for this book. For information on how to do it, I recommend *Linux Kernel in a Nutshell* (O'Reilly) by Greg Kroah-Hartman, one of the main Linux maintainers and project lead. He covers the entire range of tasks, from downloading the source code to configuration and installation steps, to kernel options at runtime.

Let's start with something easy: how do you know what kernel version you're using? You can use the following command to determine this:

```
$ uname -srm
Linux 5.11.0-25-generic x86_64 ❶
```

❶ From the `uname` output here, you can tell that at the time of writing, I'm using a 5.11 kernel (*https://oreil.ly/FJdA1*) on an `x86_64` machine (see also "x86 Architecture" on page 15).

Now that we know the kernel version, we can address the question of how to extend the kernel out-of-tree—that is, without having to add features to the kernel source code and then build it. For this extension we can use modules, so let's have a look at that.

Modules

In a nutshell, a *module* is a program that you can load into a kernel on demand. That is, you do not necessarily have to recompile the kernel and/or reboot the machine. Nowadays, Linux detects most of the hardware automatically, and with it Linux loads its modules automatically. But there are cases where you want to manually load a module. Consider the following case: the kernel detects a video card and loads a generic module. However, the video card manufacturer offers a better third-party module (not available in the Linux kernel) that you may choose to use instead.

To list available modules, run the following command (output has been edited down, as there are over one thousand lines on my system):

```
$ find /lib/modules/$(uname -r) -type f -name '*.ko*'
/lib/modules/5.11.0-25-generic/kernel/ubuntu/ubuntu-host/ubuntu-host.ko
/lib/modules/5.11.0-25-generic/kernel/fs/nls/nls_iso8859-1.ko
/lib/modules/5.11.0-25-generic/kernel/fs/ceph/ceph.ko
/lib/modules/5.11.0-25-generic/kernel/fs/nfsd/nfsd.ko
...
/lib/modules/5.11.0-25-generic/kernel/net/ipv6/esp6.ko
/lib/modules/5.11.0-25-generic/kernel/net/ipv6/ip6_vti.ko
/lib/modules/5.11.0-25-generic/kernel/net/sctp/sctp_diag.ko
/lib/modules/5.11.0-25-generic/kernel/net/sctp/sctp.ko
/lib/modules/5.11.0-25-generic/kernel/net/netrom/netrom.ko
```

That's great! But which modules did the kernel actually load? Let's take a look (output shortened):

```
$ lsmod
Module                 Size  Used by
...
linear                20480  0
crct10dif_pclmul      16384  1
crc32_pclmul          16384  0
ghash_clmulni_intel   16384  0
virtio_net            57344  0
net_failover          20480  1 virtio_net
ahci                  40960  0
aesni_intel          372736  0
crypto_simd           16384  1 aesni_intel
cryptd                24576  2 crypto_simd,ghash_clmulni_intel
glue_helper           16384  1 aesni_intel
```

Note that the preceding information is available via */proc/modules*. This is thanks to the kernel exposing this information via a pseudo-filesystem interface; more on this topic is presented in Chapter 6.

Want to learn more about a module or have a nice way to manipulate kernel modules? Then modprobe is your friend. For example, to list the dependencies:

```
$ modprobe --show-depends async_memcpy
insmod /lib/modules/5.11.0-25-generic/kernel/crypto/async_tx/async_tx.ko
insmod /lib/modules/5.11.0-25-generic/kernel/crypto/async_tx/async_memcpy.ko
```

Next up: an alternative, modern way to extend the kernel.

A Modern Way to Extend the Kernel: eBPF

An increasingly popular way to extend kernel functionality is eBPF. Originally known as *Berkeley Packet Filter* (BPF), nowadays the kernel project and technology is commonly known as *eBPF* (a term that does not stand for anything).

Technically, eBPF is a feature of the Linux kernel, and you'll need the Linux kernel version 3.15 or above to benefit from it. It enables you to safely and efficiently extend the Linux kernel functions by using the bpf (*https://oreil.ly/cltxg*) syscall. eBPF is implemented as an in-kernel virtual machine using a custom 64-bit RISC instruction set.

If you want to learn more about what is enabled in which kernel version for eBPF, you can use the iovisor/bcc docs on GitHub (*https://oreil.ly/HtKO8*).

In Figure 2-5 you see a high-level overview taken from Brendan Gregg's book *BPF Performance Tools: Linux System and Application Observability* (*https://oreil.ly/sfYKK*) (Addison Wesley).

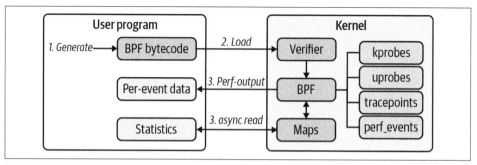

Figure 2-5. eBPF overview in the Linux kernel

eBPF is already used in a number of places and for use cases such as the following:

As a CNI plug-in to enable pod networking in Kubernetes
> For example, in Cilium (*https://oreil.ly/BS0iz*) and Project Calico. Also, for service scalability.

For observability
> For Linux kernel tracing, such as with iovisor/bpftrace (*https://oreil.ly/0M0oV*), as well as in a clustered setup with Hubble (*https://oreil.ly/7yzhq*) (see Chapter 8).

As a security control
> For example, to perform container runtime scanning as you can use with projects such as CNCF Falco (*https://falco.org*).

For network load balancing
> Such as in Facebook's L4 katran (*https://oreil.ly/HqMZg*) library.

In mid-2021, the Linux Foundation announced that Facebook, Google, Isovalent, Microsoft, and Netflix joined together to create the eBPF Foundation (*https://oreil.ly/ g2buM*), and with it giving the eBPF project a vendor-neutral home. Stay tuned!

If you want to stay on top of things, have a look at *ebpf.io*.

Conclusion

The Linux kernel is the core of the Linux operating system, and no matter what distribution or environment you are using Linux in—be it on your desktop or in the cloud—you should have a basic idea of its components and functionality.

In this chapter, we reviewed the overall Linux architecture, the role of the kernel, and its interfaces. Most importantly, the kernel abstracts away the differences of the hardware—CPU architectures and peripheral devices—and makes Linux very portable. The most important interface is the syscall interface, through which the kernel exposes its functionality—be it opening a file, allocating memory, or listing network interfaces.

We have also looked a bit at the inner workings of the kernel, including modules and eBPF. If you want to extend the kernel functionality or implement performant tasks in the kernel (controlled from the user space), then eBPF is definitely worth taking a closer look at.

If you want to learn more about certain aspects of the kernel, the following resources should provide you with some starting points:

General
- *The Linux Programming Interface* (*https://oreil.ly/HCLmX*) by Michael Kerrisk (No Starch Press).
- Linux Kernel Teaching (*https://oreil.ly/lMzbW*) provides a nice introduction with deep dives across the board.
- "Anatomy of the Linux Kernel" (*https://oreil.ly/it2jK*) gives a quick high-level intro.
- "Operating System Kernels" (*https://oreil.ly/9d93Y*) has a nice overview and comparison of kernel design approaches.
- KernelNewbies (*https://oreil.ly/OSfbA*) is a great resource if you want to dive deeper into hands-on topics.
- kernelstats (*https://oreil.ly/kSov7*) shows some interesting distributions over time.
- The Linux Kernel Map (*https://oreil.ly/G55tF*) is a visual representation of kernel components and dependencies.

Memory management

- *Understanding the Linux Virtual Memory Manager* (*https://oreil.ly/uKjtQ*)
- "The Slab Allocator in the Linux Kernel" (*https://oreil.ly/dBLkt*)
- Kernel docs (*https://oreil.ly/sTBhM*)

Device drivers

- *Linux Device Drivers* (*https://oreil.ly/Kn7CZ*) by Jonathan Corbet
- "How to Install a Device Driver on Linux" (*https://oreil.ly/a0chO*)
- Character Device Drivers (*https://oreil.ly/EGXIh*)
- *Linux Device Drivers: Tutorial for Linux Driver Development* (*https://oreil.ly/jkiwB*)

syscalls

- "Linux Interrupts: The Basic Concepts" (*https://oreil.ly/yCdTi*)
- The Linux Kernel: System Calls (*https://oreil.ly/A3XMT*)
- Linux System Call Table (*https://oreil.ly/mezjr*)
- *syscalls.h* source code (*https://oreil.ly/tf6CW*)
- syscall lookup for x86 and x86_64 (*https://oreil.ly/K7Zid*)

eBPF

- "Introduction to eBPF" (*https://oreil.ly/Afdsx*) by Matt Oswalt
- eBPF maps documentation (*https://oreil.ly/Fnj5t*)

Equipped with this knowledge, we're now ready to climb up the abstraction ladder a bit and move to the primary user interface we consider in this book: the shell, both in manual usage as well as automation through scripts.

## CHAPTER 3

Shells and Scripting

In this chapter, we'll focus on interacting with Linux on the terminal, that is, via the shell that exposes a command-line interface (CLI). It is vitally important to be able to use the shell effectively to accomplish everyday tasks, and to that end we focus on usability here.

First, we review some terminology and provide a gentle and concise introduction to shell basics. Then we have a look at modern, human-friendly shells, such as the Fish shell. We'll also look at configuration and common tasks in the shell. Then, we move on to the topic of how to effectively work on the CLI using a terminal multiplexer, enabling you to work with multiple sessions, local or remote. In the last part of this chapter, we switch gears and focus on automating tasks in the shell using scripts, including best practices for writing scripts in a safe, secure, and portable manner and also how to lint and test scripts.

There are two major ways to interact with Linux, from a CLI perspective. The first way is manually—that is, a human user sits in front of the terminal, interactively typing commands and consuming the output. This ad-hoc interaction works for most of the things you want to do in the shell on a day-to-day basis, including the following:

- Listing directories, finding files, or looking for content in files
- Copying files between directories or to remote machines
- Reading emails or the news or sending a Tweet from the terminal

Further, we'll learn how to conveniently and efficiently work with multiple shell sessions at the same time.

The other mode of operation is the automated processing of a series of commands in a special kind of file that the shell interprets for you and in turn executes. This mode is usually called *shell scripting* or just *scripting*. You typically want to use a script rather than manually repeating certain tasks. Also, scripts are the basis of many config and install systems. Scripts are indeed very convenient. However, they can also pose a danger if used without precautions. So, whenever you think about writing a script, keep the XKCD web comic shown in Figure 3-1 in mind.

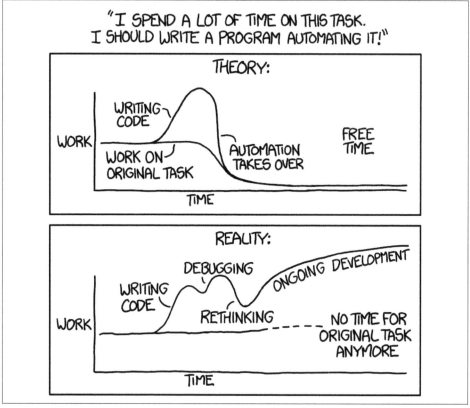

Figure 3-1. XKCD on automation (https://oreil.ly/GSKUb). Credit: Randall Munroe (shared under CC BY-NC 2.5 license)

I strongly recommend that you have a Linux environment available and try out the examples shown here right away. With that, are you ready for some (inter)action? If so, then let's start with some terminology and basic shell usage.

Basics

Before we get into different options and configurations, let's focus on some basic terms such as *terminal* and *shell*. In this section I'll define the terminology and show you how to accomplish everyday tasks in the shell. We'll also review modern commands and see them in action.

Terminals

We start with the terminal, or terminal emulator, or soft terminal, all of which refer to the same thing: a *terminal* is a program that provides a textual user interface. That is, a terminal supports reading characters from the keyboard and displaying them on the screen. Many years ago, these used to be integrated devices (keyboard and screen together), but nowadays terminals are simply apps.

In addition to the basic character-oriented input and output, terminals support so-called *escape sequences*, or *escape codes* (*https://oreil.ly/AT5qC*), for cursor and screen handling and potentially support for colors. For example, pressing Ctrl+H causes a backspace, which deletes the character to the left of the cursor.

The environment variable TERM has the terminal emulator in use, and its configuration is available via infocmp as follows (note that the output has been shortened):

```
$ infocmp ❶
#       Reconstructed via infocmp from file: /lib/terminfo/s/screen-256color
screen-256color|GNU Screen with 256 colors,
        am, km, mir, msgr, xenl,
        colors#0x100, cols#80, it#8, lines#24, pairs#0x10000,
        acsc=++\,\,--..00``aaffgghhiijjkkllmmnnooppqqrrssttuuvvwwxxyyzz{{||}}~~,
        bel=^G, blink=\E[5m, bold=\E[1m, cbt=\E[Z, civis=\E[?25l,
        clear=\E[H\E[J, cnorm=\E[34h\E[?25h, cr=\r,
        ...
```

❶ The output of infocmp is not easy to digest. If you want to learn about the capabilities in detail, consult the terminfo (*https://oreil.ly/qjwiv*) database. For example, in my concrete output, the terminal supports 80 columns (cols#80) and 24 lines (lines#24) for output as well as 256 colors (colors#0x100, in hexadecimal notation).

Examples of terminals include not only xterm, rxvt, and the Gnome terminator but also new generation ones that utilize the GPU, such as Alacritty (*https://oreil.ly/zm9M9*), kitty (*https://oreil.ly/oxyMn*), and warp (*https://oreil.ly/WBG9S*).

In "Terminal Multiplexer" on page 55, we will come back to the topic of the terminal.

Shells

Next up is the *shell*, a program that runs inside the terminal and acts as a command interpreter. The shell offers input and output handling via streams, supports variables, has some built-in commands you can use, deals with command execution and status, and usually supports both interactive usage as well as scripted usage ("Scripting" on page 62).

The shell is formally defined in sh (*https://oreil.ly/ISxwU*), and we often come across the term POSIX shell (*https://oreil.ly/rkfqG*), which will become more important in the context of scripts and portability.

Originally, we had the Bourne shell sh, named after the author, but nowadays it's usually replaced with the bash (*https://oreil.ly/C9coL*) shell—a wordplay on the original version, short for "Bourne Again Shell"—which is widely used as the default.

If you are curious about what you're using, use the file -h /bin/sh command to find out, or if that fails, try echo $0 or echo $SHELL.

In this section, we assume the bash shell (bash), unless we call it out explicitly.

There are many more implementations of sh as well as other variants, such as the Korn shell, ksh, and C shell, csh, which are not widely used today. We will, however, review modern bash replacements in "Human-Friendly Shells" on page 48.

Let's start our shell basics with two fundamental features: streams and variables.

Streams

Let's start with the topic of input (streams) and output (streams), or I/O for short. How can you feed a program some input? How do you control where the output of a program lands, say, on the terminal or in a file?

First off, the shell equips every process with three default file descriptors (FDs) for input and output:

- stdin (FD 0)
- stdout (FD 1)
- stderr (FD 2)

These FDs are, as depicted in Figure 3-2, by default connected to your screen and keyboard, respectively. In other words, unless you specify something else, a command you enter in the shell will take its input (stdin) from your keyboard, and it will deliver its output (stdout) to your screen.

The following shell interaction demonstrates this default behavior:

```
$ cat
This is some input I type on the keyboard and read on the screen^C
```

In the preceding example using `cat`, you see the defaults in action. Note that I used Ctrl+C (shown as `^C`) to terminate the command.

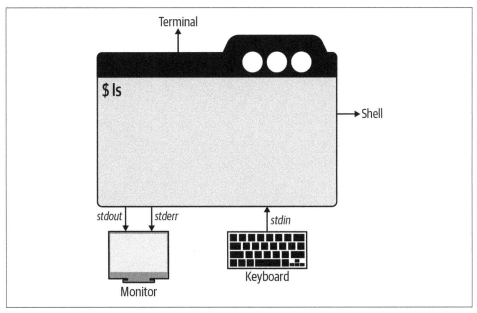

Figure 3-2. Shell I/O default streams

If you don't want to use the defaults the shell gives you—for example, you don't want `stderr` to be outputted on the screen but want to save it in a file—you can redirect (*https://oreil.ly/pOIjp*) the streams.

You redirect the output stream of a process using `$FD>` and `<$FD`, with `$FD` being the file descriptor—for example, `2>` means redirect the `stderr` stream. Note that `1>` and `>` are the same since `stdout` is the default. If you want to redirect both `stdout` and `stderr`, use `&>`, and when you want to get rid of a stream, you can use `/dev/null`.

Let's see how that works in the context of a concrete example, downloading some HTML content via `curl`:

```
$ curl https://example.com &> /dev/null ❶

$ curl https://example.com > /tmp/content.txt 2> /tmp/curl-status ❷
$ head -3 /tmp/content.txt
<!doctype html>
<html>
<head>
$ cat /tmp/curl-status
  % Total    % Received % Xferd  Average Speed   Time    Time     Time  Current
                                 Dload  Upload   Total   Spent    Left  Speed
100  1256  100  1256    0     0   3187      0 --:--:-- --:--:-- --:--:--  3195
```

```
$ cat > /tmp/interactive-input.txt ❸

$ tr < /tmp/curl-status [A-Z] [a-z] ❹
  % total    % received % xferd  average speed   time    time     time  current
                                  dload  upload   total   spent    left  speed
100  1256  100  1256    0     0    3187       0 --:--:-- --:--:-- --:--:--  3195
```

❶ Discard all output by redirecting both stdout and stderr to */dev/null*.

❷ Redirect the output and status to different files.

❸ Interactively enter input and save to file; use Ctrl+D to stop capturing and store the content.

❹ Lowercase all words, using the tr command that reads from stdin.

Shells usually understand a number of special characters, such as:

Ampersand (&)
> Placed at the end of a command, executes the command in the background (see also "Job control" on page 40)

Backslash (\)
> Used to continue a command on the next line, for better readability of long commands

Pipe (|)
> Connects stdout of one process with the stdin of the next process, allowing you to pass data without having to store it in files as a temporary place

---

Pipes and the UNIX Philosophy

While pipes (*https://oreil.ly/ipSgr*) might seem not too exciting at first glance, there's much more to them. I once had a nice interaction with Doug McIlroy, the inventor of pipes. I wrote an article, "Revisiting the Unix Philosophy in 2018" (*https://oreil.ly/ KTU4q*), in which I drew parallels between UNIX and microservices. Someone commented on the article, and that comment led to Doug sending me an email (very unexpectedly, and I had to verify to believe it) to clarify things.

Again, let's see some of the theoretical content in action. Let's try to figure out how many lines an HTML file contains by downloading it using curl and then piping the content to the wc tool:

```
$ curl https://example.com 2> /dev/null | \ ❶
  wc -l ❷
46
```

❶ Use `curl` to download the content from the URL, and discard the status that it outputs on `stderr`. (Note: in practice, you'd use the `-s` option of `curl`, but we want to learn how to apply our hard-gained knowledge, right?)

❷ The `stdout` of `curl` is fed to `stdin` of `wc`, which counts the number of lines with the `-l` option.

Now that you have a basic understanding of commands, streams, and redirection, let's move on to another core shell feature, the handling of variables.

Variables

A term you will come across often in the context of shells is *variables*. Whenever you don't want to or cannot hardcode a value, you can use a variable to store and change a value. Use cases include the following:

- When you want to handle configuration items that Linux exposes—for example, the place where the shell looks for executables captured in the `$PATH` variable. This is kind of an interface where a variable might be read/write.

- When you want to interactively query the user for a value, say, in the context of a script.

- When you want to shorten input by defining a long value once—for example, the URL of an HTTP API. This use case roughly corresponds to a `const` value in a program language since you don't change the value after you have declared the variable.

We distinguish between two kinds of variables:

Environment variables
: Shell-wide settings; list them with `env`.

Shell variables
: Valid in the context of the current execution; list with `set` in bash. Shell variables are not inherited by subprocesses.

You can, in bash, use `export` to create an environment variable. When you want to access the value of a variable, put a `$` in front of it, and when you want to get rid of it, use `unset`.

OK, that was a lot of information. Let's see how that looks in practice (in bash):

```
$ set MY_VAR=42 ❶
$ set | grep MY_VAR ❷
_=MY_VAR=42

$ export MY_GLOBAL_VAR="fun with vars" ❸

$ set | grep 'MY_*' ❹
MY_GLOBAL_VAR='fun with vars'
_=MY_VAR=42

$ env | grep 'MY_*' ❺
MY_GLOBAL_VAR=fun with vars

$ bash ❻
$ echo $MY_GLOBAL_VAR ❼
fun with vars

$ set | grep 'MY_*' ❽
MY_GLOBAL_VAR='fun with vars'

$ exit ❾
$ unset $MY_VAR
$ set | grep 'MY_*'
MY_GLOBAL_VAR='fun with vars'
```

❶ Create a shell variable called MY_VAR, and assign a value of 42.

❷ List shell variables and filter out MY_VAR. Note the _=, indicating it's not exported.

❸ Create a new environment variable called MY_GLOBAL_VAR.

❹ List shell variables and filter out all that start with MY_. We see, as expected, both of the variables we created in the previous steps.

❺ List environment variables. We see MY_GLOBAL_VAR, as we would hope.

❻ Create a new shell session—that is, a child process of the current shell session that doesn't inherit MY_VAR.

❼ Access the environment variable MY_GLOBAL_VAR.

❽ List the shell variables, which gives us only MY_GLOBAL_VAR since we're in a child process.

❾ Exit the child process, remove the MY_VAR shell variable, and list our shell variables. As expected, MY_VAR is gone.

In Table 3-1 I put together common shell and environment variables. You will find those variables almost everywhere, and they are important to understand and to use. For any of the variables, you can have a look at the respective value using echo $XXX, with XXX being the variable name.

Table 3-1. Common shell and environment variables

Variable	Type	Semantics
EDITOR	Environment	The path to program used by default to edit files
HOME	POSIX	The path of the home directory of the current user
HOSTNAME	bash shell	The name of the current host
IFS	POSIX	List of characters to separate fields; used when the shell splits words on expansion
PATH	POSIX	Contains a list of directories in which the shell looks for executable programs (binaries or scripts)
PS1	Environment	The primary prompt string in use
PWD	Environment	The full path of the working directory
OLDPWD	bash shell	The full path of the directory before the last cd command
RANDOM	bash shell	A random integer between 0 and 32767
SHELL	Environment	Contains the currently used shell
TERM	Environment	The terminal emulator used
UID	Environment	Current user unique ID (integer value)
USER	Environment	Current user name
_	bash shell	Last argument to the previous command executed in the foreground
?	bash shell	Exit status; see "Exit status" on page 39
$	bash shell	The ID of the current process (integer value)
0	bash shell	The name of the current process

Further, check out the full list of bash-specific variables (*https://oreil.ly/EIgVc*), and also note that the variables from Table 3-1 will come in handy again in the context of "Scripting" on page 62.

Exit status

The shell communicates the completion of a command execution to the caller using what is called the *exit status*. In general, it is expected that a Linux command returns a status when it terminates. This can either be a normal termination (happy path) or an abnormal termination (something went wrong). A 0 exit status means that the command was successfully run, without any errors, whereas a nonzero value between 1 and 255 signals a failure. To query the exit status, use echo $?.

Be careful with exit status handling in a pipeline, since some shells make only the last status available. You can work around that limitation by using $PIPESTATUS (*https:// oreil.ly/mMz9k*).

Built-in commands

Shells come with a number of built-in commands. Some useful examples are yes, echo, cat, or read (depending on the Linux distro, some of those commands might not be built-ins but located in */usr/bin*). You can use the help command to list built-ins. Do remember, however, that everything else is a shell-external program that you usually can find in */usr/bin* (for user commands) or in */usr/sbin* (for administrative commands).

How do you know where to find an executable? Here are some ways:

```
$ which ls
/usr/bin/ls

$ type ls
ls is aliased to `ls --color=auto'
```

 One of the technical reviewers of this book rightfully pointed out that which is a non-POSIX, external program that may not always be available. Also, they suggested using *command* -v rather than which to get the program path and or shell alias/function. See also the shellcheck docs (*https://oreil.ly/5toUM*) for further details on the matter.

Job control

A feature most shells support is called *job control* (*https://oreil.ly/zeMsU*). By default, when you enter a command, it takes control of the screen and the keyboard, which we usually call *running in the foreground*. But what if you don't want to run something interactively, or, in case of a server, what if there is no input from stdin at all? Enter job control and background jobs: to launch a process in the background, put an & at the end, or to send a foreground process to the background, press Ctrl+Z.

The following example shows this in action, giving you a rough idea:

```
$ watch -n 5 "ls" & ❶

$ jobs ❷
Job     Group   CPU     State   Command
1       3021    0%      stopped watch -n 5 "ls" &

$ fg ❸
Every 5.0s: ls                          Sat Aug 28 11:34:32 2021
```

```
Dockerfile
app.yaml
example.json
main.go
script.sh
test
```

❶ By putting the & at the end, we launch the command in the background.

❷ List all jobs.

❸ With the `fg` command, we can bring a process to the foreground. If you want to quit the `watch` command, use Ctrl+C.

If you want to keep a background process running, even after you close the shell you can prepend the `nohup` command. Further, for a process that is already running and wasn't prepended with `nohup`, you can use `disown` after the fact to achieve the same effect. Finally, if you want to get rid of a running process, you can use the `kill` command with various levels of forcefulness (see "Signals" on page 214 for more details).

Rather than job control, I recommend using terminal multiplexer, as discussed in "Terminal Multiplexer" on page 55. These programs take care of the most common use cases (shell closes, multiple processes running and need coordination, etc.) and also support working with remote systems.

Let's move on to discuss modern replacements for frequently used core commands that have been around forever.

Modern Commands

There are a handful of commands you will find yourself using over and over again on a daily basis. These include commands for navigating directories (`cd`), listing the content of a directory (`ls`), finding files (`find`), and displaying the content of files (`cat`, `less`). Given that you are using these commands so often, you want to be as efficient as possible—every keystroke counts.

Modern variations exist for some of these often-used commands. Some of them are drop-in replacements, and others extend the functionality. All of them offer somewhat sane default values for common operations and rich output that is generally easier to comprehend, and they usually lead to you typing less to accomplish the same task. This reduces the friction when you work with the shell, making it more enjoyable and improving the flow. If you want to learn more about modern tooling, check out Appendix B. In this context, a word of caution, especially if you're applying this knowledge in an enterprise environment: I have no stake in any of these tools and purely recommend them because I have found them useful myself. A good way to go about installing and using any of these tools is to use a version of the tool that has been vetted by your Linux distro of choice.

Listing directory contents with exa

Whenever you want to know what a directory contains, you use `ls` or one of its variants with parameters. For example, in bash I used to have `l` aliased to `ls -GAhltr`. But there's a better way: `exa` (*https://oreil.ly/5lPAl*), a modern replacement for `ls`, written in Rust, with built-in support for Git and tree rendering. In this context, what would you guess is the most often used command after you've listed the directory content? In my experience it's to clear the screen, and very often people use `clear`. That's typing five characters and then hitting ENTER. You can have the same effect much faster—simply use Ctrl+L.

Viewing file contents with bat

Let's assume that you listed a directory's contents and found a file you want to inspect. You'd use `cat`, maybe? There's something better I recommend you have a look at: `bat` (*https://oreil.ly/w3K76*). The `bat` command, shown in Figure 3-3, comes with syntax highlighting, shows nonprintable characters, supports Git, and has an integrated pager (the page-wise viewing of files longer than what can be displayed on the screen).

Finding content in files with rg

Traditionally, you would use `grep` to find something in a file. However, there's a modern command, `rg` (*https://oreil.ly/u3Sfw*), that is fast and powerful.

We're going to compare `rg` to a `find` and `grep` combination in this example, where we want to find YAML files that contain the string "sample":

```
$ find . -type f -name "*.yaml" -exec grep "sample" '{}' \; -print ❶
    app: sample
        app: sample
./app.yaml

$ rg -t "yaml" sample ❷
app.yaml
9:      app: sample
14:         app: sample
```

❶ Use `find` and `grep` together to find a string in YAML files.

❷ Use `rg` for the same task.

If you compare the commands and the results in the previous example, you see that not only is rg easier to use but the results are more informative (providing context, in this case the line number).

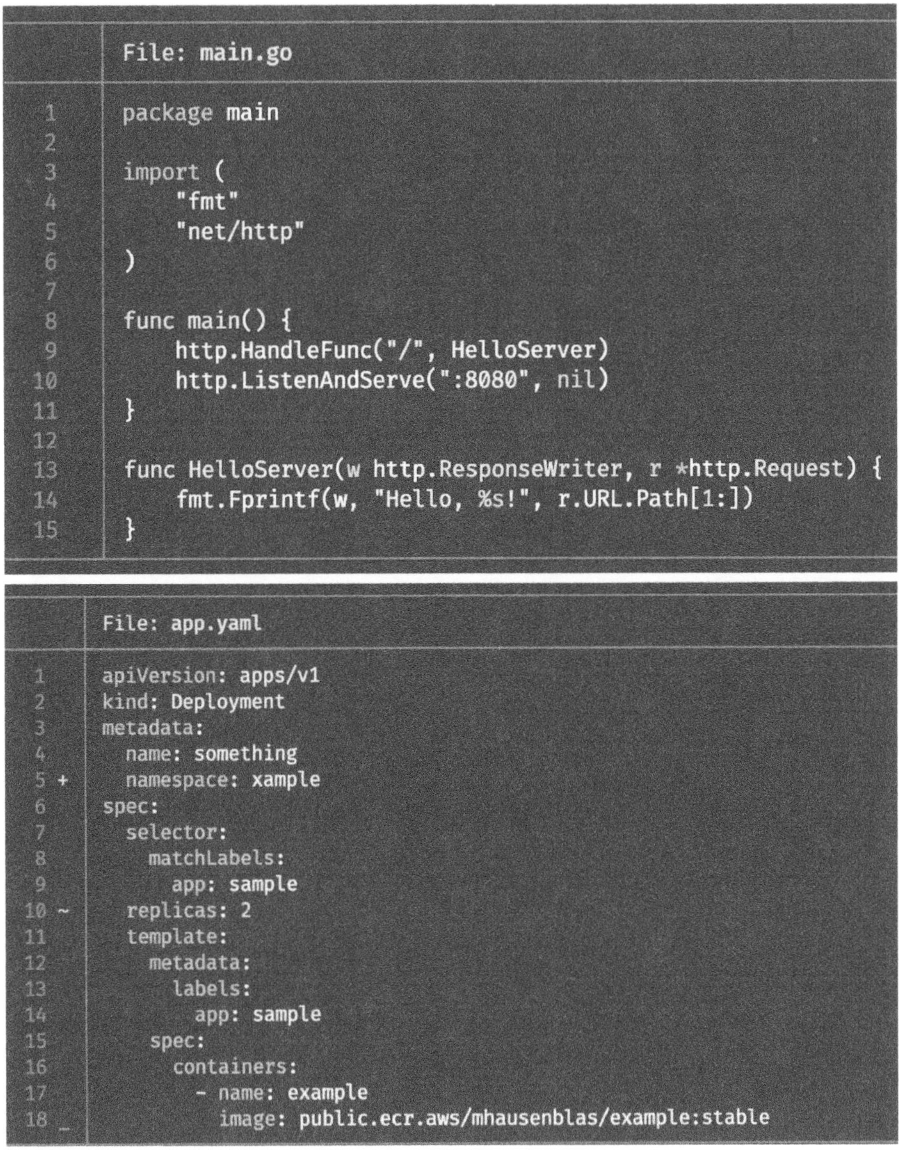

```
      File: main.go

  1   package main
  2
  3   import (
  4       "fmt"
  5       "net/http"
  6   )
  7
  8   func main() {
  9       http.HandleFunc("/", HelloServer)
 10       http.ListenAndServe(":8080", nil)
 11   }
 12
 13   func HelloServer(w http.ResponseWriter, r *http.Request) {
 14       fmt.Fprintf(w, "Hello, %s!", r.URL.Path[1:])
 15   }
```

```
      File: app.yaml

  1     apiVersion: apps/v1
  2     kind: Deployment
  3     metadata:
  4       name: something
  5 +     namespace: xample
  6     spec:
  7       selector:
  8         matchLabels:
  9           app: sample
 10 ~     replicas: 2
 11       template:
 12         metadata:
 13           labels:
 14             app: sample
 15         spec:
 16           containers:
 17             - name: example
 18               image: public.ecr.aws/mhausenblas/example:stable
```

Figure 3-3. Rendering of a Go file (top) and a YAML file (bottom) by bat

JSON data processing with jq

And now for a bonus command. This one, jq, is not an actual replacement but more like a specialized tool for JSON, a popular textual data format. You find JSON in HTTP APIs and configuration files alike.

So, use jq (*https://oreil.ly/9s7yh*) rather than awk or sed to pick out certain values. For example, by using a JSON generator (*https://oreil.ly/bcT9d*) to generate some random data, I have a 2.4 kB JSON file *example.json* that looks something like this (only showing the first record here):

```
[
  {
    "_id": "612297a64a057a3fa3a56fcf",
    "latitude": -25.750679,
    "longitude": 130.044327,
    "friends": [
      {
        "id": 0,
        "name": "Tara Holland"
      },
      {
        "id": 1,
        "name": "Giles Glover"
      },
      {
        "id": 2,
        "name": "Pennington Shannon"
      }
    ],
    "favoriteFruit": "strawberry"
  },
  ...
```

Let's say we're interested in all "first" friends—that is, entry 0 in the friends array—of people whose favorite fruit is "strawberry." With jq you would do the following:

```
$ jq 'select(.[].favoriteFruit=="strawberry") | .[].friends[0].name' example.json
"Tara Holland"
"Christy Mullins"
"Snider Thornton"
"Jana Clay"
"Wilma King"
```

That was some CLI fun, right? If you're interested in finding out more about the topic of modern commands and what other candidates there might be for you to replace, check out the modern-unix repo (*https://oreil.ly/cBAXt*), which lists suggestions. Let's now move our focus to some common tasks beyond directory navigation and file content viewing and how to go about them.

Common Tasks

There are a number of things you likely find yourself doing often, and there are certain tricks you can use to speed up your tasks in the shell. Let's review these common tasks and see how we can be more efficient.

Shorten often-used commands

One fundamental insight with interfaces is that commands that you are using very often should take the least effort—they should be quick to enter. Now apply this idea to the shell: rather than `git diff --color-moved`, I type d (a single character), since I'm viewing changes in my repositories many hundreds of times per day. Depending on the shell, there are different ways to achieve this: in bash this is called an *alias* (*https://oreil.ly/fbBvm*), and in Fish ("Fish Shell" on page 49) there are abbreviations (*https://oreil.ly/rrmNI*) you can use.

Navigating

When you enter commands on the shell prompt, there are a number of things you might want to do, such as navigating the line (for example, moving the cursor to the start) or manipulating the line (say, deleting everything left of the cursor). Table 3-2 lists common shell shortcuts.

Table 3-2. Shell navigation and editing shortcuts

Action	Command	Note
Move cursor to start of line	Ctrl+a	-
Move cursor to end of line	Ctrl+e	-
Move cursor forward one character	Ctrl+f	-
Move cursor back one character	Ctrl+b	-
Move cursor forward one word	Alt+f	Works only with left Alt
Move cursor back one word	Alt+b	-
Delete current character	Ctrl+d	-
Delete character left of cursor	Ctrl+h	-
Delete word left of cursor	Ctrl+w	-
Delete everything right of cursor	Ctrl+k	-
Delete everything left of cursor	Ctrl+u	-
Clear screen	Ctrl+l	-
Cancel command	Ctrl+c	-
Undo	Ctrl+_	bash only
Search history	Ctrl+r	Some shells
Cancel search	Ctrl+g	Some shells

Note that not all shortcuts may be supported in all shells, and certain actions such as history management may be implemented differently in certain shells. In addition, you might want to know that these shortcuts are based on Emacs editing keystrokes. Should you prefer vi, you can use set -o vi in your *.bashrc* file, for example, to perform command-line editing based on vi keystrokes. Finally, taking Table 3-2 as a starting point, try out what your shell supports and see how you can configure it to suit your needs.

File content management

You don't always want to fire up an editor such as vi to add a single line of text. And sometimes you can't do it—for example, in the context of writing a shell script ("Scripting" on page 62).

So, how can you manipulate textual content? Let's have a look at a few examples:

```
$ echo "First line" > /tmp/something ❶

$ cat /tmp/something ❷
First line

$ echo "Second line" >> /tmp/something && \ ❸
  cat /tmp/something
First line
Second line

$ sed 's/line/LINE/' /tmp/something ❹
First LINE
Second LINE

$ cat << 'EOF' > /tmp/another ❺
First line
Second line
Third line
EOF

$ diff -y /tmp/something /tmp/another ❻
First line                                          First line
Second line                                         Second line
                                                  > Third line
```

❶ Create a file by redirecting the echo output.

❷ View content of file.

❸ Append a line to file using the >> operator and then view content.

❹ Replace content from file using sed and output to stdout.

❺   Create a file using the here document (*https://oreil.ly/FPWqT*).

❻   Show differences between the files we created.

Now that you know the basic file content manipulation techniques, let's have a look at the advanced viewing of file contents.

Viewing long files

For long files—that is, files that have more lines than the shell can display on your screen—you can use pagers like `less` or `bat` (`bat` comes with a built-in pager). With paging, a program splits the output into pages where each page fits into what the screen can display and some commands to navigate the pages (view next page, previous page, etc.).

Another way to deal with long files is to display only a select region of the file, like the first few lines. There are two handy commands for this: `head` and `tail`.

For example, to display the beginning of a file:

```
$ for i in {1..100} ; do echo $i >> /tmp/longfile ; done ❶

$ head -5 /tmp/longfile ❷
1
2
3
4
5
```

❶   Create a long file (100 lines here).

❷   Display the first five lines of the long file.

Or, to get live updates of a file that is constantly growing, we could use:

```
$ sudo tail -f /var/log/Xorg.0.log ❶
[ 36065.898] (II) event14 - ALPS01:00 0911:5288 Mouse: device is a pointer
[ 36065.900] (II) event15 - ALPS01:00 0911:5288 Touchpad: device is a touchpad
[ 36065.901] (II) event4  - Intel HID events: is tagged by udev as: Keyboard
[ 36065.901] (II) event4  - Intel HID events: device is a keyboard
...
```

❶   Display the end of a log file using `tail`, with the `-f` option meaning to follow, or to update automatically.

Lastly, in this section we look at dealing with date and time.

Date and time handling

The `date` command can be a useful way to generate unique file names. It allows you to generate dates in various formats, including the Unix time stamp (*https://oreil.ly/ xB7UG*), as well as to convert between different date and time formats.

```
$ date +%s ❶
1629582883

$ date -d @1629742883 '+%m/%d/%Y:%H:%M:%S' ❷
08/21/2021:21:54:43
```

❶   Create a UNIX time stamp.

❷   Convert a UNIX time stamp to a human-readable date.

On the UNIX Epoch Time

The UNIX epoch time (or simply UNIX time) is the number of seconds elapsed since 1970-01-01T00:00:00Z. UNIX time treats every day as exactly 86,400 seconds long.

If you're dealing with software that stores UNIX time as a signed 32-bit integer, you might want to pay attention since this will cause issues on 2038-01-19, as then the counter will overflow, which is also known as the Year 2038 problem (*https://oreil.ly/ dKiWx*).

You can use online converters (*https://oreil.ly/Z1a4A*) for more advanced operations, supporting microseconds and milliseconds resolutions.

With that we wrap up the shell basics section. By now you should have a good understanding of what terminals and shells are and how to use them to do basic tasks such as navigating the filesystem, finding files, and more. We now move on to the topic of human-friendly shells.

Human-Friendly Shells

While the bash shell (*https://oreil.ly/9GNyA*) is likely still the most widely used shell, it is not necessarily the most human-friendly one. It has been around since the late 1980s, and its age sometimes shows. There are a number of modern, human-friendly shells I strongly recommend you evaluate and use instead of bash.

We'll first examine in detail one concrete example of a modern, human-friendly shell called the Fish shell and then briefly discuss others, just to make sure you have an idea about the range of choices. We wrap up this section with a quick recommendation and conclusion in "Which Shell Should I Use?" on page 55.

Fish Shell

The Fish shell (*https://fishshell.com/*) describes itself as a smart and user-friendly command-line shell. Let's have a look at some basic usage first and then move on to configuration topics.

Basic usage

For many daily tasks, you won't notice a big difference from bash in terms of input; most of the commands provided in Table 3-2 are valid. However, there are two areas where fish is different from and much more convenient than bash:

There is no explicit history management.
> You simply type and you get previous executions of a command shown. You can use the up and down key to select one (see Figure 3-4).

Autosuggestions are available for many commands.
> This is shown in Figure 3-5. In addition, when you press Tab, the Fish shell will try to complete the command, argument, or path, giving you visual hints such as coloring your input red if it doesn't recognize the command.

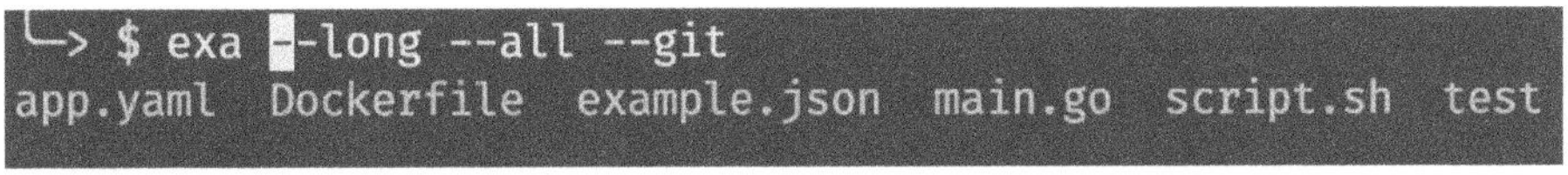

Figure 3-4. Fish history handling in action

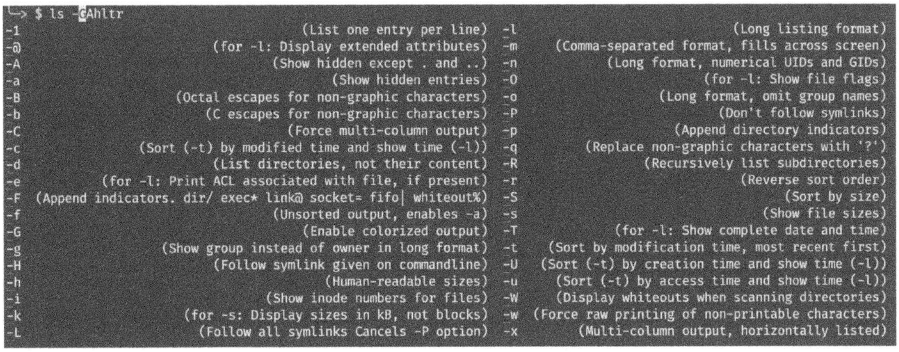

Figure 3-5. Fish autosuggestion in action

Table 3-3 lists some common `fish` commands. In this context, note specifically the handling of environment variables.

Table 3-3. Fish shell reference

Task	Command
Export environment variable KEY with value VAL	`set -x KEY VAL`
Delete environment variable KEY	`set -e KEY`
Inline env var KEY for command cmd	`env KEY=VAL cmd`
Change path length to 1	`set -g fish_prompt_pwd_dir_length 1`
Manage abbreviations	`abbr`
Manage functions	`functions` and `funcd`

Unlike other shells, `fish` stores the exit status of the last command in a variable called `$status` instead of in `$?`.

If you're coming from bash, you may also want to consult the Fish FAQ (*https://oreil.ly/Nk2S2*), which addresses most of the gotchas.

Configuration

To configure the Fish shell (*https://oreil.ly/FCSne*), you simply enter the `fish_config` command (you might need to add the `browse` subcommand, depending on your distro), and `fish` will launch a server via *http://localhost:8000* and automatically open your default browser with a fancy UI, shown in Figure 3-6, which allows you to view and change settings.

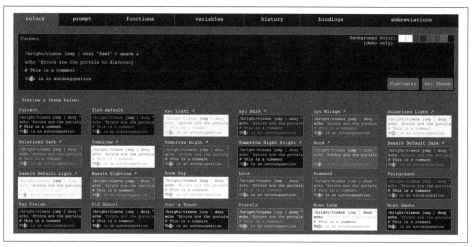

Figure 3-6. Fish shell configuration via browser

To switch between vi and Emacs (default) key bindings for command-line navigation, use the fish_vi_key_bindings to start vi mode, and use fish_default_key_bindings to reset it to Emacs. Note that the changes will take place in all active shell sessions immediately.

Let's now see how I have configured my environment. In fact, my config is rather short; in *config.fish* I have the following:

```
set -x FZF_DEFAULT_OPTS "-m --bind='ctrl-o:execute(nvim {})+abort'"
set -x FZF_DEFAULT_COMMAND 'rg --files'
set -x EDITOR nvim
set -x KUBE_EDITOR nvim
set -ga fish_user_paths /usr/local/bin
```

My prompt, defined in *fish_prompt.fish*, looks as follows:

```
function fish_prompt
    set -l retc red
    test $status = 0; and set retc blue

    set -q __fish_git_prompt_showupstream
    or set -g __fish_git_prompt_showupstream auto

    function _nim_prompt_wrapper
        set retc $argv[1]
        set field_name $argv[2]
        set field_value $argv[3]

        set_color normal
        set_color $retc
        echo -n '-'
        set_color -o blue
        echo -n '['
        set_color normal
        test -n $field_name
        and echo -n $field_name:
        set_color $retc
        echo -n $field_value
        set_color -o blue
        echo -n ']'
    end

    set_color $retc
    echo -n '┬─'
    set_color -o blue
    echo -n [
    set_color normal
    set_color c07933
    echo -n (prompt_pwd)
    set_color -o blue
    echo -n ']'
```

```
        # Virtual Environment
        set -q VIRTUAL_ENV_DISABLE_PROMPT
        or set -g VIRTUAL_ENV_DISABLE_PROMPT true
        set -q VIRTUAL_ENV
        and _nim_prompt_wrapper $retc V (basename "$VIRTUAL_ENV")

        # git
        set prompt_git (fish_git_prompt | string trim -c ' ()')
        test -n "$prompt_git"
        and _nim_prompt_wrapper $retc G $prompt_git

        # New line
        echo

        # Background jobs
        set_color normal
        for job in (jobs)
            set_color $retc
            echo -n '| '
            set_color brown
            echo $job
        end
        set_color blue
        echo -n ' ↳> '
            set_color -o blue
        echo -n '$ '
        set_color normal
    end
```

The preceding prompt definition yields the prompt shown in Figure 3-7; note the difference between a directory that contains a Git repo and one that does not, a built-in visual cue to speed up your flow. Also, notice the current time on the righthand side.

Figure 3-7. Fish shell prompt

My abbreviations—think of these as **alias** replacements, as found in other shells—look as follows:

```
$ abbr
abbr -a -U -- :q exit
abbr -a -U -- cat bat
abbr -a -U -- d 'git diff --color-moved'
abbr -a -U -- g git
abbr -a -U -- grep 'grep --color=auto'
abbr -a -U -- k kubectl
```

```
abbr -a -U -- l 'exa --long --all --git'
abbr -a -U -- ll 'ls -GAhltr'
abbr -a -U -- m make
abbr -a -U -- p 'git push'
abbr -a -U -- pu 'git pull'
abbr -a -U -- s 'git status'
abbr -a -U -- stat 'stat -x'
abbr -a -U -- vi nvim
abbr -a -U -- wget 'wget -c'
```

To add a new abbreviation, use `abbr --add`. Abbreviations are handy for simple commands that take no arguments. What if you have a more complicated construct you want to shorten? Say you want to shorten a sequence involving `git` that also takes an argument. Meet functions in Fish.

Let's now take a look at an example function, which is defined in the file named *c.fish*. We can use the `functions` command to list all defined functions, the `function` command to create a new function, and in this case the command `function c` to edit it as follows:

```
function c
    git add --all
    git commit -m "$argv"
end
```

With that we have reached the end of the Fish section, in which we walked through a usage tutorial and configuration tips. Now let's have a quick look at other modern shells.

Z-shell

Z-shell (*https://oreil.ly/6y06N*), or `zsh`, is a Bourne-like shell with a powerful completion (*https://oreil.ly/bqS8y*) system and rich theming support. With Oh My Zsh (*https://ohmyz.sh*), you can pretty much configure and use `zsh` in the way you've seen earlier on with `fish` while retaining wide backward compatibility with `bash`.

`zsh` uses five startup files, as shown in the following example (note that if `$ZDOTDIR` is not set, `zsh` uses `$HOME` instead):

```
$ZDOTDIR/.zshenv ❶
$ZDOTDIR/.zprofile ❷
$ZDOTDIR/.zshrc ❸
$ZDOTDIR/.zlogin ❹
$ZDOTDIR/.zlogout ❺
```

❶ Sourced on all invocations of the shell. It should contain commands to set the search path, plus other important environment variables. But it should not contain commands that produce output or assume the shell is attached to a `tty`.

❷ Meant as an alternative to *.zlogin* for `ksh` fans (these two are not intended to be used together); similar to *.zlogin*, except that it is sourced before *.zshrc*.

❸ Sourced in interactive shells. It should contain commands to set up aliases, functions, options, key bindings, and so on.

❹ Sourced in login shells. It should contain commands that should be executed only in login shells. Note that *.zlogin* is not the place for alias definitions, options, environment variable settings, and the like.

❺ Sourced when login shells exit.

For more `zsh` plug-ins, see also the awesome-zsh-plugins repo on GitHub (*https://oreil.ly/XHwBd*). If you want to learn `zsh`, consider reading "An Introduction to the Z Shell" (*https://oreil.ly/cMfnw*) by Paul Falstad and Bas de Bakker.

Other Modern Shells

In addition to `fish` and `zsh`, there are a number of other interesting—but not necessarily always bash-compatible—shells available out there. When you have a look at those, ask yourself what the focus of the respective shell is (interactive usage vs. scripting) and how active the community around it is.

Some examples of modern shells for Linux I came across and can recommend you have a look at include the following:

Oil shell (https://www.oilshell.org)
Targets Python and JavaScript users. Put in other words, the focus is less on interactive use but more on scripting.

murex (https://murex.rocks)
A POSIX shell that sports interesting features such as an integrated testing framework, typed pipelines, and event-driven programming.

Nushell (https://www.nushell.sh)
An experimental new shell paradigm, featuring tabular output with a powerful query language. Learn more via the detailed Nu Book (*https://oreil.ly/jIa5w*).

PowerShell (https://oreil.ly/bYKnd)
A cross-platform shell that started off as a fork of the Windows PowerShell and offers a different set of semantics and interactions than POSIX shells.

There are many more options out there. Keep looking and see what works best for you. Try thinking beyond bash and optimize for your use case.

Which Shell Should I Use?

At this point in time, every modern shell—other than bash—seems like a good choice, from a human-centric perspective. Smooth auto-complete, easy config, and smart environments are no luxury in 2022, and given the time you usually spend on the command line, you should try out different shells and pick the one you like most. I personally use the Fish shell, but many of my peers are super happy with the Z-shell.

You may have issues that make you hesitant to move away from bash, such as the following:

- You work in remote systems and/or cannot install your own shell.
- You've stayed with bash due to compatibility and/or muscle memory. It can be hard to get rid of certain habits.
- Almost all instructions (implicitly) assume bash. For example, you'll see instructions like `export FOO=BAR`, which is bash specific.

It turns out that these issues are by and large not relevant to most users. While you may have to temporarily use bash in a remote system, most of the time you will be working in an environment that you control. There is a learning curve, but the investment pays off in the long run.

With that, let's focus on another way to boost your productivity in the terminal: multiplexer.

Terminal Multiplexer

We came across terminals at the beginning of this chapter, in "Terminals" on page 33. Now let's dive deeper into the topic of how to improve your terminal usage, building on a concept that is both simple and powerful: multiplexing.

Think of it in this way: you usually work on different things that can be grouped together. For example, you may work on an open source project, author a blog post or docs, access a server remotely, interact with an HTTP API to test things, and so forth. These tasks may each require one or more terminal windows, and often you want or need to do potentially interdependent tasks in two windows at the same time. For example:

- You are using the `watch` command to periodically execute a directory listing and at the same time edit a file.
- You start a server process (a web server or application server) and want to have it running in the foreground (see also "Job control" on page 40) to keep an eye on the logs.

- You want to edit a file using `vi` and at the same time use `git` to query the status and commit changes.
- You have a VM running in the public cloud and want to `ssh` into it while having the possibility to manage files locally.

Think of all these examples as things that logically belong together and that in terms of time duration can range from short term (a few minutes) to long term (days and weeks). The grouping of those tasks is usually called a *session*.

Now, there are a number of challenges if you want to achieve this grouping:

- You need multiple windows, so one solution is to launch multiple terminals or, if the UI supports it, multiple instances (tabs).
- You would like to have all the windows and paths around, even if you close the terminal or the remote side closes down.
- You want to expand or zoom in and out to focus on certain tasks while keeping an overview of all your sessions and being able to navigate between them.

To enable these tasks, people came up with the idea of overlaying a terminal with multiple windows (and sessions, to group windows)—in other words, multiplexing the terminal I/O.

Let's have a brief look at the original implementation of terminal multiplexing, called `screen`. Then we'll focus in-depth on a widely used implement called `tmux` and wrap up with other options in this space.

screen

`screen` (*https://oreil.ly/xx3ik*) is the original terminal multiplexer and is still used. Unless you're in a remote environment where nothing else is available and/or you can't install another multiplexer, you should probably not be using `screen`. One reason is that it's not actively maintained anymore, and another is that it's not very flexible and lacks a number of features modern terminal multiplexers have.

tmux

`tmux` (*https://oreil.ly/kVg7M*) is a flexible and rich terminal multiplexer that you can bend to your needs. As you can see in Figure 3-8, there are three core elements you're interacting with in `tmux`, from coarse-grained to fine-grained units:

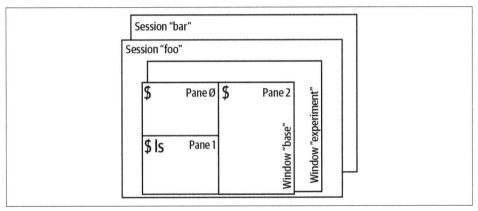

Figure 3-8. The tmux elements: sessions, windows, and panes

Sessions
> A logical unit that you can think of as a working environment dedicated to a specific task such as "working on project X" or "writing blog post Y." It's the container for all other units.

Windows
> You can think of a window as a tab in a browser, belonging to a session. It's optional to use, and often you only have one window per session.

Panes
> These are your workhorses, effectively a single shell instance running. A pane is part of a window, and you can easily split it vertically or horizontally, as well as expand/collapse it (think: zoom) and close panes as you need them.

Just like `screen`, in `tmux` you have the ability to attach and detach a session. Let's assume we start from scratch, let's launch it with a session called `test`:

```
$ tmux new -s test
```

With the preceding command, `tmux` is running as a server, and you find yourself in a shell you've configured in `tmux`, running as the client. This client/server model allows you to create, enter, leave, and destroy sessions and use the shells running in it without having to think of the processes running (or failing) in it.

`tmux` uses Ctrl+b as the default keyboard shortcut, also called *prefix* or *trigger*. So for example, to list all windows, you would press Ctrl+b and then w, or to expand the current (active) pane, you would use Ctrl+b and then z.

In tmux the default trigger is Ctrl+b. To improve the flow, I mapped the trigger to an unused key, so a single keystroke is sufficient. I did this by first mapping the trigger to the Home key in tmux and then mapping that Home key to the Caps Lock key by changing its mapping in */usr/share/X11/xkb/symbols/pc* to key <CAPS> { [Home] };.

This double-mapping was a workaround I needed to do. Depending on your target key or terminal, you might not have to do this, but I encourage you to map Ctrl+b to an unused key you can easily reach since you will press it many times a day.

You can now use any of the commands listed in Table 3-4 to manage further sessions, windows, and panes. Also, when pressing Ctrl+b+d, you can detach sessions. This means effectively that you put tmux into the background.

When you then start a new terminal instance or, say, you ssh to your machine from a remote place, you can then attach to an existing session, so let's do that with the test session we created earlier:

```
$ tmux attach -t test ❶
```

❶   Attach to existing session called test. Note that if you want to detach the session from its previous terminal, you would also supply the -d parameter.

Table 3-4 lists common tmux commands grouped by the units discussed, from widest scope (session) to narrowest (pane).

Table 3-4. tmux reference

Target	Task	Command
Session	Create new	:new -s NAME
Session	Rename	trigger + $
Session	List all	trigger + s
Session	Close	trigger
Window	Create new	trigger + c
Window	Rename	trigger + ,
Window	Switch to	trigger + 1 ... 9
Window	List all	trigger + w
Window	Close	trigger + &
Pane	Split horizontal	trigger + "
Pane	Split vertical	trigger + %
Pane	Toggle	trigger + z
Pane	Close	trigger + x

Now that you have a basic idea of how to use tmux, let's turn our attention to configuring and customizing it. My *.tmux.conf* looks as follows:

```
unbind C-b ❶
set -g prefix Home
bind Home send-prefix
bind r source-file ~/.tmux.conf \; display "tmux config reloaded :)" ❷
bind \\ split-window -h -c "#{pane_current_path}" ❸
bind - split-window -v -c "#{pane_current_path}"
bind X confirm-before kill-session ❹
set -s escape-time 1 ❺
set-option -g mouse on ❻
set -g default-terminal "screen-256color" ❼
set-option -g status-position top ❽
set -g status-bg colour103
set -g status-fg colour215
set -g status-right-length 120
set -g status-left-length 50
set -g window-status-style fg=colour215
set -g pane-active-border-style fg=colour215
set -g @plugin 'tmux-plugins/tmux-resurrect' ❾
set -g @plugin 'tmux-plugins/tmux-continuum'
set -g @continuum-restore 'on'
run '~/.tmux/plugins/tpm/tpm'
```

❶ This line and the next two lines change the trigger to Home.

❷ Reload config via trigger + r.

❸ This line and the next redefine pane splitting; retain current directory of existing pane.

❹ Adds shortcuts for new and kill sessions.

❺ No delays.

❻ Enable mouse selections.

❼ Set the default terminal mode to 256-color mode.

❽ Theme settings (next six lines).

❾ From here to the end: plug-in management.

First install tpm (*https://oreil.ly/hsoau*), the tmux plug-in manager, and then trigger + I for the plug-ins. The plug-ins used here are the following:

tmux-resurrect (https://oreil.ly/JugvE)
> Allows you to restore sessions with Ctrl+s (safe) and Ctrl+r (restore)

tmux-continuum (https://oreil.ly/KvT7l)
> Automatically saves/restores a session (15-minute interval)

Figure 3-9 shows my Alacritty terminal running `tmux`. You can see the sessions with the shortcuts 0 to 9, located in the left upper corner.

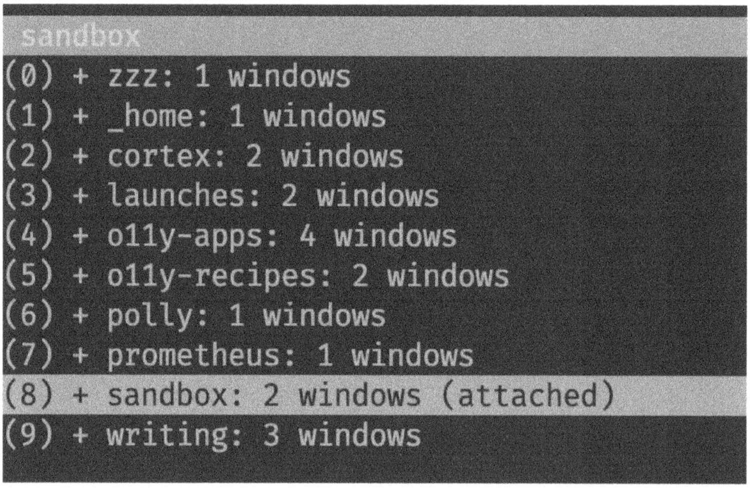

```
sandbox
(0) + zzz: 1 windows
(1) + _home: 1 windows
(2) + cortex: 2 windows
(3) + launches: 2 windows
(4) + o11y-apps: 4 windows
(5) + o11y-recipes: 2 windows
(6) + polly: 1 windows
(7) + prometheus: 1 windows
(8) + sandbox: 2 windows (attached)
(9) + writing: 3 windows
```

Figure 3-9. An example `tmux` instance in action, showing available sessions

While `tmux` certainly is an excellent choice, there are indeed other options than `tmux`, so let's have a peek.

Other Multiplexers

Other terminal multiplexers you can have a look at and try out include the following:

tmuxinator (https://oreil.ly/JyWmA)
> A meta-tool allowing you to manage `tmux` sessions

Byobu (https://oreil.ly/pJLa2)
> A wrapper around either `screen` or `tmux`; it's especially interesting if you're using the Ubuntu- or Debian-based Linux distros

Zellij (https://oreil.ly/ZRHnX)
> Calls itself a terminal workspace, is written in Rust, and goes beyond what `tmux` offers, including a layout engine and a powerful plug-in system

dvtm (https://oreil.ly/yaTan)
> Brings the concept of tiling window management to the terminal; it's powerful but has a learning curve like `tmux`

3mux (https://oreil.ly/S6nvV)
> A simple terminal multiplexer written in Go; it's easy to use but not as powerful as `tmux`

With this quick review of multiplexer options out of the way, let's talk about selecting one.

Bringing It All Together: Terminal, mux, and shell

I'm using Alacritty as my terminal. It's fast, and best of all, to configure it I'm using a YAML configuration file that I can version in Git, allowing me to use it on any target system in seconds. This config file called *alacritty.yml* defines all my settings for the terminal, from colors to key bindings to font sizes.

Most of the settings apply right away (hot-reload), others when I save the file. One setting, called `shell`, defines the integration between the terminal multiplexer I use (`tmux`) and the shell I use (`fish`) and looks as follows:

```
...
shell:
  program: /usr/local/bin/fish
  args:
  - -l
  - -i
  - -c
  - "tmux new-session -A -s zzz"
...
```

In the preceding snippet, I configure Alacritty to use `fish` as the default shell, but also, when I launch the terminal, it automatically attaches to a specific session. Together with the `tmux-continuum` plug-in, this gives me peace of mind. Even if I switch off the computer, once I restart I find my terminal with all its sessions, windows, and panes (almost) exactly in the state it was in before a crash, besides the shell variables.

Which Multiplexer Should I Use?

Unlike with shells for human users, I do have a concrete preference here in the context of terminal multiplexer: use `tmux`. The reasons are manifold: it is mature, stable, rich (has many available plug-ins), and flexible. Many folks are using it, so there's plenty of material out there to read up on as well as help available. The other multiplexers are exciting but relatively new or are, as is the case with `screen`, no longer in their prime.

With that, I hope I was able to convince you to consider using a terminal multiplexer to improve your terminal and shell experience, speed up your tasks, and make the overall flow smoother.

Now, we turn our attention to the last topic in this chapter, automating tasks with shell scripts.

Scripting

In the previous sections of this chapter, we focused on the manual, interactive usage of the shell. Once you've done a certain task over and over again manually on the prompt, it's likely time to automate the task. This is where scripts come in.

Here we focus on writing scripts in bash. This is due to two reasons:

- Most of the scripts out there are written in bash, and hence you will find a lot of examples and help available for bash scripts.
- The likelihood of finding bash available on a target system is high, making your potential user base bigger than if you used a (potentially more powerful but esoteric or not widely used) alternative to bash.

Just to provide you with some context before we start, there are shell scripts out there that clock in at several thousands (*https://oreil.ly/0oWzI*) of lines of code. Not that I encourage you to aim for this—quite the opposite: if you find yourself writing long scripts, ask yourself if a proper scripting language such as Python or Ruby is the better choice.

Let's step back now and develop a short but useful example, applying good practices along the way. Let's assume we want to automate the task of displaying a single statement on the screen that, given a user's GitHub handle, shows when the user joined, using their full name, something along the lines of the following:

```
XXXX XXXXX joined GitHub in YYYY
```

How do we go about automating this task with a script? Let's start with the basics, then review portability, and work our way up to the "business logic" of the script.

Scripting Basics

The good news is that by interactively using a shell, you already know most of the relevant terms and techniques. In addition to variables, streams and redirection, and common commands, there are a few specific things you want to be familiar with in the context of scripts, so let's review them.

Advanced data types

While shells usually treat everything as strings (if you want to perform some more complicated numerical tasks, you should probably not use a shell script), they do support some advanced data types such as arrays.

Let's have a look at arrays in action:

```
os=('Linux' 'macOS' 'Windows') ❶
echo "${os[0]}" ❷
numberofos="${#os[@]}" ❸
```

❶ Define an array with three elements.

❷ Access the first element; this would print Linux.

❸ Get the length of the array, resulting in numberofos being 3.

Flow control

Flow control allows you to branch (if) or repeat (for and while) in your script, making the execution dependent on a certain condition.

Some usage examples of flow control:

```
for afile in /tmp/* ; do ❶
  echo "$afile"
done

for i in {1..10}; do ❷
    echo "$i"
done

while true; do ❸
  ...
done ❸
```

❶ Basic loop iterating over a directory, printing each file name

❷ Range loop

❸ Forever loop; break out with Ctrl+C

Functions

Functions allow you to write more modular and reusable scripts. You have to define the function before you use it since the shell interprets the script from top to bottom.

A simple function example:

```
sayhi() { ❶
    echo "Hi $1 hope you are well!"
}

sayhi "Michael" ❷
```

❶ Function definition; parameters implicitly passed via $n

❷ Function invocation; the output is "Hi Michael hope you are well!"

Advanced I/O

With `read` you can read user input from `stdin` that you can use to elicit runtime input—for example, with a menu of options. Further, rather than using `echo`, consider `printf`, which allows you fine-grained control over the output, including colors. `printf` is also more portable than `echo`.

Following is an example usage of the advanced I/O in action:

```
read name ❶
printf "Hello %s" "$name" ❷
```

❶ Read value from user input.

❷ Output value read in the previous step.

There are other, more advanced concepts available for you, such as signals and traps (*https://oreil.ly/JsV1v*). Given that we want to provide only an overview and introduction to the scripting topic here, I will refer you to the excellent bash Scripting Cheatsheet (*https://oreil.ly/nVjhN*) for a comprehensive reference of all the relevant constructs. If you are serious about writing shell scripts, I recommend you read *bash Cookbook* by Carl Albing, JP Vossen, and Cameron Newham, which contains lots and lots of great snippets you can use as a starting point.

Writing Portable bash Scripts

We'll now look at what it means to write portable scripts in bash. But wait. What does *portable* mean, and why should you care?

At the beginning of "Shells" on page 33, we defined what *POSIX* means, so let's build on that. When I say "portable," I mean that we are not making too many assumptions—implicitly or explicitly—about the environment a script will be executed in. If a script is portable, it runs on many different systems (shells, Linux distros, etc.).

But remember that, even if you pin down the type of shell, in our case to bash, not all features work the same way across different versions of a shell. At the end of the day, it boils down to the number of different environments you can test your script in.

Executing portable scripts

How are scripts executed? First, let's state that scripts really are simply text files; the extension doesn't matter, although often you find *.sh* used as a convention. But there are two things that turn a text file into a script that is executable and able to be run by the shell:

- The text file needs to declare the interpreter in the first line, using what is called *shebang* (*https://oreil.ly/88BcE*) (or *hashbang*), which is written as #! (see also the first line of the template that follows).

- Then, you need to make the script executable using, for example, chmod +x, which allows everyone to run it, or, even better, chmod 750, which is more along the lines of the least privileges principle, as it allows only the user and group associated with the script to run it. We'll dive deep into this topic in Chapter 4.

Now that you know the basics, let's have a look at a concrete template we can use as a starting point.

A skeleton template

A skeleton template for a portable bash shell script that you can use as a seed looks as follows:

```
#!/usr/bin/env bash ❶
set -o errexit ❷
set -o nounset ❸
set -o pipefail ❹

firstargument="${1:-somedefaultvalue}" ❺

echo "$firstargument"
```

❶ The hashbang (*https://oreil.ly/l6xNO*) instructs the program loader that we want it to use bash to interpret this script.

❷ Define that we want to stop the script execution if an error happens.

❸ Define that we treat unset variables as an error (so the script is less likely to fail silently).

❹ Define that when one part of a pipe fails, the whole pipe should be considered failed. This helps to avoid silent failures.

❺ An example command-line parameter with a default value.

We will use this template later in this section to implement our GitHub info script.

Good practices

I'm using *good* practices instead of *best* practices because what you should do depends on the situation and how far you want to go. There is a difference between a script you write for yourself and one that you ship to thousands of users, but in general, high-level good practices writing scripts are as follows:

Fail fast and loud
> Avoid silent fails, and fail fast; things like `errexit` and `pipefail` do that for you. Since bash tends to fail silently by default, failing fast is almost always a good idea.

Sensitive information
> Don't hardcode any sensitive information such as passwords into the script. Such information should be provided at runtime, via user input or calling out to an API. Also, consider that a `ps` reveals program parameters and more, which is another way that sensitive information can be leaked.

Input sanitization
> Set and provide sane defaults for variables where possible, and sanitize the input you receive from users or other sources. For example, launch parameters provided or interactively ingested via the `read` command to avoid situations where an innocent-looking `rm -rf "$PROJECTHOME/"*` wipes your drive because the variable wasn't set.

Check dependencies
> Don't assume that a certain tool or command is available, unless it's a build-in or you know your target environment. Just because your machine has `curl` installed doesn't mean the target machine has. If possible, provide fallbacks—for example, if no `curl` is available, use `wget`.

Error handling
> When your script fails (and it's not a matter of if but when and where), provide actionable instructions for your users. For example, rather than `Error 123`, say what has failed and how your user can fix the situation, such as `Tried to write to /project/xyz/ but seems this is read-only for me`.

Documentation
> Document your scripts inline (using `# Some doc here`) for main blocks, and try to stick to 80-column width for readability and diffing.

Versioning
> Consider versioning your scripts using Git.

Testing

Lint and *test* the scripts. Since this is such an important practice, we will discuss it in greater detail in the next section.

Let's now move on to making scripts safe(r) by linting them while developing and testing them before you distribute them.

Linting and Testing Scripts

While you're developing, you want to check and lint your scripts, making sure that you're using commands and instructions correctly. There's a nice way to do that, depicted in Figure 3-10, with the program ShellCheck (*https://oreil.ly/Z3blD*); you can download and install it locally, or you can also use the online version via *shell check.net*. Also, consider formatting your script with shfmt (*https://oreil.ly/obaKQ*). It automatically fixes issues that can be reported later by shellcheck.

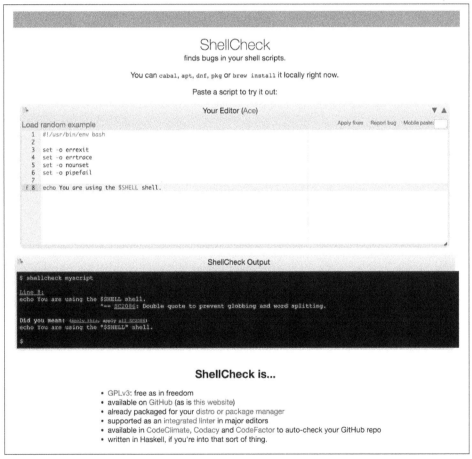

Figure 3-10. A screenshot of the online ShellCheck tool

And further, before you check your script into a repo, consider using bats to test it. bats (*https://oreil.ly/uVNgh*), short for Bash Automated Testing System, allows you to define test files as a bash script with special syntax for test cases. Each test case is simply a bash function with a description, and you would typically invoke these scripts as part of a CI pipeline—for example, as a GitHub action.

Now we'll put our good practices for script writing, linting, and testing into use. Let's implement the example script we specified in the beginning of this section.

End-to-End Example: GitHub User Info Script

In this end-to-end example, we bring all of the preceding tips and tooling together to implement our example script that is supposed to take a GitHub user handle and print out a message that contains what year the user joined, along with their full name.

This is how one implementation looks, taking the good practices into account. Store the following in a file called *gh-user-info.sh*, and make it executable:

```
#!/usr/bin/env bash

set -o errexit
set -o errtrace
set -o nounset
set -o pipefail

### Command line parameter:
targetuser="${1:-mhausenblas}" ❶

### Check if our dependencies are met:
if ! [ -x "$(command -v jq)" ]
then
  echo "jq is not installed" >&2
  exit 1
fi

### Main:
githubapi="https://api.github.com/users/"
tmpuserdump="/tmp/ghuserdump_$targetuser.json"

result=$(curl -s $githubapi$targetuser) ❷
echo $result > $tmpuserdump

name=$(jq .name $tmpuserdump -r) ❸
created_at=$(jq .created_at $tmpuserdump -r)

joinyear=$(echo $created_at | cut -f1 -d"-") ❹
echo $name joined GitHub in $joinyear ❺
```

❶ Provide a default value to use if user doesn't supply one.

❷ Using `curl`, access the GitHub API (*https://oreil.ly/A7CLS*) to download the user information as a JSON file, and store it in a temporary file (next line).

❸ Using `jq`, pull out the fields we need. Note that the `created_at` field has a value that looks something like `"2009-02-07T16:07:32Z"`.

❹ Using `cut`, extract the year from the `created_at` field in the JSON file.

❺ Assemble the output message and print to screen.

Now let's run it with the defaults:

```
$ ./gh-user-info.sh
Michael Hausenblas joined GitHub in 2009
```

Congratulations, you now have everything at your disposal to use the shell, both interactively on the prompt and for scripting. Before we wrap up, take a moment to think about the following concerning our *gh-user-info.sh* script:

- What if the JSON blob the GitHub API returns is not valid? What if we encounter a 500 HTTP error? Maybe adding a message along the lines of "try later" is more useful if there's nothing the user can do themselves.

- For the script to work, you need network access, otherwise the `curl` call will fail. What could you do about a lack of network access? Informing the user about it and suggesting what they can do to check networking may be an option.

- Think about improvements around dependency checks—for example, we implicitly assume here that `curl` is installed. Can you maybe add a check that makes the binary variable and falls back to `wget`?

- How about adding some usage help? If the script is called with an `-h` or `--help` parameter, perhaps show a concrete usage example and the options that users can use to influence the execution (ideally, including defining default values used).

You see now that, although this script looks good and works in most cases, there's always something you can improve, such as making the script more robust and providing actionable error messages. In this context, consider using frameworks such as bashing (*https://oreil.ly/gLmlB*), rerun (*https://oreil.ly/t8U9u*), or rr (*https://oreil.ly/7F2lT*) to improve modularity.

Conclusion

In this chapter, we focused on working with Linux in the terminal, a textual user interface. We discussed shell terminology, provided a hands-on introduction to using the shell basics, and reviewed common tasks and how you can improve your shell productivity using modern variants of certain commands (such as `exa` rather than `ls`).

Then, we looked at modern, human-friendly shells, specifically at `fish`, and how to configure and use them. Further, we covered the terminal multiplexer by using `tmux` as the hands-on example, enabling you to work with multiple local or remote sessions. Using modern shells and multiplexers can dramatically improve your efficiency on the command line, and I strongly recommend you consider adopting them.

Lastly, we discussed automating tasks by writing safe and portable shell scripts, including linting and testing said scripts. Remember that shells are effectively command interpreters, and as with any kind of language, you have to practice to get fluent. Having said this, now that you're equipped with the basics of using Linux from the command line, you can already work with the majority of Linux-based systems out there, be it an embedded system or a cloud VM. In any case, you'll find a way to get hold of a terminal and issue commands interactively or via executing scripts.

If you want to dive deeper into the topics discussed in this chapter, here are some additional resources:

Terminals
- "Anatomy of a Terminal Emulator" (*https://oreil.ly/u2CFr*)
- "The TTY Demystified" (*https://oreil.ly/8GT6s*)
- "The Terminal, the Console and the Shell—What Are They?" (*https://oreil.ly/vyVAV*)
- "What Is a TTY on Linux? (and How to Use the tty Command)" (*https://oreil.ly/E0EGG*)
- "Your Terminal Is Not a Terminal: An Introduction to Streams" (*https://oreil.ly/xIEoZ*)

Shells
- "Unix Shells: bash, Fish, ksh, tcsh, zsh" (*https://oreil.ly/4pepC*)
- "Comparison of Command Shells" (*https://oreil.ly/RQfS6*)
- "bash vs zsh" thread on reddit (*https://oreil.ly/kseEe*)
- "Ghost in the Shell—Part 7—ZSH Setup" (*https://oreil.ly/1KGz6*)

Terminal multiplexer
- "A tmux Crash Course" (*https://oreil.ly/soqPv*)
- "A Quick and Easy Guide to tmux" (*https://oreil.ly/0hVCS*)
- "How to Use tmux on Linux (and Why It's Better Than screen)" (*https://oreil.ly/Q75TR*)
- *The Tao of tmux* (*https://oreil.ly/QDsYI*)
- *tmux 2: Productive Mouse-Free Development* (*https://oreil.ly/eO9y2*)
- Tmux Cheat Sheet & Quick Reference website (*https://oreil.ly/SWCa5*)

Shell scripts
- "Shell Style Guide" (*https://oreil.ly/3cxAw*)
- "bash Style Guide" (*https://oreil.ly/zfy1v*)
- "bash Best Practices" (*https://oreil.ly/eC1ol*)
- "bash Scripting Cheatsheet" (*https://oreil.ly/nVroM*)
- "Writing bash Scripts That Are Not Only bash: Checking for bashisms and Testing with Dash" (*https://oreil.ly/D0zwe*)

With the shell basics at our disposal, we now turn our focus to access control and enforcement in Linux.

## CHAPTER 4

Access Control

After the wide scope in the previous chapter on all things shell and scripting, we now focus on one specific and crucial security aspect in Linux. In this chapter, we discuss the topic of users and controlling access to resources in general and files in particular.

One question that immediately comes to mind in such a multiuser setup is ownership. A user may own, for example, a file. They are allowed to read from the file, write to the file, and also, say, delete it. Given that there are other users on the system as well, what are those users allowed to do, and how is this defined and enforced? There are also activities that you might not necessarily associate with files in the first place. For example, a user may (or may not) be allowed to change networking-related settings.

To get a handle on this topic, we'll first take a look at the fundamental relationship between users, processes, and files, from an access perspective. We'll also review sandboxing and access control types. Next, we'll focus on the definition of a Linux user, what users can do, and how to manage users either locally or alternatively from a central place.

Then, we'll move on to the topic of permissions, where we'll look at how to control access to files and how processes are impacted by such restrictions.

We'll wrap up this chapter covering a range of advanced Linux features in the access control space, including capabilities, seccomp profiles, and ACLs. To round things off, we'll provide some security good practices around permissions and access control.

With that, let's jump right into the topic of users and resource ownership, laying the basis for the rest of the chapter.

Basics

Before we get into access control mechanisms, let's step back a little and take a bird's-eye view on the topic. This will help us to establish some terminology and clarify relationships between the main concepts.

Resources and Ownership

Linux is a multiuser operating system and as such has inherited the concept of a user (see "Users" on page 76) from UNIX. Each user account is associated with a user ID that can be given access to executables, files, devices, and other Linux assets. A human user can log in with a user account, and a process can run as a user account. Then, there are resources (which we will simply refer to as *files*), which are any hardware or software components available to the user. In the general case, we will refer to resources as files, unless we explicitly talk about access to other kinds of resources, such as with syscalls. In Figure 4-1 and the passage that follows, you see the high-level relationships between users, processes, and files in Linux.

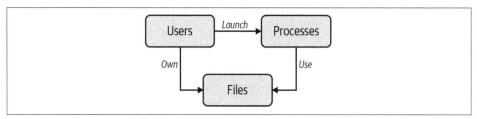

Figure 4-1. Users, processes, and files in Linux

Users
> Launch processes and own files. A *process* is a program (executable file) that the kernel has loaded into main memory and runs.

Files
> Have owners; by default, the user who creates the file owns it.

Processes
> Use files for communication and persistency. Of course, users indirectly also use files, but they need to do so via processes.

This depiction of the relationships between users, processes, and files is of course a very simplistic view, but it allows us to understand the actors and their relationships and will come in handy later on when we discuss the interaction between these different players in greater detail.

Let's first look at the execution context of a process, addressing the question of how restricted the process is. A term that we often come across when talking about access to resources is *sandboxing*.

Sandboxing

Sandboxing is a vaguely defined term and can refer to a range of different methods, from jails to containers to virtual machines, which can be managed either in the kernel or in user land. Usually there is something that runs in the sandbox—typically some application—and the supervising mechanism enforces a certain degree of isolation between the sandboxed process and the hosting environment. If all of that sounds rather theoretical, I ask you for a little bit of patience. We will see sandboxing in action later in this chapter, in "seccomp Profiles" on page 89, and then again in Chapter 9 when we talk about VMs and containers.

With a basic understanding of resources, ownership, and access to said resources in your mind, let's talk briefly about some conceptual ways to go about access control.

Types of Access Control

One aspect of access control is the nature of the access itself. Does a user or process directly access a resource, maybe in an unrestricted manner? Or maybe there is a clear set of rules about what kind of resources (files or syscalls) a process can access, under what circumstances. Or maybe the access itself is even recorded.

Conceptually, there are different access control types. The two most important and relevant to our discussion in the context of Linux are *discretionary* and *mandatory* access control:

Discretionary access control
> With discretionary access control (DAC), the idea is to restrict access to resources based on the identity of the user. It's discretionary in the sense that a user with certain permissions can pass them on to other users.

Mandatory access control
> Mandatory access control is based on a hierarchical model representing security levels. Users are assigned a clearance level, and resources are assigned a security label. Users can only access resources corresponding to a clearance level equal to (or lower than) their own. In a mandatory access control model, an admin strictly and exclusively controls access, setting all permissions. In other words, users cannot set permissions themselves, even when they own the resource.

In addition, Linux traditionally has an all-or-nothing attitude—that is, you are either a superuser who has the power to change everything or you are a normal user with limited access. Initially, there was no easy and flexible way to assign a user or process certain privileges. For example, in the general case, to enable that "process X is allowed to change networking settings," you had to give it `root` access. This, naturally, has a concrete impact on a system that is breached: an attacker can misuse these wide privileges easily.

To qualify the "all-or-nothing attitude" in Linux a bit: the defaults in most Linux systems allow read access to almost every file and executable by "others"—that is, all users on the system. For example, with SELinux enabled, mandatory access control restricts access to only those assets that are explicitly given permission. So, for example, a web server can only use ports 80 and 443, only share files and scripts from specific directories, only write logs to specific places, and so on.

We'll revisit this topic in "Advanced Permission Management" on page 87 and see how modern Linux features can help overcome this binary worldview, allowing for more fine-grained management of privileges.

Probably the best-known implementation of mandatory access control for Linux is SELinux (*https://oreil.ly/HAOBS*). It was developed to meet the high security requirements of government agencies and is usually used in these environments since the usability suffers from the strict rules. Another option for mandatory access control, included in the Linux kernel since version 2.6.36 and rather popular in the Ubuntu family of Linux distributions, is AppArmor (*https://oreil.ly/rp4Fq*).

Let's now move on to the topic of users and how to manage them in Linux.

Users

In Linux we often distinguish between two types of user accounts, from a purpose or intended usage point of view:

So-called system users, or system accounts
   Typically, programs (sometimes called *daemons*) use these types of accounts to run background processes. The services provided by these programs can be part of the operating system, such as networking (`sshd`, for example), or on the application layer (for example, `mysql`, in the case of a popular relational database).

Regular users
   For example, a human user that interactively uses Linux via the shell.

The distinction between system and regular users is less of a technical one and more an organizational construct. To understand that, we first have to introduce the concept of a user ID (UID), a 32-bit numerical value managed by Linux.

Linux identifies users via a UID, with a user belonging to one or more groups identified via a group ID (GID). There is a special kind of user with the UID 0, usually called `root`. This "superuser" is allowed to do anything, that is, no restriction apply. Usually, you want to avoid working as the `root` user, because it's just too much power to have. You can easily destroy a system if you're not careful (believe me, I've done this). We'll get back to this later in the chapter.

Different Linux distributions have their own ways to decide how to manage the UID range. For example, `systemd`-powered distributions (see "systemd" on page 119), have the following convention (*https://oreil.ly/c0DuO*) (simplified here):

UID 0
    Is `root`

UID 1 to 999
    Are reserved for system users

UID 65534
    Is user `nobody`—used, for example, for mapping remote users to some well-known ID, as is the case with "Network File System" on page 181

UID 1000 to 65533 and 65536 to 4294967294
    Are regular users

To figure out your own UIDs, you can use the (surprise!) `id` command like so:

```
$ id -u
2016796723
```

Now that you know the basics about Linux users, let's see how you can manage users.

Managing Users Locally

The first option, and traditionally the only one available, is managing users locally. That is, only information local to the machine is used, and user-related information is not shared across a network of machines.

For local user management, Linux uses a simple file-based interface with a somewhat confusing naming scheme that is a historic artifact we have to live with, unfortunately. Table 4-1 lists the four files that, together, implement user management.

Table 4-1. Reference of local user management files

Purpose	File
User database	/etc/passwd
Group database	/etc/group
User passwords	/etc/shadow
Group passwords	/etc/gshadow

Think of */etc/passwd* as a kind of mini user database keeping track of user names, UIDs, group membership, and other data, such as home directory and login shell used, for regular users. Let's have a look at a concrete example:

```
$ cat /etc/passwd
root:x:0:0:root:/root:/bin/bash ❶
```

```
daemon:x:1:1:daemon:/usr/sbin:/usr/sbin/nologin ❷
bin:x:2:2:bin:/bin:/usr/sbin/nologin
sys:x:3:3:sys:/dev:/usr/sbin/nologin
nobody:x:65534:65534:nobody:/nonexistent:/usr/sbin/nologin
syslog:x:104:110::/home/syslog:/usr/sbin/nologin
mh9:x:1000:1001::/home/mh9:/usr/bin/fish ❸
```

❶ The root user has UID 0.

❷ A system account (the nologin gives it away; see more below).

❸ My user account.

Let's have a closer look at one of the lines in */etc/passwd* to understand the structure of a user entry in detail:

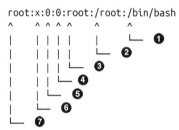

❶ The login shell to use. To prevent interactive logins, use */sbin/nologin*.

❷ The user's home directory; this defaults to /.

❸ User information such as full name or contact data like phone number. Often also known as GECOS (*https://oreil.ly/ZWQ0f*) field. Note that GECOS formatting is not used, but rather the field itself is used typically for the full name of the person associated with the account.

❹ The user's primary group (GID); see also */etc/group*.

❺ The UID. Note that Linux reserves UIDs below 1000 for system usage.

❻ The user's password, with the x character meaning that the (encrypted) password is stored in */etc/shadow*, which is the default these days.

❼ The username, which must be 32 characters or fewer.

One thing we notice is absent in */etc/passwd* is the one thing we would expect to find there, based on its name: the password. Passwords are, for historic reasons, stored in a file called */etc/shadow*. While every user can read */etc/passwd*, you usually need root privileges to read for */etc/shadow*.

To add a user, you can use the adduser (*https://oreil.ly/HQVZK*) command as follows:

```
$ sudo adduser mh9
Adding user `mh9' ...
Adding new group `mh9' (1001) ...
Adding new user `mh9' (1000) with group `mh9' ...
Creating home directory `/home/mh9' ... ❶
Copying files from `/etc/skel' ... ❷
New password: ❸
Retype new password:
passwd: password updated successfully
Changing the user information for mh9
Enter the new value, or press ENTER for the default ❹
        Full Name []: Michael Hausenblas
        Room Number []:
        Work Phone []:
        Home Phone []:
        Other []:
Is the information correct? [Y/n] Y
```

❶ The adduser command creates a home directory.

❷ It also copies a bunch of default config files into the home directory.

❸ Need to define a password.

❹ Provide optional GECOS information.

If you want to create a system account, pass in the -r option. This will disable the ability to use a login shell and also avoid home directory creation. For configuration details, see also */etc/adduser.conf*, including options such as the UID/GID range to be used.

In addition to users, Linux also has the concept of groups, which in a sense is just a collection of one or more users. Any regular user belongs to one default group but can be a member of additional groups. You can find out about groups and mappings via the */etc/group* file:

```
$ cat /etc/group ❶
root:x:0:
daemon:x:1:
bin:x:2:
sys:x:3:
adm:x:4:syslog
...
ssh:x:114:
landscape:x:115:
admin:x:116:
netdev:x:117:
lxd:x:118:
```

```
systemd-coredump:x:999:
mh9:x:1001:  ❷
```

❶ Display the content of the group mapping file.

❷ An example group of my user with the GID 1001. Note that you can add a comma-separated list of user names after the last colon to allow multiple users to have that group permission.

With this basic user concept and management under our belt, we move on to a potentially better way to manage users in a professional setup, allowing for scale.

Centralized User Management

If you have more than one machine or server for which you have to manage users—say, in a professional setup—then managing users locally quickly becomes old. You want a centralized way to manage users that you can apply locally, to one specific machine. There are a few approaches available to you, depending on your requirements and (time) budget:

Directory based
Lightweight Directory Access Protocol (LDAP) (*https://oreil.ly/Ll5AU*), a decades-old suite of protocols now formalized by IETF, defines how to access and maintain a distributed directory over Internet Protocol (IP). You can run an LDAP server yourself—for example, using projects like Keycloak (*https://oreil.ly/j6qm2*)—or outsource this to a cloud provider, such as Azure Active Directory.

Via a network
Users can be authenticated in this manner with Kerberos. We'll look at Kerberos in detail in "Kerberos" on page 222.

Using config management systems
These systems, which include Ansible, Chef, Puppet, or SaltStack, can be used to consistently create users across machines.

The actual implementation is often dictated by the environment. That is, a company might already be using LDAP, and hence the choices might be limited. The details of the different approaches and pros and cons are, however, beyond the scope of this book.

Permissions

In this section, we first go into detail concerning Linux file permissions, which are central to how access control works, and then we look at permissions around processes. That is, we review runtime permissions and how they are derived from file permissions.

File Permissions

File permissions are core to Linux's concept of access to resources, since everything is a file in Linux, more or less. Let's first review some terminology and then discuss the representation of the metadata around file access and permissions in detail.

There are three types or scopes of permissions, from narrow to wide:

User
> The owner of the file

Group
> Has one or more members

Other
> The category for everyone else

Further, there are three types of access:

Read (r)
> For a normal file, this allows a user to view the contents of the file. For a directory, it allows a user to view the names of files in the directory.

Write (w)
> For a normal file, this allows a user to modify and delete the file. For a directory, it allows a user to create, rename, and delete files in the directory.

Execute (x)
> For a normal file, this allows a user to execute the file if the user also has read permissions on it. For a directory, it allows a user to access file information in the directory, effectively permitting them to change into it (cd) or list its content (ls).

Other File Access Bits

I listed r/w/x as the three file access types, but in practice you will find others as well when you do an ls:

- s is the setuid/setgid permission applied to an executable file. A user running it inherits the effective privileges of the owner or group of the file.

- t is the sticky bit, which is only relevant for directories. If set, it prevents nonroot users from deleting files in it, unless said user owns the directory/file.

There are also special settings in Linux available via the chattr (change attribute) command, but this is beyond the scope of this chapter.

Let's see file permissions in action (note that the spaces you see here in the output of the ls command have been expanded for better readability):

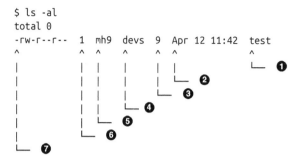

```
$ ls -al
total 0
-rw-r--r-- 1 mh9 devs 9 Apr 12 11:42 test
```

❶ File name

❷ Last modified time stamp

❸ File size in bytes

❹ Group the file belongs to

❺ File owner

❻ Number of hard links (*https://oreil.ly/9Gfzu*)

❼ File mode

When zooming in on the *file mode*—that is, the file type and permissions referred to as ❼ in the preceding snippet—we have fields with the following meaning:

```
. rwx rwx rwx
```

❶ Permissions for others

❷ Permissions for the group

❸ Permissions for the file owner

❹ The file type (Table 4-2)

The first field in the file mode represents the file type; see Table 4-2 for details. The remainder of the file mode encodes the permissions set for various targets, from owner to everyone, as listed in Table 4-3.

Table 4-2. File types used in mode

Symbol	Semantics
-	A regular file (such as when you do `touch abc`)
b	Block special file
c	Character special file
C	High-performance (contiguous data) file
d	A directory
l	A symbolic link
p	A named pipe (create with `mkfifo`)
s	A socket
?	Some other (unknown) file type

There are some other (older or obsolete) characters such as M or P used in the position 0, which you can by and large ignore. If you're interested in what they mean, run `info ls -n "What information is listed"`.

In combination, these permissions in the file mode define what is allowed for each element of the target set (user, group, everyone else), as shown in Table 4-3, checked and enforced through access (*https://oreil.ly/wwLsV*).

Table 4-3. File permissions

Pattern	Effective permission	Decimal representation
---	None	0
--x	Execute	1
-w-	Write	2
-wx	Write and execute	3
r--	Read	4
r-x	Read and execute	5
rw-	Read and write	6
rwx	Read, write, execute	7

Let's have a look at a few examples:

755

Full access for its owner; read and execute for everyone else

700

Full access by its owner; none for everyone else

664

Read/write access for owner and group; read-only for others

644

Read/write for owner; read-only for everyone else

400

Read-only by its owner

The 664 has a special meaning on my system. When I create a file, that's the default permission it gets assigned. You can check that with the umask command (*https:// oreil.ly/H9ksX*), which in my case gives me 0002.

The setuid permissions are used to tell the system to run an executable as the owner, with the owner's permissions. If a file is owned by root, that can cause issues.

You can change the permissions of a file using chmod. Either you specify the desired permission settings explicitly (such as 644) or you use shortcuts (for example, +x to make it executable). But how does that look in practice?

Let's make a file executable with chmod:

```
$ ls -al /tmp/masktest
-rw-r--r-- 1 mh9 dev 0 Aug 28 13:07 /tmp/masktest ❶

$ chmod +x /tmp/masktest ❷

$ ls -al /tmp/masktest
-rwxr-xr-x 1 mh9 dev 0 Aug 28 13:07 /tmp/masktest ❸
```

❶ Initially the file permissions are r/w for the owner and read-only for everyone else, aka 644.

❷ Make the file executable.

❸ Now the file permissions are r/w/x for the owner and r/x for everyone else, aka 755.

In Figure 4-2 you see what is going on under the hood. Note that you might not want to give everyone the right to execute the file, so a chmod 744 might have been better here, giving only the owner the correct permissions while not changing it for the rest. We will discuss this topic further in "Good Practices" on page 89.

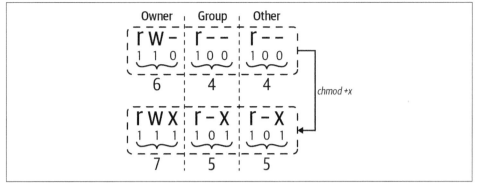

Figure 4-2. Making a file executable and how the file permissions change with it

You can also change the ownership using chown (and chgrp for the group):

```
$ touch myfile
$ ls -al myfile
-rw-rw-r-- 1 mh9 mh9 0 Sep 4 09:26 myfile ❶

$ sudo chown root myfile ❷
-rw-rw-r-- 1 root mh9 0 Sep 4 09:26 myfile
```

❶ The file *myfile*, which I created and own.

❷ After chown, root owns that file.

Having discussed basic permission management, let's take a look at some more advanced techniques in this space.

Process Permissions

So far we've focused on how human users access files and what the respective permissions in play are. Now we shift the focus to processes. In "Resources and Ownership" on page 74, we talked about how users own files as well as how processes use files. This raises the question: what are the relevant permissions, from a process point of view?

As documented on the credentials(7) manual page (*https://oreil.ly/o7gf6*), there are different user IDs relevant in the context of runtime permissions:

Real UID
    The *real* UID is the UID of the user that launched the process. It represents process ownership in terms of human user. The process itself can obtain its real UID via getuid(2) (*https://oreil.ly/Efi4H*), and you can query it via the shell using stat -c "%u %g" /proc/$pid/.

Effective UID

The Linux kernel uses the *effective* UID to determine permissions the process has when accessing shared resources such as message queues. On traditional UNIX systems, they are also used for file access. Linux, however, previously used a dedicated filesystem UID (see the following discussion) for file access permissions. This is still supported for compatibility reasons. A process can obtain its effective UID via `geteuid(2)` (*https://oreil.ly/b69OQ*).

Saved set-user-ID

Saved set-user-IDs are used in `suid` cases where a process can assume privileges by switching its effective UID between the real UID and the saved set-user-ID. For example, in order for a process to be allowed to use certain network ports (see "Ports" on page 160), it needs elevated privileges, such as being run as `root`. A process can get its saved set-user-IDs via `getresuid(2)` (*https://oreil.ly/01QVp*).

Filesystem UID

These Linux-specific IDs are used to determine permissions for file access. This UID was initially introduced to support use cases where a file server would act on behalf of a regular user while isolating the process from signals by said user. Programs don't usually directly manipulate this UID. The kernel keeps track of when the effective UID is changed and automatically changes the filesystem UID with it. This means that usually the filesystem UID is the same as the effective UID but can be changed via `setfsuid(2)` (*https://oreil.ly/NhhNr*). Note that technically this UID is no longer necessary since kernel v2.0 but is still supported, for compatibility.

Initially, when a child process is created via `fork(2)`, it inherits copies of its parent's UIDs, and during an `execve(2)` syscall, the process's real UID is preserved, whereas the effective UID and saved set-user-ID may change.

For example, when you run the `passwd` command, your effective UID is your UID, let's say 1000. Now, `passwd` has `suid` set enabled, which means when you run it, your effective UID is 0 (aka `root`). There are also other ways to influence the effective UID —for example, using `chroot` and other sandboxing techniques.

 POSIX threads (*https://oreil.ly/kJFaJ*) require that credentials are shared by all threads in a process. However, at the kernel level, Linux maintains separate user and group credentials for each thread.

In addition to file access permissions, the kernel uses process UIDs for other things, including but not limited to the following:

- Establishing permissions for sending signals—for example, to determine what happens when you do a `kill -9` for a certain process ID. We'll get back to this in Chapter 6.

- Permission handling for scheduling and priorities (for example, `nice`).

- Checking resource limits, which we'll discuss in detail in the context of containers in Chapter 9.

While it can be straightforward to reason with effective UID in the context of `suid`, once capabilities come into play it can be more challenging.

Advanced Permission Management

While so far we've focused on widely used mechanisms, the topics in this section are in a sense advanced and not necessarily something you would consider in a casual or hobby setup. For professional usage—that is, production use cases where business critical workloads are deployed—you should definitely be at least aware of the following advanced permission management approaches.

Capabilities

In Linux, as is traditionally the case in UNIX systems, the `root` user has no restrictions when running processes. In other words, the kernel only distinguishes between two cases:

- Privileged processes, bypassing the kernel permission checks, with an effective UID of 0 (aka `root`)

- Unprivileged processes, with a nonzero effective UID, for which the kernel does permission checks, as discussed in "Process Permissions" on page 85

With the introduction of the capabilities syscall (*https://oreil.ly/1Fma7*) in kernel v2.2, this binary worldview has changed: the privileges traditionally associated with `root` are now broken down into distinct units that can be independently assigned on a per-thread level.

In practice, the idea is that a normal process has zero capabilities, controlled by the permissions discussed in the previous section. You can assign capabilities to executables (binaries and shell scripts) as well as processes to gradually add privileges necessary to carry out a task (see the discussion in "Good Practices" on page 89).

Now, a word of caution: capabilities are generally relevant only for system-level tasks. In other words: most of the time you won't necessarily depend on them.

In Table 4-4 you can see some of the more widely used capabilities.

Table 4-4. Examples of useful capabilities

Capability	Semantics
CAP_CHOWN	Allows user to make arbitrary changes to files' UIDs/GIDs
CAP_KILL	Allows sending of signals to processes belonging to other users
CAP_SETUID	Allows changing the UID
CAP_SETPCAP	Allows setting the capabilities of a running process
CAP_NET_ADMIN	Allows various network-related actions, such as interface config
CAP_NET_RAW	Allows using RAW and PACKET sockets
CAP_SYS_CHROOT	Allows calling chroot
CAP_SYS_ADMIN	Allows system admin operations, including mounting filesystems
CAP_SYS_PTRACE	Allows using strace to debug processes
CAP_SYS_MODULE	Allows loading kernel modules

Let's now see the capabilities in action. For starters, to view the capabilities, you can use commands as shown in the following (output edited to fit):

```
$ capsh --print ❶
Current: =
Bounding set =cap_chown,cap_dac_override,cap_dac_read_search,
cap_fowner,cap_fsetid,cap_kill,cap_setgid,cap_setuid,cap_setpcap,
...

$ grep Cap /proc/$$/status ❷
CapInh:  0000000000000000
CapPrm:  0000000000000000
CapEff:  0000000000000000
CapBnd:  000001ffffffffff
CapAmb:  0000000000000000
```

❶ Overview of all capabilities on the system

❷ Capabilities for the current process (the shell)

You can manage capabilities in a fine-grained manner—that is, on a per-file basis—with getcap (*https://oreil.ly/03bkF*) and setcap (*https://oreil.ly/cuBwc*) (the details and good practices are beyond the scope of this chapter).

Capabilities help to transition from an all-or-nothing approach to finer-grained privileges on a file basis. Let's now move on to a different advanced access control topic: the sandboxing technique of seccomp.

seccomp Profiles

Secure computing mode (seccomp) (*https://oreil.ly/p5iuR*) is a Linux kernel feature available since 2005. The basic idea behind this sandboxing technique is that, using a dedicated syscall called `seccomp(2)`, you can restrict the syscalls a process can use.

While you might find it inconvenient to manage seccomp yourself directly, there are ways to use it without too much hassle. For example, in the context of containers (see "Containers" on page 131), both Docker (*https://oreil.ly/A78pm*) and Kubernetes (*https://oreil.ly/oYFsK*) support seccomp.

Let's now have a look at an extension of the traditional, granular file permission.

Access Control Lists

With access control lists (ACLs), we have a flexible permission mechanism in Linux that you can use on top of or in addition to the more "traditional" permissions discussed in "File Permissions" on page 81. ACLs address a shortcoming of traditional permissions in that they allow you to grant permissions for a user or a group not in the group list of a user.

To check if your distribution supports ACLs, you can use `grep -i acl /boot/config*` where you'd hope to find a `POSIX_ACL=Y` somewhere in the output to confirm it. In order to use ACL for a filesystem, it must be enabled at mount time, using the `acl` option. The docs reference on acl (*https://oreil.ly/Ngr0m*) has a lot of useful details.

We won't go into greater detail here on ACLs since they're slightly outside the scope of this book; however, being aware of them and knowing where to start can be beneficial, should you come across them in the wild.

With that, let's review some good practices for access control.

Good Practices

Here are some security "good practices" in the wider context of access control. While some of them might be more applicable in professional environments, everyone should at least be aware of them.

Least privileges
>   The least privileges principle says, in a nutshell, that a person or process should only have the necessary permissions to achieve a given task. For example, if an app doesn't write to a file, then it only needs read access. In the context of access control, you can practice least privileges in two ways:

- In "File Permissions" on page 81, we saw what happens when using `chmod +x`. In addition to the permissions you intended, it also assigns some additional permissions to other users. Using explicit permissions via the numeral mode is better than symbolic mode. In other words: while the latter is more convenient, it's less strict.
- Avoid running as root as much as you can. For example, when you need to install something, you should be using `sudo` rather than logging in as `root`.

Note that if you're writing an application, you can use an SELinux policy to restrict access to only selected files, directories, and other features. In contrast, the default Linux model could potentially give the application access to any files left open on the system.

Avoid setuid
Take advantage of capabilities rather than relying on `setuid`, which is like a sledgehammer and offers attackers a great way to take over your system.

Auditing
Auditing is the idea that you record actions (along with who carried them out) in a way that the resulting log can't be tampered with. You can then use this read-only log to verify who did what, when. We'll dive into this topic in Chapter 8.

Conclusion

Now that you know how Linux manages users, files, and access to resources, you have everything at your disposal to carry out routine tasks safely and securely.

For any practical work with Linux, remember the relationship between users, processes, and files. This is crucial, in the context of the multiuser operating system that Linux is, for a safe and secure operation and to avoid damages.

We reviewed access control types, defined what users in Linux are, what they can do, and how to manage them both locally and centrally. The topic of file permissions and how to manage them can be tricky, and mastering it is mostly a matter of practice.

Advanced permissions techniques including capabilities and seccomp profiles are super relevant in the context of containers.

In the last section, we discussed good practices around access control–related security, especially applying least privileges.

If you want to dive deeper into the topics discussed in this chapter, here are some resources:

General
- "A Survey of Access Control Policies" (*https://oreil.ly/0PpnS*) by Amanda Crowell
- Lynis (*https://oreil.ly/SXSkp*), an auditing and compliance testing tool

Capabilities
- "Linux Capabilities in Practice" (*https://oreil.ly/NIdPu*)
- "Linux Capabilities: Making Them Work" (*https://oreil.ly/qsYJN*)

seccomp
- "A seccomp Overview" (*https://oreil.ly/2cKGI*)
- "Sandboxing in Linux with Zero Lines of Code" (*https://oreil.ly/U5bYG*)

Access Control Lists
- "POSIX Access Control Lists on Linux" (*https://oreil.ly/gbc4A*)
- "Access Control Lists" (*https://oreil.ly/owpYE*) via ArchLinux
- "An Introduction to Linux Access Control Lists (ACLs)" (*https://oreil.ly/WCjpN*) via Red Hat

Remember that security is an ongoing process, so you want to make sure to keep an eye on users and files, something we'll go into greater detail on in Chapters 8 and 9, but for now let's move on to the topic of filesystems.

## CHAPTER 5

Filesystems

In this chapter, we focus on files and filesystems. The UNIX concept of "everything is a file" lives on in Linux, and while that's not true 100% of the time, most resources in Linux are indeed files. Files can be everything from the content of the letter you write to your school to the funny GIF you download (from an obviously safe and trusted site).

There are other things that are also exposed as files in Linux—for example, devices and pseudo-devices such as in `echo "Hello modern Linux users" > /dev/pts/0`, which prints "Hello modern Linux users" to the screen. While you may not associate these resources with files, you can access them with the same methods and tools you know from regular files. For example, the kernel exposes certain runtime information (as discussed in "Process Management" on page 17) about a process, such as its PID or the binary used to run the process.

What all these things have in common is a standardized, uniform interface: opening a file, gathering information about a file, writing to a file, and so forth. In Linux, filesystems (*https://oreil.ly/9CEdn*) provide this uniform interface. This interface, together with the fact that Linux treats files as a stream of bytes, without any expectations about the structure, enables us to build tools that work with a range of different file types.

In addition, the uniform interface that filesystems provide reduces your cognitive load, making it faster for you to learn how to use Linux.

In this chapter, we first define some relevant terms. Then, we look at how Linux implements the "everything is a file" abstraction. Next, we review special-purpose filesystems the kernel uses to expose information about processes or devices. We then move on to regular files and filesystems, something you would typically associate with documents, data, and programs. We compare filesystem options and discuss common operations.

Basics

Before we get into the filesystem terminology, let's first make some implicit assumptions and expectations about filesystems more explicit:

- While there are exceptions, most of the widely used filesystems today are hierarchical. That is, they provide the user with a single filesystem tree, starting at the root (/).

- In the filesystem tree, you find two different types of objects: directories and files. Think of directories as an organizational unit, allowing you to group files. If you'd like to apply the tree analogy, directories are the nodes in the tree, whereas the leaves are either files or directories.

- You can navigate a filesystem by listing the content of a directory (ls), changing into that directory (cd), and printing the current working directory (pwd).

- Permissions are built-in: as discussed in "Permissions" on page 80, one of the attributes a filesystem captures is ownership. Consequently, ownership enforces access to files and directories via the assigned permissions.

- Generally, filesystems are implemented in the kernel.

While filesystems are usually, for performance reasons, implemented in the kernel space, there's also an option to implement them in user land. See the Filesystem in Userspace (FUSE) documentation (*https://oreil.ly/hIVgq*) and the libfuse project site (*https://oreil.ly/cEZyY*).

With this informal high-level explanation out of the way, we now focus on some more crisp definitions of terms that you'll need to understand:

Drive
A (physical) block device such as a hard disk drive (HDD) or a solid-state drive (SSD). In the context of virtual machines, a drive also can be emulated—for example, */dev/sda* (SCSI device) or */dev/sdb* (SATA device) or */dev/hda* (IDE device).

Partition
You can logically split up drives into partitions, a set of storage sectors. For example, you may decide to create two partitions on your HDD, which then would show up as */dev/sdb1* and */dev/sdb2*.

Volume

A volume is somewhat similar to a partition, but it is more flexible, and it is also formatted for a specific filesystem. We'll discuss volumes in detail in "Logical Volume Manager" on page 99.

Super block

When formatted, filesystems have a special section in the beginning that captures the metadata of the filesystem. This includes things like filesystem type, blocks, state, and how many inodes per block.

Inodes

In a filesystem, inodes store metadata about files, such as size, owner, location, date, and permissions. However, inodes do not store the filename and the actual data. This is kept in directories, which really are just a special kind of regular file, mapping inodes to filenames.

That was a lot of theory, so let's see these concepts in action. First, here's how to see what drives, partitions, and volumes are present in your system:

```
$ lsblk --exclude 7 ❶
NAME                        MAJ:MIN RM   SIZE RO TYPE MOUNTPOINTS
sda                             8:0  0 223.6G  0 disk               ❷
├─sda1                          8:1  0   512M  0 part /boot/efi      ❸
└─sda2                          8:2  0 223.1G  0 part               ❹
  ├─elementary--vg-root     253:0  0 222.1G  0 lvm  /
  └─elementary--vg-swap_1 253:1  0   976M  0 lvm  [SWAP]
```

❶ List all block devices but exclude pseudo (loop) devices.

❷ We have a disk drive called *sda* with some 223 GB overall.

❸ There are two partitions here, with *sda1* being the boot partition.

❹ The second partition, called *sda2*, contains two volumes (see "Logical Volume Manager" on page 99 for details).

Now that we have an overall idea of the physical and logical setup, let's have a closer look at the filesystems in use:

```
$ findmnt -D -t nosquashfs ❶
SOURCE                            FSTYPE    SIZE  USED  AVAIL USE% TARGET
udev                              devtmpfs  3.8G     0   3.8G  0% /dev
tmpfs                             tmpfs   778.9M  1.6M 777.3M  0% /run
/dev/mapper/elementary--vg-root   ext4    217.6G 13.8G 192.7G  6% /
tmpfs                             tmpfs     3.8G 19.2M   3.8G  0% /dev/shm
tmpfs                             tmpfs       5M    4K     5M  0% /run/lock
tmpfs                             tmpfs     3.8G     0   3.8G  0% /sys/fs/cgroup
/dev/sda1                         vfat      511M    6M 504.9M  1% /boot/efi
tmpfs                             tmpfs   778.9M   76K 778.8M  0% /run/user/1000
```

❶ List filesystems but exclude squashfs types (*https://oreil.ly/vS88y*) (specialized read-only compressed filesystem originally developed for CDs, now also for snapshots).

We can go a step further and look at individual filesystem objects such as directories or files:

```
$ stat myfile
  File: myfile
  Size: 0               Blocks: 0          IO Block: 4096    regular empty file ❶
Device: fc01h/64513d    Inode: 555036      Links: 1 ❷
Access: (0664/-rw-rw-r--)  Uid: ( 1000/    mh9)  Gid: ( 1001/    mh9)
Access: 2021-08-29 09:26:36.638447261 +0000
Modify: 2021-08-29 09:26:36.638447261 +0000
Change: 2021-08-29 09:26:36.638447261 +0000
 Birth: 2021-08-29 09:26:36.638447261 +0000
```

❶ File type information

❷ Information about device and inode

In the previous command, if we used `stat .` (note the dot), we would have gotten the respective directory file information, including its inode, number of blocks used, and so forth.

Table 5-1 lists some basic filesystem commands that allow you to explore the concepts we introduced earlier.

Table 5-1. Selection of low-level filesystem and block device commands

Command	Use case
lsblk	List all block devices
fdisk, parted	Manage disk partitions
blkid	Show block device attributes such as UUID
hwinfo	Show hardware information
file -s	Show filesystem and partition information
stat, df -i, ls -i	Show and list inode-related information

Another term you'll come across in the context of filesystems is that of *links*. Sometimes you want to refer to files with different names or provide shortcuts. There are two types of links in Linux:

Hard links

Reference inodes and can't refer to directories. They also do not work across filesystems.

Symbolic links, or symlinks (https://oreil.ly/yRWYA)

Special files with their content being a string representing the path of another file.

Now let's see links in action (some outputs shortened):

```
$ ln myfile somealias ❶
$ ln -s myfile somesoftalias ❷

$ ls -al *alias ❸
-rw-rw-r-- 2 mh9 mh9 0 Sep  5 12:15 somealias
lrwxrwxrwx 1 mh9 mh9 6 Sep  5 12:45 somesoftalias -> myfile

$ stat somealias ❹
  File: somealias
  Size: 0              Blocks: 0          IO Block: 4096    regular empty file
Device: fd00h/64768d    Inode: 6302071     Links: 2
...
$ stat somesoftalias ❺
  File: somesoftalias -> myfile
  Size: 6              Blocks: 0          IO Block: 4096    symbolic link
Device: fd00h/64768d    Inode: 6303540     Links: 1
...
```

❶ Create a hard link to *myfile*.

❷ Create a soft link to the same file (notice the `-s` option).

❸ List the files. Notice the different file types and the rendering of the name. We could also have used `ls -ali *alias`, which would show that the inodes were the same on the two names associated with the hard link.

❹ Show the file details of the hard link.

❺ Show the file details of the soft link.

Now that you're familiar with filesystem terminology let's explore how Linux makes it possible to treat any kind of resource as a file.

The Virtual File System

Linux manages to provide a file-like access to many sorts of resources (in-memory, locally attached, or networked storage) through an abstraction called the virtual file system (VFS) (*https://oreil.ly/3sZQ1*). The basic idea is to introduce a layer of indirection between the clients (syscalls) and the individual filesystems implementing operations for a concrete device or other kind of resource. This means that VFS separates the generic operation (open, read, seek) from the actual implementation details.

VFS is an abstraction layer in the kernel that provides clients a common way to access resources, based on the file paradigm. A file, in Linux, doesn't have any prescribed structure; it's just a stream of bytes. It's up to the client to decide what the bytes mean. As shown in Figure 5-1, VFS abstracts access to different kinds of filesystems:

Local filesystems, such as ext3, *XFS, FAT, and NTFS*
    These filesystems use drivers to access local block devices such as HDDs or SSDs.

In-memory filesystems, such as tmpfs, *that are not backed by long-term storage devices but live in main memory (RAM)*
    We'll cover these and the previous category in "Regular Files" on page 108.

Pseudo filesystems like procfs, *as discussed in "Pseudo Filesystems" on page 104*
    These filesystems are also in-memory in nature. They're used for kernel interfacing and device abstractions.

Networked filesystems, such as NFS, Samba, Netware (nee Novell), and others
    These filesystems also use a driver; however, the storage devices where the actual data resides is not locally attached but remote. This means that the driver involves network operations. For this reason, we'll cover them in Chapter 7.

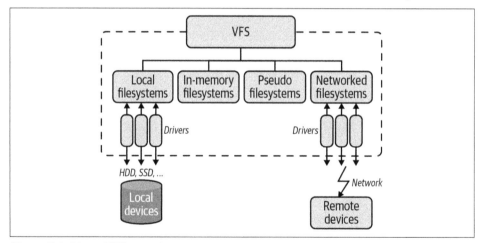

Figure 5-1. Linux VFS overview

Describing the makeup of the VFS isn't easy. There are over 100 syscalls related to files; however, in its core, the operations can be grouped into a handful of categories, as listed in Table 5-2.

Table 5-2. Select syscalls making up the VFS interface

Category	Example syscalls
Inodes	chmod, chown, stat
Files	open, close, seek, truncate, read, write
Directories	chdir, getcwd, link, unlink, rename, symlink
Filesystems	mount, flush, chroot
Others	mmap, poll, sync, flock

Many VFS syscalls dispatch to the filesystem-specific implementation. For other syscalls, there are VFS default implementations. Further, the Linux kernel defines relevant VFS data structures—see *include/linux/fs.h* (*https://oreil.ly/Fkq8i*)—such as the following:

inode
> The core filesystem object, capturing type, ownership, permissions, links, pointers to blocks containing the file data, creation and access statistics, and more

file
> Representing an open file (including path, current position, and inode)

dentry *(directory entry)*
> Stores its parent and children

super_block
> Representing a filesystem including mount information

Others
> Including vfsmount and file_system_type

With the VFS overview done, let's have a closer look at the details, including volume management, filesystem operations, and common file system layouts.

Logical Volume Manager

We previously talked about carving up drives using partitions. While doing this is possible, partitions are hard to use, especially when resizing (changing the amount of storage space) is necessary.

Logical volume manager (LVM) uses a layer of indirection between physical entities (such as drives or partitions) and the file system. This yields a setup that allows for risk-free, zero-downtime expanding and automatic storage extension through the pooling of resources. The way LVM works is depicted in Figure 5-2, with key concepts explained in the passage that follows.

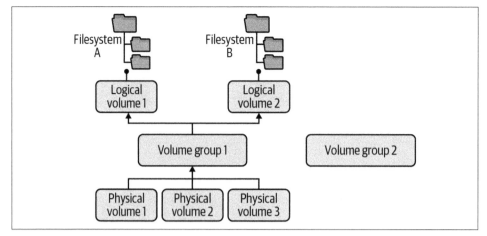

Figure 5-2. Linux LVM overview

Physical volumes (PV)
    Can be a disk partition, an entire disk drive, and other devices.

Logical volumes (LV)
    Are block devices created from VGs. These are conceptually comparable to partitions. You have to create a filesystem on an LV before you can use it. You can easily resize LVs while in use.

Volume groups (VG)
    Are a go-between between a set of PVs and LVs. Think of a VG as pools of PVs collectively providing resources.

To manage volumes with LVM (*https://oreil.ly/rYXVI*), a number of tools are required; however, they are consistently named and relatively easy to use:

PV management tools
- lvmdiskscan
- pvdisplay
- pvcreate
- pvscan

VG management tools
- vgs
- vgdisplay
- vgcreate
- vgextend

LV management tools
- lvs

- lvscan

- lvcreate

Let's see some LVM commands in action, using a concrete setup:

```
$ sudo lvscan ❶
  ACTIVE              '/dev/elementary-vg/root' [<222.10 GiB] inherit
  ACTIVE              '/dev/elementary-vg/swap_1' [976.00 MiB] inherit

$ sudo vgs ❷
  VG            #PV #LV #SN Attr   VSize    VFree
  elementary-vg   1   2   0 wz--n- <223.07g 16.00m

$ sudo pvdisplay ❸
  --- Physical volume ---
  PV Name               /dev/sda2
  VG Name               elementary-vg
  PV Size               <223.07 GiB / not usable 3.00 MiB
  Allocatable           yes
  PE Size               4.00 MiB
  Total PE              57105
  Free PE               4
  Allocated PE          57101
  PV UUID               2OrEfB-77zU-jun3-a0XC-QiJH-erDP-1ujfAM
```

❶ List logical volumes; we have two here (*root* and *swap_1*) using volume group *elementary-vg*.

❷ Display volume groups; we have one here called *elementary-vg*.

❸ Display physical volumes; we have one here (*/dev/sda2*) that's assigned to the volume group *elementary-vg*.

Whether you use a partition or an LV, two more steps, which we'll cover next, are necessary to use a filesystem.

Filesystem Operations

In the following section, we'll discuss how to create a filesystem, given a partition or a logical volume (created using LVM). There are two steps involved: creating the filesystem—in other non-Linux operating systems, this step is sometimes called *formatting*—and then mounting it, or inserting it into the filesystem tree.

Creating filesystems

In order to use a filesystem, the first step is to create one. This means that you're setting up the management pieces that make up a filesystem, taking a partition or a volume as the input. Consult Table 5-1 if you're unsure how to gather the necessary information about the input, and once you have everything together, use `mkfs` (*https://oreil.ly/uqI57*) to create a filesystem.

`mkfs` takes two primary inputs: the type of filesystem you want to create (see one of the options we discuss in "Common Filesystems" on page 109) and the device you want to create the filesystem on (for example, a logical volume):

```
mkfs -t ext4 \ ❶
    /dev/some_vg/some_lv ❷
```

❶   Create a filesystem of type `ext4`.

❷   Create the filesystem on the logical volume */dev/some_vg/some_lv*.

As you can see from the previous command, there's not much to it to create a filesystem, so the main work for you is to figure out what filesystem type to use.

Once you have created the filesystem with `mkfs`, you can then make it available in the filesystem tree.

Mounting filesystems

Mounting a filesystem means attaching it to the filesystem tree (which starts at /). Use the `mount` command (*https://oreil.ly/c6ryR*) to attach a filesystem. `mount` takes two main inputs: the device you want to attach and the place in the filesystem tree. In addition, you can provide other inputs, including mount options (via -o) such as read-only, and bind mounts—via `--bind` (*https://oreil.ly/C2QuV*)—for mounting directories into the filesystem tree. We'll revisit this latter option in the context of containers.

You can use `mount` on its own as well. Here's how to list existing mounts:

```
$ mount -t ext4,tmpfs ❶
tmpfs on /run type tmpfs (rw,nosuid,noexec,relatime,size=797596k,mode=755)
/dev/mapper/elementary--vg-root on / type ext4 (rw,relatime,errors=remount-ro) ❷
tmpfs on /dev/shm type tmpfs (rw,nosuid,nodev)
tmpfs on /run/lock type tmpfs (rw,nosuid,nodev,noexec,relatime,size=5120k)
tmpfs on /sys/fs/cgroup type tmpfs (ro,nosuid,nodev,noexec,mode=755)
```

❶   List mounts but only show certain filesystem types (`ext4` and `tmpfs` here).

❷   An example mount: the LVM VG */dev/mapper/elementary--vg-root* of type `ext4` is mounted at the root.

You must make sure that you mount a filesystem using the type it has been created with. For example, if you're trying to mount an SD card using `mount -t vfat /dev/sdX2 /media`, you have to know the SD card is formatted using `vfat`. You can let `mount` try all filesystems until one works using the `-a` option.

Further, the mounts are valid only for as long as the system is running, so in order to make it permanent, you need to use the fstab file (*/etc/fstab*) (*https://oreil.ly/zoSE1*). For example, here is mine (output slightly edited to fit):

```
$ cat /etc/fstab
# /etc/fstab: static file system information.
#
# Use 'blkid' to print the universally unique identifier for a
# device; this may be used with UUID= as a more robust way to name devices
# that works even if disks are added and removed. See fstab(5).
#
# <file system> <mount point> <type> <options> <dump> <pass>
/dev/mapper/elementary--vg-root / ext4 errors=remount-ro 0 1
# /boot/efi was on /dev/sda1 during installation
UUID=2A11-27C0  /boot/efi vfat umask=0077 0 1
/dev/mapper/elementary--vg-swap_1 none swap sw 0 0
```

Now you know how to manage partitions, volumes, and filesystems. Next up, we review common ways to organize filesystems.

Common Filesystem Layouts

Once you have a filesystem in place, an obvious challenge is to come up with a way to organize its content. You may want to organize things like where programs are stored, configuration data, system data, and user data. We will refer to this organization of directories and their content as the *filesystem layout*. Formally, the layout is called the Filesystem Hierarchy Standard (FHS) (*https://oreil.ly/q0c4a*). It defines directories, including their structure and recommended content. The Linux Foundation maintains the FHS, and it's a good starting point for Linux distributions to follow.

The idea behind FHS is laudable. However, in practice you will find that the filesystem layout very much depends on the Linux distribution you're using. Thus, I strongly recommend you use the `man hier` command to learn about your concrete setup.

To provide you with a high-level idea of what you can expect when you see certain top-level directories, I compiled a list of common ones in Table 5-3.

Table 5-3. Common top-level directories

Directory	Semantics
bin, sbin	System programs and commands (usually links to */usr/bin* and */usr/sbin*)
boot	Kernel images and related components

Directory	Semantics
dev	Devices (terminals, drives, etc.)
etc	System configuration files
home	User home directories
lib	Shared system libraries
mnt, media	Mount points for removable media (e.g., USB sticks)
opt	Distro specific; can host package manager files
proc, sys	Kernel interfaces; see also "Pseudo Filesystems" on page 104
tmp	For temporary files
usr	User programs (usually read-only)
var	User programs (logs, backups, network caches, etc.)

With that, let's move on to some special kinds of filesystems.

Pseudo Filesystems

Filesystems are a great way to structure and access information. By now you have likely already internalized the Linux motto that "everything is a file." We looked at how Linux provides a uniform interface via VFS in "The Virtual File System" on page 97. Now, let's take a closer look at how an interface is provided in cases where the VFS implementor is not a block device (such as an SD card or an SSD drive).

Meet pseudo filesystems: they only pretend to be filesystems so that we can interact with them in the usual manner (`ls`, `cd`, `cat`), but really they are wrapping some kernel interface. The interface can be a range of things, including the following:

- Information about a process
- An interaction with devices such as keyboards
- Utilities such as special devices you can use as data sources or sinks

Let's have a closer look at the three major pseudo filesystems Linux has, starting with the oldest.

procfs

Linux inherited the */proc (https://oreil.ly/QEdmm)* filesystem (`procfs`) from UNIX. The original intention was to publish process-related information from the kernel, to make it consumable for system commands such as `ps` or `free`. It has very few rules around structure, allows read-write access, and over time many things found their way into it. In general, you find two types of information there:

- Per-process information in */proc/PID/*. This is process-relevant information that the kernel exposes via directories with the PID as the directory name. Details concerning the information available there are listed in Table 5-4.

- Other information such as mounts, networking-related information, TTY drivers, memory information, system version, and uptime.

You can glean per-process information as listed in Table 5-4 simply by using commands like `cat`. Note that most are read-only; the write semantics depend on the underlying resource.

Table 5-4. Per-process information in procfs (most notable)

Entry	Type	Information
attr	Directory	Security attributes
cgroup	File	Control groups
cmdline	File	Command line
cwd	Link	Current working directory
environ	File	Environment variables
exe	Link	Executable of the process
fd	Directory	File descriptors
io	File	Storage I/O (bytes/char read and written)
limits	File	Resource limits
mem	File	Memory used
mounts	File	Mounts used
net	Directory	Network stats
stat	File	Process status
syscall	File	Syscall usage
task	Directory	Per-task (thread) information
timers	File	Timers information

To see this in action, let's inspect the process status. We're using `status` here rather than `stat`, which doesn't come with human-readable labels:

```
$ cat /proc/self/status | head -10 ❶
Name:    cat
Umask:   0002
State:   R (running) ❷
Tgid:    12011
Ngid:    0
Pid:     12011 ❸
PPid:    3421 ❹
TracerPid:    0
```

```
Uid:    1000    1000    1000    1000
Gid:    1000    1000    1000    1000
```

❶ Get the process status about the currently running command, showing only the first 10 lines.

❷ The current state (running, on-CPU).

❸ The PID of the current process.

❹ The process ID of the parent process of the command; in this case, it's the shell where I ran the cat command in.

Here is one more example of using procfs to glean information, this time from the networking space:

```
$ cat /proc/self/net/arp
IP address      HW type    Flags    HW address          Mask    Device
192.168.178.1   0x1        0x2      3c:a6:2f:8e:66:b3   *       wlp1s0
192.168.178.37  0x1        0x2      dc:54:d7:ef:90:9e   *       wlp1s0
```

As shown in the previous command, we can glean ARP information about the current process from this special */proc/self/net/arp*.

procfs is very useful if you're low-level debugging (*https://oreil.ly/nJ01w*) or developing system tooling. It is relatively messy, so you'll need the kernel docs or, even better, the kernel source code at hand to understand what each file represents and how to interpret the information in it.

Let's move on to a more recent, more orderly way the kernel exposes information.

sysfs

Where procfs is pretty Wild West, the */sys* (*https://oreil.ly/EHJEJ*) filesystem (sysfs) is a Linux-specific, structured way for the kernel to expose select information (such as about devices) using a standardized layout.

Here are the directories in sysfs:

block/
 This directory symbolic links to discovered block devices.

bus/
 In this directory, you find one subdirectory for each physical bus type supported in the kernel.

class/
 This directory contains device classes.

dev/
> This directory contains two subdirectories: *block/* for block devices and *char/* for character devices on the system, structured with `major-ID:minor-ID`.

devices/
> In this directory, the kernel provides a representation of the device tree.

firmware/
> Via these directories, you can manage firmware-specific attributes.

fs/
> This directory contains subdirectories for some filesystems.

module/
> In these directories you find subdirectories for each module loaded in the kernel.

There are more subdirectories in `sysfs`, but some are newish and/or would benefit from better documentation. You'll find certain information duplicated in `sysfs` that is also available in `procfs`, but other information (such as memory information) is only available in `procfs`.

Let's see `sysfs` in action (output edited to fit):

```
$ ls -al /sys/block/sda/ | head -7 ❶
total 0
drwxr-xr-x 11 root root    0 Sep  7 11:49 .
drwxr-xr-x  3 root root    0 Sep  7 11:49 ..
-r--r--r--  1 root root 4096 Sep  8 16:22 alignment_offset
lrwxrwxrwx  1 root root    0 Sep  7 11:51 bdi -> ../../../virtual/bdi/8:0 ❷
-r--r--r--  1 root root 4096 Sep  8 16:22 capability ❸
-r--r--r--  1 root root 4096 Sep  7 11:49 dev ❹
```

❶ List information about block device `sda`, showing only the first seven lines.

❷ The `backing_dev_info` link using `MAJOR:MINOR` format.

❸ Captures device capabilities (*https://oreil.ly/GFUid*), such as if it is removable.

❹ Contains the device major and minor number (`8:0`); see also the block device drivers reference (*https://oreil.ly/DK9GT*) for what the numbers mean.

Next up in our little pseudo filesystem review are devices.

devfs

The */dev* (*https://oreil.ly/EkO8V*) filesystem (`devfs`) hosts device special files, representing devices ranging from physical devices to things like a random number generator or a write-only data sink.

The devices available and managed via `devfs` are:

Block devices
Handle data in blocks—for example, storage devices (drives)

Character devices
Handle things character by character, such as a terminal, a keyboard, or a mouse

Special devices
Generate data or allow you to manipulate it, including the famous */dev/null* or */dev/random*

Let's now see `devfs` in action. For example, assume you want to get a random string. You could do something like the following:

```
tr -dc A-Za-z0-9 < /dev/urandom | head -c 42
```

The previous command generates a 42-character random sequence containing uppercase and lowercase as well as numerical characters. And while */dev/urandom* looks like a file and can be used like one, it indeed is a special file that, using a number of sources, generates (more or less) random output.

What do you think about the following command:

```
echo "something" > /dev/tty
```

That's right! The string "something" appeared on your display, and that is by design. */dev/tty* stands for the terminal, and with that command we sent something (quite literally) to it.

With a good understanding of filesystems and their features, let's now turn our attention to filesystems that you want to use to manage regular files such as documents and data files.

Regular Files

In this section, we focus on regular files and filesystems (*https://oreil.ly/LOuvP*) for such file types. Most of the day-to-day files we're dealing with when working fall into this category: office documents, YAML and JSON configuration files, images (PNG, JPEG, etc.), source code, plain text files, and so on.

Linux comes with a wealth of options. We'll focus on local filesystems, both those native for Linux as well as those in other operating systems (such as Windows/DOS) that Linux allows you to use. First, let's have a look at some common filesystems.

Common Filesystems

The term *common filesystem* doesn't have a formal definition. It's simply an umbrella term for filesystems that are either the defaults used in Linux distributions or widely used in storage devices such as removable devices (USB sticks and SD cards) or read-only devices, like CDs and DVDs.

In Table 5-5 I provide a quick overview and comparison of some common filesystems that enjoy in-kernel support. Later in this section, we'll review some popular filesystems in greater detail.

Table 5-5. Common filesystems for regular files

Filesystem	Linux support since	File size	Volume size	Number of files	Filename length
ext2 (*https://oreil.ly/cL9W7*)	1993	2 TB	32 TB	10^{18}	255 characters
ext3 (*https://oreil.ly/lEnxW*)	2001	2 TB	32 TB	variable	255 characters
ext4 (*https://oreil.ly/482ku*)	2008	16 TB	1 EB	4 billion	255 characters
btrfs (*https://oreil.ly/gJQex*)	2009	16 EB	16 EB	2^{18}	255 characters
XFS (*https://oreil.ly/5LHGl*)	2001	8 EB	8 EB	2^{64}	255 characters
ZFS (*https://oreil.ly/HH1Lb*)	2006	16 EB	2^{128} Bytes	10^{14} files per directory	255 characters
NTFS	1997	16 TB	256 TB	2^{32}	255 characters
vfat	1995	2 GB	N/A	2^{16} per directory	255 characters

> The information provided in Table 5-5 is meant to give you a rough idea about the filesystems. Sometimes it's hard to pinpoint the exact time a filesystem would be officially considered part of Linux; sometimes the numbers make sense only with the relevant context applied. For example, there are differences between theoretical limits and implementation.

Now let's take a closer look at some widely used filesystems for regular files:

ext4 (*https://oreil.ly/Ot9DI*)
: A widely used filesystem, used by default in many distributions nowadays. It's a backward-compatible evolution of ext3. Like ext3, it offers journaling—that is, changes are recorded in a log so that in the worst-case scenario (think: power outage), the recovery is fast. It's a great general-purpose choice. See the ext4 manual (*https://oreil.ly/9kSXn*) for usage.

XFS (https://oreil.ly/WzHIZ)
: A journaling filesystem that was originally designed by Silicon Graphics (SGI) for their workstations in the early 1990s. Offering support for large files and high-speed I/O, it's now used, for example, in the Red Hat distributions family.

ZFS (https://oreil.ly/ApA2z)

> Originally developed by Sun Microsystems in 2001, ZFS combines filesystem and volume manager functionality. While now there is the OpenZFS project (*https://oreil.ly/7itzs*), offering a path forward in an open source context, there are some concerns about ZFS's integration with Linux (*https://oreil.ly/mM8du*).

FAT (https://oreil.ly/sfUa3)

> This is really a family of FAT filesystems for Linux, with `vfat` being used most often. The main use case is interoperability with Windows systems, as well as removable media that uses FAT. Many of the native considerations around volumes do not apply.

Drives are not the only place one can store data, so let's have a look at in-memory options.

In-Memory Filesystems

There are a number of in-memory filesystems available; some are general purpose and others have very specific use cases. In the following, we list some widely used in-memory filesystems (in alphabetical order):

`debugfs` *(https://oreil.ly/j30dd)*

> A special-purpose filesystem used for debugging; usually mounted with `mount -t debugfs none /sys/kernel/debug`.

`loopfs` *(https://oreil.ly/jZi4I)*

> Allows mapping a filesystem to blocks rather than devices. See also a mail thread on the background (*https://oreil.ly/kMZ7j*).

`pipefs`

> A special (pseudo) filesystem mounted on `pipe:` that enables pipes.

`sockfs`

> Another special (pseudo) filesystem that makes network sockets look like files, sitting between the syscalls and the sockets (*https://oreil.ly/ANDjr*).

`swapfs` *(https://oreil.ly/g1WsU)*

> Used to realize swapping (not mountable).

`tmpfs` *(https://oreil.ly/ICkgj)*

> A general-purpose filesystem that keeps file data in kernel caches. It's fast but nonpersistent (power off means data is lost).

Let's move on to a special category of filesystems, specifically relevant in the context of "Containers" on page 131.

Copy-on-Write Filesystems

Copy-on-write (CoW) is a nifty concept to increase I/O speed and at the same time use less space. The way it works is depicted in Figure 5-3, with further explanation in the passage that follows.

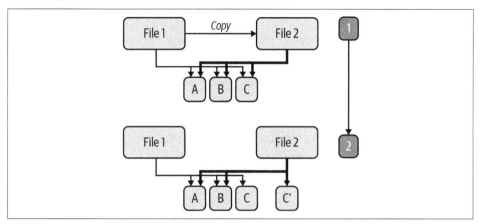

Figure 5-3. The CoW principle in action

1. The original file, File 1, consisting of blocks A, B, and C, is copied to a file called File 2. Rather than copying the actual blocks, only the metadata (pointers to the blocks) is copied. This is fast and doesn't use up much space since only metadata is created.

2. When File 2 is modified (let's say something in block C is changed), only then is block C copied: a new block called C′ is created, and while File 2 still points to (uses) the unmodified blocks A and B, it now uses a new block (C′) to capture new data.

Before we get to implementations, we need to understand a second concept relevant in this context: union mounts (*https://oreil.ly/dh6vW*). This is the idea that you can combine (mount) multiple directories into one location so that, to the user of the resulting directory, it appears that said directory contains the combined content (or: union) of all the participating directories. With union mounts, you often come across the terms *upper filesystem* and *lower filesystem*, hinting at the layering order of the mounts. You'll find more details in the article "Unifying Filesystems with Union Mounts" (*https://oreil.ly/yqV9H*).

With union mounts, the devil is in the details. You have to come up with rules around what happens when a file exists in multiple places or what writing to or removing files means.

Let's have a quick look at implementations of CoW in the context of Linux filesystems. We'll have a closer look at some of these in the context of Chapter 6, when we discuss their use as a building block for container images.

Unionfs (https://oreil.ly/rWKZO)
Originally developed at Stony Brook University, Unionfs implements a union mount for CoW filesystems. It allows you to transparently overlay files and directories from different filesystems using priorities at mount time. It was widely popular and used in the context of CD-ROMs and DVDs.

OverlayFS (https://oreil.ly/5HzmC)
A union mount filesystem implementation for Linux introduced in 2009 and added to the kernel in 2014. With OverlayFS, once a file is opened, all operations are directly handled by the underlying (lower or upper) filesystems.

AUFS (https://oreil.ly/kdjge)
Another attempt to implement an in-kernel union mount, AUFS (short for advanced multilayered unification filesystem; originally AnotherUnionFS) has not been merged into the kernel yet. It is used to default in Docker (see "Docker" on page 138; nowadays Docker defaults to OverlayFS with storage driver `overlay2`).

`btrfs` *(https://oreil.ly/z1uxq)*
Short for b-tree filesystem (and pronounced *butterFS* or *betterFS*), `btrfs` is a CoW initially designed by Oracle Corporation. Today, a number of companies contribute to the `btrfs` development, including Facebook, Intel, SUSE, and Red Hat.

It comes with a number of features such as snapshots (for software-based RAID) and automatic detection of silent data corruptions. This makes `btrfs` very suitable for professional environments—for example, on a server.

Conclusion

In this chapter, we discussed files and filesystems in Linux. Filesystems are a great and flexible way to organize access to information in a hierarchical manner. Linux has many technologies and projects around filesystems. Some are open source based, but there is also a range of commercial offerings.

We discussed the basic building blocks, from drives to partitions and volumes. Linux realizes the "everything is a file" abstraction using VFS, supporting virtually any kind of filesystem, local or remote.

The kernel uses pseudo filesystems such as */proc* and */sys* to expose information about processes or devices. You can interact with these (in-memory) filesystems that represent kernel APIs just like with filesystems such as `ext4` (that you use to store files).

We then moved on to regular files and filesystems, where we compared common local filesystem options, as well as in-memory and CoW filesystem basics. Linux's filesystem support is comprehensive, allowing you to use (at least read) a range of filesystems, including those originating from other operating systems such as Windows.

You can dive deeper into the topics covered in this chapter with the following resources:

Basics
- "UNIX File Systems: How UNIX Organizes and Accesses Files on Disk" (*https://oreil.ly/8a3Zr*)
- "KHB: A Filesystems Reading List" (*https://oreil.ly/aFqjg*)

VFS
- "Overview of the Linux Virtual File System" (*https://oreil.ly/pnvQ4*)
- "Introduction to the Linux Virtual Filesystem (VFS)" (*https://oreil.ly/sqSHK*)
- "LVM" on ArchWiki (*https://oreil.ly/kOfU1*)
- "LVM2 Resource Page" (*https://oreil.ly/Ds7me*)
- "How to Use GUI LVM Tools" (*https://oreil.ly/UTFpL*)
- "Linux Filesystem Hierarchy" (*https://oreil.ly/osXbo*)
- "Persistent BPF Objects" (*https://oreil.ly/sFdVo*)

Regular files
- "Filesystem Efficiency—Comparison of EXT4, XFS, BTRFS, and ZFS" thread on reddit (*https://oreil.ly/Y3rAh*)
- "Linux Filesystem Performance Tests" (*https://oreil.ly/ZrPci*)
- "Comparison of File Systems for an SSD" thread on Linux.org (*https://oreil.ly/DBboM*)
- "Kernel Korner—Unionfs: Bringing Filesystems Together" (*https://oreil.ly/Odkls*)
- "Getting Started with btrfs for Linux" (*https://oreil.ly/TLylF*)

Equipped with knowledge around filesystems, we're now ready to bring things together and focus on how to manage and launch applications.

## CHAPTER 6

Applications, Package Management, and Containers

In this chapter, we talk about applications in Linux. Sometimes, the term *application* (or simply *app*) is used interchangeably with *program*, *binary*, or *executable*. We'll explain the differences between these terms and initially will be focusing on terminology, including the definition of applications and packages.

We discuss how Linux starts up and brings all the services we depend on into being. This is also known as the *boot process*. We will focus on init systems, specifically on the de-facto standard, the systemd ecosystem.

We then move on to package management, where we first review the application supply chain in general terms and see what the different moving parts are about. Then, to give you some context about existing mechanisms and challenges, we focus on how apps were traditionally distributed and installed. We discuss package management in traditional Linux distros, from Red Hat to Debian-based systems, and also have a peek at programming language–specific package managers such as Python or Rust.

In the next part of the chapter, we focus on containers: what they are and how they work. We'll review the building blocks of containers, what tooling you have available, and good practices around using containers.

To round off this chapter, we look at modern ways to manage Linux apps, especially in desktop environments. Most of those modern package manager solutions are also making use of containers in some form or another.

Running Example: greeter

To demonstrate certain technologies in this chapter, we'll use a running example called `greeter`. It's a simple shell script that echoes the name provided or a fallback greeting if nothing is provided.

If you want to follow along, now is a good time to paste the following bash script into a file called *greeter.sh*. Make it executable using `chmod 750 greeter.sh` (and if you don't recall what this means, read up on it in "File Permissions" on page 81):

```bash
#!/usr/bin/env bash

set -o errexit
set -o errtrace
set -o pipefail

name="${1}"

if [ -z "$name" ]
then
  printf "You are awesome!\n"
else
  printf "Hello %s, you are awesome!\n" ${name}
fi
```

And now, without further ado, let's see what an application is and what other related terms there are.

Basics

Before we get into the nitty-gritty details of application management, init systems, and containers, let's start with relevant definitions for this chapter and beyond. The reason why we only now go into details concerning apps is that there are a number of prerequisites (such as the Linux kernel, shell, filesystems, and security aspects) that you need to fully understand apps, and now that we're in a position to build on what we've learned so far, we can tackle apps:

Program
> This is usually either a binary file or a shell script that Linux can load into memory and execute. Another way to refer to this entity is *executable*. The type of the executable determines what exactly takes care of running it—for example, a shell (see "Shells" on page 33) would interpret and execute a shell script.

Process

A running entity based on a program, loaded into main memory and either using the CPU or I/O, when not sleeping. See also "Process Management" on page 17 and Chapter 3.

Daemon

Short for *daemon process*, sometimes called *service*, this is a background process that provides a certain function to other processes. For example, a printer daemon allows you to print. There are also daemons for web services, logging, time, and many more utilities you rely on on a daily basis.

Application

A program including its dependencies. Usually a substantial program, including a user interface. We usually associate the term *application* with the entire life cycle of a program, its configuration, and its data: from finding and installing to upgrading to removing it.

Package

A file that contains programs and configurations; used to distribute software applications.

Package manager

A program that takes a package as an input and, based on its content and the user instruction, installs it, upgrades it, or removes it from a Linux environment.

Supply Chain

A collection of software producers and distributors that enable you to find and use applications based on packages; see "Linux Application Supply Chains" on page 124 for details.

Booting

The startup sequence in Linux that involves hardware and operating system initialization steps, including loading the kernel and launching service (or daemon) programs with the goal to bring Linux into a state that it can be used; see "The Linux Startup Process" on page 117 for details.

Equipped with these high-level definitions, we quite literally start at the beginning: let's have a look at how Linux starts up and how all the daemons get launched so that we can use Linux to do our work.

The Linux Startup Process

The Linux boot process (*https://oreil.ly/fbnk3*) is typically a multiphase effort in which hardware and the kernel work together.

In Figure 6-1, you can see the boot process end to end, with the following five steps:

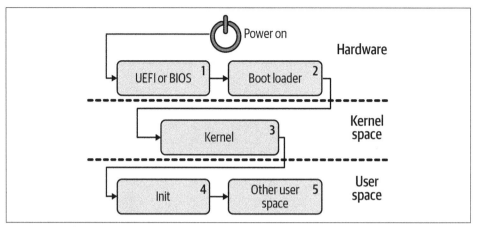

Figure 6-1. The Linux startup process

1. In modern environments, the Unified Extensible Firmware Interface (*https://uefi.org*) (UEFI) spec defines the boot configuration (stored in NVRAM) and the boot loader. In older systems, in this step, after the Power On Self Test (POST) is completed, the Basic I/O System (BIOS; see "The BIOS and UEFI" on page 14) would initialize hardware (managing I/O ports and interrupts) and hand over control to the boot loader.

2. The boot loader has one goal: to bootstrap the kernel. Depending on the boot medium, the details may differ slightly. There are a range of boot loader options, both current (e.g., GRUB 2, systemd-boot, SYSLINUX, rEFInd) and legacy (e.g., LILO, GRUB 1).

3. The kernel is usually located in the */boot* directory in a compressed form. That means the first step is to extract and load the kernel into main memory. After the initialization of its subsystems, filesystems, and drivers (as discussed in Chapter 2 and "Mounting filesystems" on page 102), the kernel hands over control to the init system, and with that the boot process proper ends.

4. The init system is responsible for launching daemons (service processes) system-wide. This init process is the root of the process hierarchy and with it has the process ID (PID) 1. In other words, the process with PID 1 runs until you power off the system. Besides being responsible for launching other daemons, the PID 1 process traditionally also takes care of orphaned processes (processes that don't have a parent process anymore).

5. Usually, some other user-space-level initialization takes place after this, depending on the environment:

   - There is usually a terminal, environment, and shell initialization going on, as discussed in Chapter 3.

- Display manager, graphical server, and the like, for desktop environments with a GUI are launched, taking user preferences and configurations into account.

With this high-level overview of the Linux startup process, we conclude our introductory section and focus on a vital, user-facing component: the init systems. This part (the preceding steps 4 and 5) is the most relevant for you, in the context of this book, allowing you to customize and extend your Linux installation.

There is a good comparison of init systems (*https://oreil.ly/Vn6pu*) available via the Gentoo wiki. We'll restrict our discussion to systemd, which almost all current Linux distributions are using.

System V Init

System V–style init programs (*https://oreil.ly/ho4eI*) (or *SysV init* for short) were the traditional init system in Linux. Linux inherited SysV from Unix, which defines so-called *runlevels* (think: system states such as halt, single-user, multi-user mode, or GUI mode) with the configuration usually stored in */etc/init.d*. However, the sequential way of starting up daemons and the distro-specific handling of the configuration made this a not-very-portable option.

Here's a fun fact: one of the book reviewers, Chris, was the first person to document SysV init in about 1984 (which an engineer designed over a weekend, reportedly).

---

systemd

systemd (*https://systemd.io*) was initially an init system, a replacement for initd, but today it's a powerful supervisor that includes functions such as logging, network configuration, and network time synchronization. It provides for a flexible, portable way to define daemons and their dependencies, and a uniform interface to control the configuration.

Almost all current Linux distributions are using systemd, including Fedora since May 2011, openSUSE since September 2012, CentOS since April 2014, RHEL since June 2014, SUSE Linux since October 2014, Debian since April 2015, and Ubuntu since April 2015.

In particular, systemd addresses the shortcomings of previous init systems by doing the following:

- Providing a uniform way to manage startup across distros
- Implementing a faster, more comprehensible service configuration

- Offering a modern management suite including monitoring, resource usage control (via cgroups), and built-in auditing

Additionally, `init` starts services at initialization time in sequence (that is, in alphanumeric order), while `systemd` can start any service that has had its dependencies met, potentially speeding up the startup time.

The way you tell `systemd` what to run, when to run, and how to run is via units.

Units

A unit in `systemd` is a logical grouping with different semantics depending on its function and/or the resource it targets. `systemd` distinguishes a number of units, depending on the target resource:

`service` *units*
> Describe how to manage a service or application

`target` *units*
> Capture dependencies

`mount` *units*
> Define a mountpoint

`timer` *units*
> Define timers for cron jobs and the like

Other, less important unit types include the following:

`socket`
> Describes a network or IPC socket

`device`
> For `udev` or `sysfs` filesystems

`automount`
> Configures automatic mountpoints

`swap`
> Describes swap space

`path`
> For path-based activation

`snapshot`
> Allows for reconstructing the current state of the system after changes

```
slice
```
Associated with cgroups (see "Linux cgroups" on page 135)

```
scope
```
Manages sets of system processes created externally

To be known to `systemd`, a unit needs to be serialized into a file. `systemd` looks for unit files in multiple locations. The three most important filepaths are the following:

/lib/systemd/system
Package-installed units

/etc/systemd/system
System admin–configured units

/run/systemd/system
Nonpersistent runtime modifications

With the basic unit of work (no pun intended) in `systemd` defined, let's move on to how you control it via the command line.

Management with systemctl

The tool you use to interact with `systemd` to manage services is `systemctl` (*https:// oreil.ly/kigFH*).

In Table 6-1 I've compiled a list of often-used `systemctl` commands.

Table 6-1. Useful systemd commands

Command	Use case
`systemctl enable XXXXX.service`	Enable the service; ready to be started
`systemctl daemon-reload`	Reload all unit files and re-create entire dependency tree
`systemctl start XXXXX.service`	Start the service
`systemctl stop XXXXX.service`	Stop the service
`systemctl restart XXXXX.service`	Stop and then start the service
`systemctl reload XXXXX.service`	Issue `reload` command to service; falls back to `restart`
`systemctl kill XXXXX.service`	Stop service execution
`systemctl status XXXXX.service`	Get a short summary of service state including some log lines

Note that there are many more commands that `systemctl` offers, from dependency management and query to controlling the overall system (`reboot`, for example).

The `systemd` ecosystem has a number of other command-line tools you may find handy and that you should at least be aware of. This includes but is not limited to the following:

bootctl *(https://oreil.ly/WNKjd)*
    Allows you to check the boot loader status and manage available boot loaders.

timedatectl
    Allows you to set and view time- and date-related information (*https://oreil.ly/hmgxb*).

coredumpctl
    Enables you to process saved core dumps. Consider this tool when you're troubleshooting.

Monitoring with journalctl

The journal is a component of systemd; technically it is a binary file managed by the systemd-journald daemon, providing a centralized location for all messages logged by systemd components. We'll cover it in detail in "journalctl" on page 196. All you need to know for now is that this is the tool that allows you to view systemd-managed logs.

Example: scheduling greeter

After all that theory, let's see systemd in action. As a simple use case example, let's assume we want to launch our greeter app (see "Running Example: greeter" on page 116) every hour.

First, we define a systemd unit file of type service. This tells systemd how to start the greeter app; store the following in a file called *greeter.service* (in any directory, could be a temporary one):

```
[Unit]
Description=My Greeting Service ❶

[Service]
Type=oneshot
ExecStart=/home/mh9/greeter.sh ❷
```

❶   The description of our services, shown when we use systemctl status

❷   The location of our app

Next, we define a timer unit (*https://oreil.ly/Qv8qt*) to launch the greeter service every hour. Store the following in a file called *greeter.timer*:

```
[Unit]
Description=Runs Greeting service at the top of the hour

[Timer]
OnCalendar=hourly ❶
```

➊ Defines the schedule using the systemd time and date format (*https://oreil.ly/pinVc*)

Now we copy both unit files to */run/systemd/system* so that `systemd` recognizes them:

```
$ sudo ls -al /run/systemd/system/
total 8
drwxr-xr-x  2 root root  80 Sep 12 13:08 .
drwxr-xr-x 21 root root 500 Sep 12 13:09 ..
-rw-r--r-- 1 root root 117 Sep 12 13:08 greeter.service
-rw-r--r-- 1 root root 107 Sep 12 13:08 greeter.timer
```

We're now in a position to use the greeter timer, since `systemd` automatically picked it up when we copied it into the respective directory.

Debian-based systems such as Ubuntu enable and start service units by default. Red Hat family systems won't start the service without an explicit `systemctl start greeter.timer`. This is also true for enabling services on boot, where Debian-based distros enable services by default, whereas Red Hat distros require an explicit confirmation in the form of `systemctl enable`.

Let's check the status of our greeter timer:

```
$ sudo systemctl status greeter.timer
● greeter.timer - Runs Greeting service at the top of the hour
   Loaded: loaded (/run/systemd/system/greeter.timer; static; \
   vendor preset: enabled)
   Active: active (waiting) since Sun 2021-09-12 13:10:35 IST; 2s ago
  Trigger: Sun 2021-09-12 14:00:00 IST; 49min left
Sep 12 13:10:35 starlite systemd[1]: \
Started Runs Greeting service at the top of the hour.
```

So `systemd` confirms that it knows about our greeter and that it's scheduled to run. But how do you know if it worked? Let's check the logs (note that the output was edited and that the `stdout` output is going directly to the logs):

```
$ journalctl -f -u greeter.service ➊
-- Logs begin at Sun 2021-01-24 14:36:30 GMT. --
Sep 12 14:00:01 starlite systemd[1]: Starting My Greeting Service...
Sep 12 14:00:01 starlite greeter.sh[21071]: You are awesome!
...
```

➊ Using `journalctl` to look at and follow (`-f`) the logs of the *greeter.service* unit (selected with `-u`)

With this high-level `systemd` overview, let's move on to how to manage applications the traditional way, with general-purpose package managers. But before we get into the technicalities of packages, let's step back a bit and discuss apps, packages, and package managers in the context of a broader concept: supply chains.

Linux Application Supply Chains

Let's start with what we mean by *supply chain* (*https://oreil.ly/EegdU*): a system of organizations and individuals supplying a product to a consumer. While you may not think about supply chains a lot, you're dealing with them on a daily basis—for example, when you buy food or fuel your car. In our discussion, the products are applications made up of software artifacts, and you can think of the consumer as either yourself as the person using an app or as a tool that manages the apps for you.

On a conceptual level, Figure 6-2 shows the main actors and phases of a typical Linux application supply chain.

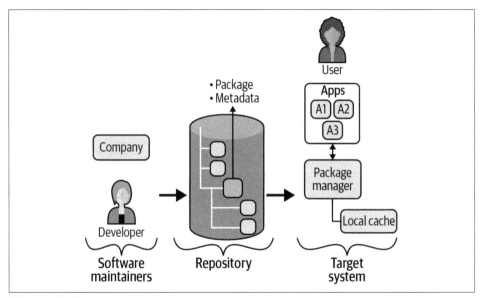

Figure 6-2. Linux app supply chain

The three distinct areas in a Linux application supply are as follows:

Software maintainers
These include individual developers, open source projects, and companies, such as independent software vendors (ISVs), that produce software artifacts and publish them, for example, as packages to a repository (repo).

Repository
This lists the package that contains all or part of an app together with metadata. The package usually captures the dependencies of an app. Dependencies are

other packages that an app needs in order to function. This can be a library, some kind of exporters or importers, or other service programs. Keeping these dependencies up to date is hard.

Tooling (a package manager)
On the target-system side, this can look up packages in the repository and install, update, and remove apps as instructed by the human user. Note that one or more packages can represent the app and its dependencies.

While the details may differ from distribution to distribution and depend on the environment (server, desktop, etc.), the app supply chains all have the elements shown in Figure 6-2 in common.

There are many options available for package and dependency management, such as traditional package managers, container-based solutions, and more recent approaches.

In Figure 6-3, I've tried to give you a high-level overview, without claiming this is a complete picture.

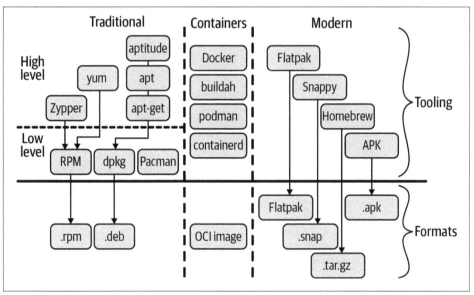

Figure 6-3. The Linux package management and application dependency management universe

A few notes on the three primary categories of options for package and dependency management:

Traditional package managers
> Within this category, we usually differentiate between low-level and high-level tooling. If a package manager can resolve dependencies and provides a high-level interface (install, update, remove), we call it a *high-level* package manager.

Container-based solutions
> These initially came out of the server and cloud computing realm. Given their capabilities, one use case, but not necessarily their primary one, is application management. In other words, as a developer you'll love containers since they enable you to easily test things and make it straightforward to ship your production-ready app. See also "Containers" on page 131.

Modern package managers
> These have their roots in desktop environments, and the main goal here is to make it as easy as possible for the end user to consume apps. See also "Modern Package Managers" on page 143.

Packages and Package Managers

In this section, we discuss package formats and package managers that have been in use for a long time, in some cases decades. These usually stem from two major Linux distribution families: Red Hat (RHEL, Fedora, CentOS, etc.) and Debian-based systems (Debian, Ubuntu, etc.).

The two concepts relevant to our discussions here are the following:

The packages themselves
> Technically a file that usually is zipped and may contain metadata.

The tooling (called package managers)
> Deals with those packages on the target system, to install and maintain apps. A package manager usually interacts with the repo on your behalf and maintains a local cache of packages.

The target system may be a desktop environment on your laptop or a server VM instance in the cloud, for example. Depending on the environment, packages may be more or less applicable—for example, a GUI app on a server is not necessarily something that makes sense.

RPM Package Manager

RPM Package Manager (*https://oreil.ly/Ef2FC*) (for which the recursive acronym RPM is used) was originally created by Red Hat but is now widely used in various distros. The *.rpm* file format is used in Linux Standard Base and can contain binary or source files. The packages can be cryptographically verified and support delta updates via patch files.

Package managers that use RPM include the following:

yum *(https://oreil.ly/sPb2H)*
In Amazon Linux, CentOS, Fedora, and RHEL

DNF (https://oreil.ly/0Pcod)
In CentOS, Fedora, and RHEL

Zypper (https://oreil.ly/OVize)
In openSUSE and SUSE Linux Enterprise

Let's see RPM in action: let's say we have a fresh developer environment and want to install the Go programming language tool chain using yum.

Note that the output in the following shell sessions has been edited and shortened to fit the space (there are many lines in the output that are not relevant to understanding the usage).

First off, we need to find the package for Go:

```
# yum search golang ❶
Loaded plugins: ovl, priorities
================= N/S matched: golang =================
golang-bin.x86_64 : Golang core compiler tools
golang-docs.noarch : Golang compiler docs
...
golang-googlecode-net-devel.noarch : Supplementary Go networking libraries
golang-googlecode-sqlite-devel.x86_64 : Trivial sqlite3 binding for Go
```

❶ Search for the Go package. Note the # prompt, suggesting we're logged in as root. Perhaps a better way would be to use sudo yum.

Equipped with this info about the package, we can now install it using the following:

```
# yum install golang ❶
Loaded plugins: ovl, priorities
Resolving Dependencies ❷
--> Running transaction check
---> Package golang.x86_64 0:1.15.14-1.amzn2.0.1 will be installed
--> Processing Dependency: golang-src = 1.15.14-1.amzn2.0.1 for package:
    golang-1.15.14-1.amzn2.0.1.x86_64
...
Transaction Summary
================================================================================
Install  1 Package (+101 Dependent packages)

Total download size: 183 M
Installed size: 624 M
Is this ok [y/d/N]: y ❸
Dependencies Resolved

================================================================================
```

```
  Package                       Arch     Version                Repository    Size
  ================================================================================
  Installing:
   golang                       x86_64   1.15.14-1.amzn2.0.1 amzn2-core      705 k
  Installing for dependencies:
   acl                          x86_64   2.2.51-14.amzn2        amzn2-core     82 k
   apr                          x86_64   1.6.3-5.amzn2.0.2      amzn2-core    118 k
   ...

    Verifying  : groff-base-1.22.2-8.amzn2.0.2.x86_64                        101/102
    Verifying  : perl-Text-ParseWords-3.29-4.amzn2.noarch                    102/102

  Installed: ❹
    golang.x86_64 0:1.15.14-1.amzn2.0.1

  Dependency Installed:
    acl.x86_64 0:2.2.51-14.amzn2     apr.x86_64 0:1.6.3-5.amzn2.0.2
    ...

  Complete!
```

❶ Install the Go package.

❷ yum's first step is to determine Go's dependencies.

❸ Here yum provides us with a summary of what it found in terms of dependencies and tells us what it plans to do. I need to confirm here interactively by entering a y. However, in a script I would use the yum install golang -y form of the command to automatically accept this.

❹ After verifying that all dependencies and the main package are installed, yum reports success.

Last but not least, we want to verify the package, checking exactly what we have installed and where:

```
# yum info golang
Loaded plugins: ovl, priorities
Installed Packages
Name        : golang
Arch        : x86_64
Version     : 1.15.14
Release     : 1.amzn2.0.1
Size        : 7.8 M
Repo        : installed
From repo   : amzn2-core
Summary     : The Go Programming Language
URL         : http://golang.org/
License     : BSD and Public Domain
Description : The Go Programming Language.
```

Next, let's have a look at the other widely used package manager using Debian packages.

Debian deb

deb (*https://oreil.ly/sctS1*) packages and the *.deb* file format originate from the Debian distro. The deb packages can also contain binary or source files. Multiple package managers use deb, including low-level, no-dependency-management ones such as dpkg, and high-level ones such as apt-get, apt, and aptitude. Given that Ubuntu is a Debian-based distro, deb packages are widely used, on the desktop and server alike.

To see deb packages in action, let's assume we want to install the curl utility with apt. This is a useful tool to interact with HTTP APIs and to download files from a range of locations. Note that we again edited the output to make it fit.

First, we search for the curl package:

```
# apt search curl ❶
Sorting... Done
Full Text Search... Done
curl/focal-updates,focal-security 7.68.0-1ubuntu2.6 amd64
  command line tool for transferring data with URL syntax

curlftpfs/focal 0.9.2-9build1 amd64
  filesystem to access FTP hosts based on FUSE and cURL

flickcurl-doc/focal 1.26-5 all
  utilities to call the Flickr API from command line - documentation

flickcurl-utils/focal 1.26-5 amd64
  utilities to call the Flickr API from command line

gambas3-gb-net-curl/focal 3.14.3-2ubuntu3.1 amd64
  Gambas advanced networking component
...
```

❶ Search for the curl package with apt. Note that there were overall dozens of more search results shown, most of them libraries and language-specific bindings (Python, Ruby, Go, Rust, etc.).

Next, we install the curl package like so:

```
# apt install curl ❶
Reading package lists... Done
Building dependency tree ❷
Reading state information... Done
The following additional packages will be installed:
  ca-certificates krb5-locales libasn1-8-heimdal libbrotli1 ...
```

```
Suggested packages:
  krb5-doc krb5-user libsasl2-modules-gssapi-mit ...

The following NEW packages will be installed:
  ca-certificates curl krb5-locales libasn1-8-heimdal ...

0 upgraded, 32 newly installed, 0 to remove and 2 not upgraded.
Need to get 5447 kB of archives.
After this operation, 16.7 MB of additional disk space will be used.
Do you want to continue? [Y/n] ❸

Get:1 http://archive.ubuntu.com/ubuntu focal-updates/main amd64
      libssl1.1 amd64 1.1.1f-1ubuntu2.8 [1320 kB]
Get:2 http://archive.ubuntu.com/ubuntu focal-updates/main amd64
      openssl amd64 1.1.1f-1ubuntu2.8 [620 kB]
...
Fetched 5447 kB in 1s (3882 kB/s)
Selecting previously unselected package libssl1.1:amd64.
(Reading database ... 4127 files and directories currently installed.)
Preparing to unpack .../00-libssl1.1_1.1.1f-1ubuntu2.8_amd64.deb ...
Unpacking libssl1.1:amd64 (1.1.1f-1ubuntu2.8) ...
...
Setting up libkeyutils1:amd64 (1.6-6ubuntu1) ...
...
Processing triggers for ca-certificates (20210119~20.04.1) ...
Updating certificates in /etc/ssl/certs...
1 added, 0 removed; done. ❹
Running hooks in /etc/ca-certificates/update.d...
Done.
```

❶ Install the curl package.

❷ apt's first step is to determine the dependencies.

❸ Here apt provides us with a dependencies summary and tells us what it will
    install. Interactive confirmation is needed here; in a script I would use apt
    install curl -y to automatically accept it.

❹ After verifying that all dependencies and the main package are installed, apt
    reports success.

And finally we verify the curl package:

```
# apt show curl
Package: curl
Version: 7.68.0-1ubuntu2.6
Priority: optional
Section: web
Origin: Ubuntu
Maintainer: Ubuntu Developers <ubuntu-devel-discuss@lists.ubuntu.com>
```

```
Original-Maintainer: Alessandro Ghedini <ghedo@debian.org>
Bugs: https://bugs.launchpad.net/ubuntu/+filebug
Installed-Size: 411 kB
Depends: libc6 (>= 2.17), libcurl4 (= 7.68.0-1ubuntu2.6), zlib1g (>= 1:1.1.4)
Homepage: http://curl.haxx.se
Task: server, cloud-image, ubuntu-budgie-desktop
Download-Size: 161 kB
APT-Manual-Installed: yes
APT-Sources: http://archive.ubuntu.com/ubuntu focal-updates/main amd64 Packages
Description: command line tool for transferring data with URL syntax

N: There is 1 additional record. Please use the '-a' switch to see it
```

Let's now move on to programming language–specific package managers.

Language-Specific Package Managers

There are also programming language–specific package managers, such as the following:

C/C++
> Have many different package managers (*https://oreil.ly/ibEK2*), including Conan and vcpkg

Go
> Has package management built in (go get, go mod)

Node.js
> Has npm and others

Java
> Has maven and nuts and others

Python
> Has pip and PyPM

Ruby
> Has rubygems and Rails

Rust
> Has cargo

With that, let's look at containers and how you can manage applications with them.

Containers

In the context of this book, we understand a *container* as a Linux process group that uses Linux namespaces, cgroups, and optionally CoW filesystems to provide application-level dependency management. Use cases for containers range from local testing and development (*https://oreil.ly/6RPcT*) to working with distributed systems —for example, working with containerized microservices in Kubernetes (*https://kubernetes.io*).

While containers are very useful for developers and sys admins, as an end user you will more likely be comfortable using higher-level tooling to manage applications—for example, the ones discussed in "Modern Package Managers" on page 143.

If Only I Had Containers

In a previous job, I once had to put together a proof of concept that involved a time series database called InfluxDB. The overall setup required a number of prerequisites (directories created, data copied) as well as dependencies installed. When it came to handing it over to a colleague for demonstration to the customer, I ended up writing up a detailed document that enumerated all the steps and checks to make sure everything worked as planned.

If only at that time container solutions such as Docker had been available, I could have saved myself and my colleague a lot of time by simply packaging up everything into a container. This would not only have made it easy to use for my colleague, but I could also guarantee that it would run in their environment exactly as it did on my laptop.

Containers are, per se, nothing new in Linux. However, they've enjoyed mainstream adoption only due to Docker, starting in roughly 2014. Before that, we had a number of attempts to introduce containers, often targeting system administrators rather than developers, including the following:

- Linux-VServer (2001) (*https://oreil.ly/A5Uri*)
- OpenVZ (2005) (*https://oreil.ly/yM3Tm*)
- LXC (2008) (*https://oreil.ly/BDSjL*)
- Let Me Contain That for You (lmctfy) (2013) (*https://oreil.ly/xpmMx*)

What all of these approaches have in common is that they use the basic building blocks the Linux kernel provides, such as namespaces or cgroups, to allow users to run applications.

Docker innovated on the concept and introduced two groundbreaking elements: a standardized way to define the packaging via container images and a human-friendly user interface (for example, `docker run`). The way container images are defined and distributed, as well as how containers are executed, formed the basis for what is now known as the Open Container Initiative (OCI) (*https://opencontainers.org*) core specifications. When we talk about containers here, we focus on OCI-compliant implementations.

The three core OCI container specifications are as follows:

Runtime specification (https://oreil.ly/vrN0V)
Defines what a runtime needs to support, including operations and life-cycle phases

Image format specification (https://oreil.ly/p0WCY)
Defines how container images are constructed, based on metadata and layers

Distribution specification (https://oreil.ly/kNNeA)
Defines how container images are shipped, effectively the way repositories work in the context of containers

Another idea associated with containers is *immutability*. This means that once a configuration is put together, you cannot change it during its usage. In other words, changes require creating a new (static) configuration and a new resource (such as a process) with it. We will revisit this in the context of container images.

Now that you're aware of what containers are on a conceptual level, let's have a closer look at the building blocks of OCI-compliant containers.

Linux Namespaces

As we discussed in Chapter 1, Linux initially had a global view on resources. To allow processes to have a local view on a resource (such as a filesystem, networking, or even users), Linux introduced namespaces.

In other words, Linux namespaces (*https://oreil.ly/3SvR1*) are all about resource visibility and can be used to isolate different aspects of the operating system resources. Isolation in this context is mostly about what a process sees, not necessarily a hard boundary (from a security perspective).

To create namespaces, you have three relevant syscalls at your disposal:

`clone` *(https://oreil.ly/JNot8)*
Used to create a child process that can share parts of its execution context with the parent process

`unshare` *(https://oreil.ly/9BXiz)*
Used to remove a shared execution context from an existing process

`setns` *(https://oreil.ly/PKGHm)*
Used to join an existing process to an existing namespace

The preceding syscalls take a range of flags as parameters, enabling you to have fine-grained control over the namespaces you want to create, join, or leave:

CLONE_NEWNS

Use for filesystem mount points (*https://oreil.ly/i1Igl*). Visible via */proc/$PID/ mounts*. Supported since Linux 2.4.19.

CLONE_NEWUTS

Use to create hostname and (NIS) domain name (*https://oreil.ly/7lB3U*) isolation. Visible via uname -n and hostname -f. Supported since Linux 2.6.19.

CLONE_NEWIPC

Use to do interprocess communication (IPC) (*https://oreil.ly/h9tlW*) resource isolation like System V IPC objects or POSIX message queues. Visible via */proc/sys/fs/mqueue*, */proc/sys/kernel*, and */proc/sysvipc*. Supported since Linux 2.6.19.

CLONE_NEWPID

Use for PID number space isolation (*https://oreil.ly/Czzu7*) (PID inside/PID outside the namespace). You can gather details about it via */proc/$PID/status*. Supported since Linux 2.6.24.

CLONE_NEWNET

Use to control visibility of network system resources (*https://oreil.ly/X9klx*) such as network devices, IP addresses, IP routing tables, and port numbers. You can view it via ip netns list, */proc/net*, and */sys/class/net*. Supported since Linux 2.6.29.

CLONE_NEWUSER

Use to map UID+GIDs (*https://oreil.ly/uClq3*) inside/outside the namespace. You can query UIDs and GIDs and their mappings via the id command and */proc/ $PID/uid_map* and */proc/$PID/gid_map*. Supported since Linux 3.8.

CLONE_NEWCGROUP

Use to manage cgroups in a namespace (*https://oreil.ly/YAGGb*). You can see it via */sys/fs/cgroup*, */proc/cgroups*, and */proc/$PID/cgroup*. Supported since Linux 4.6.

One way to view namespaces in use on your system is as follows (output edited to fit):

```
$ sudo lsns
         NS TYPE     NPROCS   PID USER          COMMAND
4026531835 cgroup      251     1 root          /sbin/init splash
4026531836 pid         245     1 root          /sbin/init splash
4026531837 user        245     1 root          /sbin/init splash
4026531838 uts         251     1 root          /sbin/init splash
4026531839 ipc         251     1 root          /sbin/init splash
```

```
4026531840 mnt       241    1 root            /sbin/init splash
4026531860 mnt         1   33 root            kdevtmpfs
4026531992 net       244    1 root            /sbin/init splash
4026532233 mnt         1  432 root            /lib/systemd/systemd-udevd
4026532250 user        1 5319 mh9             /opt/google/chrome/nacl_helper
4026532316 mnt         1  684 systemd-timesync /lib/systemd/systemd-timesyncd
4026532491 mnt         1  688 systemd-resolve /lib/systemd/systemd-resolved
...
```

The next container building block focuses on resource consumption limits and reporting on resource usage.

Linux cgroups

Where namespaces are about visibility, *cgroups* (*https://oreil.ly/m4wBr*) provide a different kind of functionality: they are a mechanism to organize process groups. Along with the hierarchical organization, you can use cgroups to control system resources usage. In addition, cgroups provide resource usage tracking; for example, they show how much RAM or CPU seconds a process (group) is using. Think of cgroups as the declarative unit and the controller as a piece of kernel code that enforces a certain resource limitation or reports on its usage.

At this time of writing, there are two versions of cgroups available in the kernel: cgroups v1 and v2. cgroup v1 is still widely used, but v2 will eventually replace v1, so you should focus on v2.

cgroup v1

With cgroup v1 (*https://oreil.ly/iOEcV*), the community had an ad hoc approach, adding new cgroups and controllers as needed. The following v1 cgroups and controllers exist (ordered from oldest to newest; note that the docs are all over the place and inconsistent):

CFS bandwidth control (https://oreil.ly/vGu0Y)
  Used via the cpu cgroup. Supported since Linux 2.6.24.

CPU accounting controller (https://oreil.ly/7NSLN)
  Used via the cpuacct cgroup. Supported since Linux 2.6.24.

cpusets *cgroup (https://oreil.ly/sJp4X)*
  Allows you to assign CPU and memory to a task. Supported since Linux 2.6.24.

Memory resource controller (https://oreil.ly/VjsXY)
  Allows you to isolate the memory behavior of tasks. Supported since Linux 2.6.25.

Device whitelist controller (https://oreil.ly/DklEJ)
  Allows you to control device file usage. Supported since Linux 2.6.26.

`freezer` *cgroup (https://oreil.ly/waLVz)*
Used for batch job management. Supported since Linux 2.6.28.

Network classifier cgroup (https://oreil.ly/fGcWg)
Used to assign different priorities to packets. Supported since Linux 2.6.29.

Block IO controller (https://oreil.ly/V3Zto)
Allows you to throttle block I/D. Supported since Linux 2.6.33.

`perf_event` *command (https://oreil.ly/AMWei)*
Allows you to collect performance data. Supported since Linux 2.6.39.

Network priority cgroup (https://oreil.ly/4e9f2)
Allows you to dynamically set the priority of network traffic. Supported since Linux 3.3.

HugeTLB controller (https://oreil.ly/dzl7L)
Allows you to limit HugeTLB usage. Supported since Linux 3.5.

Process number controller (https://oreil.ly/WkBss)
Used to allow a cgroup hierarchy to create new processes after a certain limit is reached. Supported since Linux 4.3.

cgroup v2

cgroup v2 (*https://oreil.ly/YWCEi*) is a total rewrite of cgroups with the lessons learned from v1. This is true both in terms of consistent configuration and use of the cgroups as well as the (centralized and uniform) documentation. Unlike the per-process cgroup v1 design, cgroup v2 has only single hierarchy, and all controllers are managed the same way. Here are the v2 controllers:

CPU controller
Regulates distribution of CPU cycles, supporting different models (weight, max) and includes usage reporting

Memory controller
Regulates distribution of memory with a range of control parameters, supporting user-space memory, kernel data structures such as dentries and inodes, and TCP socket buffers

I/O controller
Regulates the distribution of I/O resources with both weight-based and absolute bandwidth or I/O operations per second (IOPS) limits, reporting on bytes and IOPS read/writes

Process number (PID) controller
Is similar to the v1 version

cpuset *controller*
    Is similar to the v1 version

device *controller*
    Manages access to device files, implemented on top of eBPF

rdma *controller*
    Regulates the distribution and accounting of remote direct memory access
    (RDMA) resources (*https://oreil.ly/a5Wk3*)

HugeTLB controller
    Is similar to the v1 version

There are also miscellaneous cgroups in v2 that allow resource limits and tracking
mechanisms for scalar resources (which can't be abstracted like other cgroup
resources).

You can view all of the v2 cgroups in your Linux system in a nice tree rendering via
the systemctl command, as shown in the following example (output shortened and
edited to fit):

```
$ systemctl status ❶
starlite
    State: degraded
     Jobs: 0 queued
   Failed: 1 units
    Since: Tue 2021-09-07 11:49:08 IST; 1 weeks 1 days ago
   CGroup: /
           ├─22160 bpfilter_umh
           ├─user.slice
           │ └─user-1000.slice ❷
           │   ├─user@1000.service
           │   │ ├─gvfs-goa-volume-monitor.service
           │   │ │ └─14497 /usr/lib/gvfs/gvfs-goa-volume-monitor
    ...
```

❶ Using the systemctl tool to render cgroups

❷ An example of a specific cgroup that systemd manages

Another useful view on cgroups is interactive resource usage, as shown in the following (output edited to fit):

```
$ systemd-cgtop
Control Group                       Tasks  %CPU   Memory  Input/s Output/s
/                                     623  15.7     5.8G        -        -
/docker                                 -     -    48.3M        -        -
/system.slice                         122   6.2     1.6G        -        -
/system.slice/ModemManager.service      3     -   748.0K        -        -
...
```

```
/system.slice/rsyslog.service          4    -    420.0K    -    -
/system.slice/snapd.service           17    -    5.1M      -    -
```

Going forward, you can expect that, as modern kernel versions are more widely used, the cgroups v2 will become the standard. There are indeed certain distros, such as Arch (*https://oreil.ly/rxFF2*), Fedora 31+, and Ubuntu 21.10, that already have v2 by default.

Copy-on-Write Filesystems

The third building block of containers are CoW filesystems, as discussed in greater detail in "Copy-on-Write Filesystems" on page 111. These are used at build time. They package the application and all of its dependencies into a single, self-contained file that you can distribute. Usually the CoW filesystems are used in combination with bind mounts (*https://oreil.ly/BS4nK*) to layer the content of the different dependencies on top of each other in an efficient manner.

Docker

Docker is a human-friendly container implementation developed and popularized by Docker Inc. in 2014. With Docker, it's easy to package up programs and their dependencies and launch them in a range of environments, from desktops to the cloud. What's so unique about Docker is not the building blocks (namespaces, cgroups, CoW filesystems, and bind mounts). These existed a while before Docker came into being. What's so special is that Docker combined these building blocks in a way that makes them easy to use by hiding the complexity of managing the low-level bits like namespaces and cgroups.

As shown in Figure 6-4 and described in the passage that follows, there are two main concepts in Docker: the image and the running container.

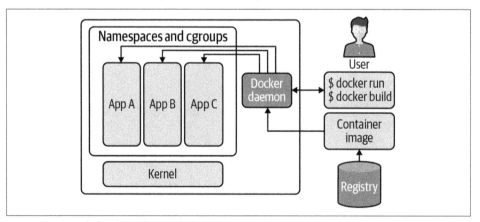

Figure 6-4. High-level Docker architecture

The container image
> A compressed archive file that contains metadata in JSON files and the layers, which are effectively directories. The Docker daemon pulls the container images as needed from a container registry.

The container as the runtime artifact (for example, app A/B/C)
> You can start, stop, kill, and remove it. You interact with the Docker daemon using a client CLI tool (`docker`). This CLI tool sends commands to the daemon, which in turn executes the respective operation, such as building or running a container.

Table 6-2 presents a short reference of often-used Docker CLI commands, covering both the build-time and the runtime phases. To get the full reference, including use cases, refer to the Docker docs (*https://oreil.ly/y1c1W*).

Table 6-2. Often-used Docker commands

Command	Description	Example
`run`	Launch a container	Run NGINX as a daemon and remove container on exit: `docker run -d --rm nginx:1.21`
`ps`	List containers	List all containers (including nonrunning): `docker ps -a`
`inspect`	Display low-level info	To query the container IP: `docker inspect -f '{{.Network Settings.IPAddress}}'`
`build`	Generate a container image locally	Build image based on current directory and tag: `docker build -t some:tag .`
`push`	Upload a container image to a registry	Push to AWS registry: `docker push public.ecr.aws/some:tag`
`pull`	Download a container image from a registry	Pull from AWS registry: `docker pull public.ecr.aws/some:tag`
`images`	List local container images	List images from a certain registry: `docker images ubuntu`
`image`	Manage container images	Remove all unused images: `docker image prune -all`

Let's now have a closer look at the build-time artifact: the container image that Docker uses.

Container Images

To define the instructions on how to build a container image, you use a plain text file format called Dockerfile (*https://oreil.ly/dM8LO*).

There are different directives you can have in a Dockerfile:

Base images
> FROM; can be multiple for build/run phases

Metadata
> LABEL for lineage

Arguments and environment variables
> ARGS, ENV

Build-time specifications
> COPY, RUN, etc., which define how the image is constructed, layer for layer

Runtime specifications
> CMD and ENTRYPOINT, which define how the container can be run

Using the docker build command, you turn a collection of files that represent your application (either as source or in binary format), along with the Dockerfile, into a container image. This container image is the artifact that you can then run or push to a registry, in order to distribute it for others to pull and eventually run.

Running containers

You can run containers with interactive input (terminal attached) or as daemons (background). The docker run (*https://oreil.ly/87YZq*) command takes a container image and a set of runtime inputs, such as environment variables, ports to expose, and volumes to mount. With this information, Docker creates the necessary namespaces and cgroups and launches the application defined in the container image (CMD or ENTRYPOINT).

With the Docker theory out of the way, let's see it in action.

Example: containerized greeter

Let's now put our greeter app (see "Running Example: greeter" on page 116) into a container and run it.

First off, we need to define the Dockerfile, which contains the instructions to build the container image:

```
FROM ubuntu:20.04 ❶
LABEL org.opencontainers.image.authors="Michael Hausenblas" ❷
COPY greeter.sh /app/ ❸
WORKDIR /app ❹
RUN chown -R 1001:1 /app ❺
USER 1001
ENTRYPOINT ["/app/greeter.sh"] ❻
```

❶ Define the base image using an explicit tag (20.04).

❷ Assign some metadata via a label (*https://oreil.ly/eYWVo*).

❸ Copy shell script. This could be a binary, a JAR file, or a Python script.

❹ Set the working directory.

❺ This and the next line define the user running the app. If you don't do this, it will unnecessarily run as root.

❻ Define what to run, in our case the shell script. The way we defined it, using ENTRYPOINT, it is possible to pass a parameter by running docker run greeter:1 _SOME_PARAMETER_.

Next, we build the container image:

```
$ sudo docker build -t greeter:1 . ❶
Sending build context to Docker daemon  3.072kB
Step 1/7 : FROM ubuntu:20.04 ❷
20.04: Pulling from library/ubuntu
35807b77a593: Pull complete
Digest: sha256:9d6a8699fb5c9c39cf08a0871bd6219f0400981c570894cd8cbea30d3424a31f
Status: Downloaded newer image for ubuntu:20.04
 ---> fb52e22af1b0
Step 2/7 : LABEL org.opencontainers.image.authors="Michael Hausenblas"
 ---> Running in 6aa921276c3b
Removing intermediate container 6aa921276c3b
 ---> def717e3352b
Step 3/7 : COPY greeter.sh /app/
 ---> 5f3eb160fea3
Step 4/7 : WORKDIR /app
 ---> Running in 698c29938a96
Removing intermediate container 698c29938a96
 ---> d73572886c13
Step 5/7 : RUN chown -R 1001:1 /app
 ---> Running in 5b5eb5d1935a
Removing intermediate container 5b5eb5d1935a
 ---> 42c35a6db6e2
Step 6/7 : USER 1001
 ---> Running in bec92deaac6e
Removing intermediate container bec92deaac6e
 ---> b6e0e27f253b
Step 7/7 : CMD ["/app/greeter.sh"]
 ---> Running in 6d3b439f7e50
Removing intermediate container 6d3b439f7e50
 ---> 433a5f10d84e
Successfully built 433a5f10d84e
Successfully tagged greeter:1
```

❶ Build the container image and label it (with `-t greeter:1`). The `.` means that it uses the current directory and assumes that a Dockerfile is present there.

❷ This and the next lines pull the base image and build it layer by layer.

Let's check if the container image is there:

```
$ sudo docker images
REPOSITORY    TAG      IMAGE ID        CREATED          SIZE
greeter       1        433a5f10d84e    35 seconds ago   72.8MB
ubuntu        20.04    fb52e22af1b0    2 weeks ago      72.8MB
```

Now we can run a container based on the `greeter:1` image, like so:

```
$ sudo docker run greeter:1
You are awesome!
```

That wraps up our Docker 101. We'll now take a quick look at related tooling.

Other Container Tooling

You don't have to use Docker to work with OCI containers; as an alternative, you can use a Red Hat–led and –sponsored combo: `podman` (*https://podman.io*) and `buildah` (*https://buildah.io*). These daemon-less tools allow you to build OCI container images (`buildah`) and run them (`podman`).

In addition, there are a number of tools that make working with OCI containers, namespaces, and cgroups easier, including but not limited to the following:

`containerd` (*https://oreil.ly/mIKkm*)
A daemon that manages the OCI container life cycle, from image transfer and storage to container runtime supervision

`skopeo` (*https://oreil.ly/UAom6*)
For container image manipulation (copying, inspecting manifest, etc.)

`systemd-cgtop` (*https://oreil.ly/aDgBa*)
A kind of cgroups-aware variant of `top` that shows resource usage interactively

`nsenter` (*https://oreil.ly/D0Gbc*)
Allows you to execute a program in a specified, existing namespace

`unshare` (*https://oreil.ly/oOigx*)
Allows you to run a program with specific namespaces (opt in via flags)

`lsns` (*https://oreil.ly/jY7Q6*)
Lists information about Linux namespaces

`cinf` *(https://oreil.ly/yaiMo)*
> Lists information about Linux namespaces and cgroups associated with process IDs

With this we end our containers tour. Let's now look at modern package managers and how they utilize containers to isolate applications from each other.

Modern Package Managers

In addition to the more traditional package managers that often are distribution-specific, there is a new sort of package manager. These modern solutions often make use of containers and aim to be cross-distribution or target specific environments. For example, they can make it easy for Linux desktop users to install GUI apps.

Snap (https://oreil.ly/n4fe6)
> A Canonical Ltd.–designed and –promoted software packaging and deployment system. It comes with a refined sandboxing (*https://oreil.ly/ImWPH*) setup and can be used in desktop, cloud, and IoT environments.

Flatpak (https://oreil.ly/sEEu1)
> Optimized for Linux desktop environments, using cgroups, namespaces, bind mounts, and seccomp as its building blocks. While initially from the Red Hat part of the Linux distro universe, it is now available for dozens of distros, including Fedora, Mint, Ubuntu, Arch, Debian, openSUSE, and Chrome OS.

AppImage (https://oreil.ly/76Uhu)
> Has been around for years and promotes the idea that one app equals one file; that is, it requires no dependencies other than what is included in the targeted Linux system. Over time, a number of interesting features have found their way into AppImage, from efficient updates to desktop integration to software catalogs.

Homebrew (https://oreil.ly/XegIz)
> Originally from the macOS world but available for Linux and enjoying increasing popularity. It's written in Ruby and has a powerful yet intuitive user interface.

Conclusion

In this chapter, we covered a wide range of topics, all related to how to install, maintain, and use applications on Linux.

We first defined basic application terms, then we looked at the Linux startup process, discussing `systemd`, the now standard way of managing startup and components.

To distribute applications, Linux uses packages and package managers. We discussed various managers in this context and how you can use containers for development and testing as well as dependency management. Docker containers use Linux primitives (cgroups, namespaces, CoW filesystems) to provide you with application-level dependency management (via container images).

Finally, we looked at custom solutions for app management, including Snap and others.

If you're interested in further reading on the topics in this chapter, have a look at the following resources:

Startup process and init systems
- "Analyzing the Linux Boot Process" (*https://oreil.ly/bYPw5*)
- "Stages of Linux Booting Process" (*https://oreil.ly/k90in*)
- "How to Configure a Linux Service to Start Automatically After a Crash or Reboot" (*https://oreil.ly/tvaMe*)

Package management
- "2021 State of the Software Supply Chain" (*https://oreil.ly/66mo5*)
- "Linux Package Management" (*https://oreil.ly/MFGlL*)
- "Understanding RPM Package Management Tutorial" (*https://oreil.ly/jiRj8*)
- Debian packages (*https://oreil.ly/DmAvc*)

Containers
- "A Practical Introduction to Container Terminology" (*https://oreil.ly/zn69i*)
- "From Docker to OCI: What Is a Container?" (*https://oreil.ly/NUxrE*)
- "Building Containers Without Docker" (*https://oreil.ly/VofA0*)
- "Why Red Hat Is Investing in CRI-O and Podman" (*https://oreil.ly/KJB9O*)
- "Demystifying Containers" (*https://oreil.ly/Anvty*)
- "Rootless Containers" (*https://oreil.ly/FLTHf*)
- "Docker Storage Drivers Deep Dive" (*https://oreil.ly/8QPPh*)
- "The Hunt for a Better Dockerfile" (*https://oreil.ly/MLAom*)

Now that you know all the basics around applications let's move on from the scope of a single Linux system to an interconnected setup and its necessary precondition: networking.

## CHAPTER 7

Networking

In this chapter, we go into detail about Linux networking. In modern environments, the network stack that Linux provides is an essential component. Without it, few things are possible. Whether you want to access an instance in your cloud provider, browse the web, or install a new app, you need connectivity, and you need a way to interact with it.

We'll first have a look at common network terms, from the hardware level all the way up to user-facing components such as HTTP and SSH. We'll also discuss the network stack, protocols, and interfaces. Specifically, we'll spend time on the naming center piece of the web and the wider internet, the so-called Domain Name System (DNS). Interestingly, this system is found not only in wide-area deployments but is also a central component used for service discovery in container environments such as Kubernetes.

Next, we'll look at application layer network protocols and tooling. This includes file sharing, the web, networked filesystems, and other methods to share data over the network.

In the last part of the chapter, we'll review some advanced network topics, from geo-mapping to managing time over the network.

To set the expectations for the content in this chapter: you can spend a lot of time with the topic of Linux networking; in fact, entire books are dedicated to the topic. We'll take a pragmatic stance here, jumping into hands-on topics from an end-user point of view. Admin topics around networking, such as configuration and setup of network devices, are by and large out of scope here.

Now, let's turn our attention to the networking basics.

Basics

Let's first discuss why networking is relevant for a number of use cases and define some common network terminology.

In modern environments, networking plays a central role. This ranges from tasks such as installing apps, browsing the web, and viewing mail or social media to working with remote machines (from the embedded system you're connecting to over a local network to servers that run in data centers of your cloud providers). Given a network's many moving parts and layers, it can be difficult to figure out if a problem is hardware-related or originates in the software stack.

Another challenge Linux networking addresses comes from abstractions: many of the things we'll cover in this chapter provide a high-level user interface, making it appear that files or applications that in reality run on a remote machine are accessible or can be manipulated on your local machine. While providing an abstraction that makes remote resources seem to be local is a useful feature, we should not forget that at the end of the day, all of this boils down to bits traveling over the wire and through the air. Keep this in mind when troubleshooting or testing.

Figure 7-1 shows how, on a high level, networking works in Linux. There is some kind of networking hardware, such as Ethernet or wireless cards; then a number of kernel-level components, such as the TCP/IP stack; and finally, in the user space, a range of tools to configure, query, and use networking.

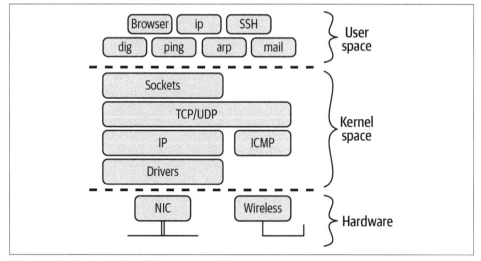

Figure 7-1. An overview of Linux networking

Let's now dive into the TCP/IP stack, the core of networking in Linux.

Unlike in other areas of Linux, where you need to either consult the source code or hope for properly documented design assumptions behind interfaces and protocols, in the networking space, almost every protocol and interface is based on publicly available specifications. The Internet Engineering Task Force (IETF) makes all of those requests for comments (RFCs) freely available via *data tracker.ietf.org*.

Make a habit out of simply reading these RFCs before you get into the details of implementations. Those RFCs are written by practitioners for practitioners and document good practices and how to implement stuff. Don't be afraid of working through them; you'll gain a much better understanding about the motivation, use cases, and reasons why things are the way they are.

The TCP/IP Stack

The TCP/IP stack, shown in Figure 7-2, is a layered network model made of a number of protocols and tools, mostly defined by IETF specs. Each layer must be aware of and able to communicate with only the layers right above and below itself. The data is encapsulated in packets, and each layer typically wraps the data in a header that contains information relevant for its function. So, if an app wants to send data, it would interact directly with the highest layer that would add a header and so on down the stack (the send path). Conversely, if an app wants to receive data, it would arrive at the lowest layer, and each layer in turn would process it based on the header information it finds and pass the payload on to the layer above (the receive path).

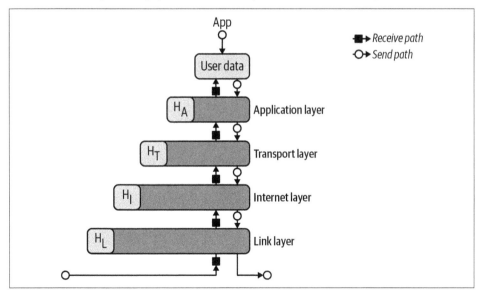

Figure 7-2. The TCP/IP layers working together to enable communication

Starting at the bottom of the stack, the four layers of the TCP/IP stack are the following:

The link layer
> Lowest in the stack, this layer covers the hardware (Ethernet, WiFi) and kernel drivers and focuses on how packets are sent between physical devices. See "The Link Layer" on page 149 for details.

The internet layer
> With the Internet Protocol (IP), this layer focuses on routing; that is, it supports sending packets between machines across networks. We'll discuss it in "The Internet Layer" on page 152.

The transport layer
> This layer controls end-to-end communications between (virtual or physical) hosts, with the Transmission Control Protocol (TCP) for session-based, reliable communication and User Datagram Protocol (UDP) for connection-less communication. It mainly deals with how packets are transmitted, including addressing individual services on a machine via ports as well as data integrity. Further, Linux supports sockets as communication endpoints. See "The Transport Layer" on page 160.

The application layer
> This layer deals with user-facing tooling and apps, such as the web, SSH, and mail. We'll discuss it in "DNS" on page 165 and "Application Layer Networking" on page 173.

The Internet and OSI

The internet has its roots in a US Department of Defense project started in the 1960s that had the goal to create a communication network that couldn't easily be destroyed. The internet is a network of networks—that is, many local networks hooked up with a backend infrastructure enabling communication between different systems.

You'll likely come across the Open Systems Interconnection (OSI) model, a theoretical model of networking that uses seven layers, with the seventh, the top-most layer, being the application layer. The TCP/IP model has only four layers, but the TCP/IP stack is what is used everywhere in practice.

Don't get confused by the layer numbering. Usually, since the hardware counts as layer 1, the link layer would be 2, the internet layer 3, the transport layer 4, and (for historical reasons, to be OSI model-aligned), the application layer would be 7.

The layering means that the header and the payload of a layer make up the payload for the next layer. For example, looking at Figure 7-2, the payload in the internet layer is the transport layer header H_T and its payload. In other words, the internet layer takes the packet it gets from the transport layer, treats it as an opaque chunk of bytes, and can focus on its function, the routing of the packet to the target machine.

Let's now work our way up the TCP/IP stack, starting with the lowest layer, the link layer.

The Link Layer

In the link layer of the TCP/IP stack, it's all about hardware or near-hardware stuff, such as bytes, wires, electromagnetic waves, device drivers, and network interfaces. You'll come across the following terms in this context:

Ethernet
A family of networking technologies using wires to connect machines; often used in local area networks (LANs).

Wireless
Also known as WiFi, a class of communication protocols and methods that, rather than using wires, uses some electromagnetic waves to transport data.

MAC addresses
Short for *media access control*, MAC is a unique 48-bit identifier for hardware, used to identify your machine (to be precise, the network interface; see the following term). The MAC address encodes the manufacturer (of the interface) via the organizationally unique identifier (OUI), usually occupying the first 24 bits.

Interface
A network connection. It can be a physical interface (see "Network interface controller" on page 149 for details) or a virtual (software) interface, like the loopback interface lo.

Equipped with these basics, let's have a closer look at the link layer.

Network interface controller

One essential piece of hardware equipment is the *network interface controller* (NIC) (*https://oreil.ly/fZeVJ*), sometimes also called the *network interface card*. The NIC provides the physical connectivity to a network through either a wired standard—for example, the IEEE 802.3-2018 standard for Ethernet (*https://oreil.ly/9g4Mu*)—or one of the many wireless standards from the IEEE 802.11 family (*https://oreil.ly/V5NiL*). Once part of a network, the NIC turns the digital representation of the bytes you want to send into electrical or electromagnetic signals. The reverse is true for the receive path, where the NIC turns whatever physical signals it receives into bits and bytes that the software can deal with.

Let's have a look at NICs in action. Traditionally, one would use the (now widely considered deprecated) ifconfig command (*https://oreil.ly/QwgOc*) to query information on the NICs available on the system (we show it here first for educational purposes; in practice, it's better to use ip, as shown in the next example):

```
$ ifconfig
lo: flags=73<UP,LOOPBACK,RUNNING>  mtu 65536  ❶
        inet 127.0.0.1  netmask 255.0.0.0
        inet6 ::1  prefixlen 128  scopeid 0x10<host>
        loop  txqueuelen 1000  (Local Loopback)
        RX packets 7218  bytes 677714 (677.7 KB)
        RX errors 0  dropped 0  overruns 0  frame 0
        TX packets 7218  bytes 677714 (677.7 KB)
        TX errors 0  dropped 0 overruns 0  carrier 0  collisions 0

wlp1s0: flags=4163<UP,BROADCAST,RUNNING,MULTICAST>  mtu 1500  ❷
        inet 192.168.178.40  netmask 255.255.255.0  broadcast 192.168.178.255
        inet6 fe80::be87:e600:7de7:e08f  prefixlen 64  scopeid 0x20<link>
        ether 38:de:ad:37:32:0f  txqueuelen 1000  (Ethernet)
        RX packets 2398756  bytes 3003287387 (3.0 GB)
        RX errors 0  dropped 7  overruns 0  frame 0
        TX packets 504087  bytes 85467550 (85.4 MB)
        TX errors 0  dropped 0 overruns 0  carrier 0  collisions 0
```

❶ The first interface here is lo, the loopback interface with the IP address 127.0.0.1 (see "IPv4" on page 153). The maximum transmission unit (MTU) is the packet size, here 65,536 bytes (with larger sizes meaning higher throughput); for historical reasons, the default for Ethernet was 1,500 bytes, but you can use jumbo frames (*https://oreil.ly/NjpnF*) that are 9,000 bytes in size.

❷ The second interface reported is wlp1s0, with an IPv4 address of 192.168.178.40 assigned. This interface is an NIC and has a MAC address (ether is 38:de:ad:37:32:0f). When looking at the flags (<UP,BROADCAST,RUN NING,MULTICAST>), it seems to be operational.

For a more modern approach of doing the same thing (querying interfaces and checking on their status), use the ip command (*https://oreil.ly/pruUF*). We'll use this approach most often in this chapter (output edited to fit):

```
$ ip link show
1: lo: <LOOPBACK,UP,LOWER_UP> mtu 65536 qdisc noqueue  ❶
    state UNKNOWN mode DEFAULT group default qlen 1000
    link/loopback 00:00:00:00:00:00 brd 00:00:00:00:00:00
2: wlp1s0: <BROADCAST,MULTICAST,UP,LOWER_UP> mtu 1500 qdisc noqueue  ❷
    state UP mode DORMANT group default qlen 1000
     link/ether 38:de:ad:37:32:0f brd ff:ff:ff:ff:ff:ff
```

❶ The loopback interface.

❷ My NIC, with a MAC address of `38:de:ad:37:32:0f`. Note that the name (`wlp1s0`) here tells you something about the interface: it's a wireless interface (`wl`) in PCI bus 1 (`p1`) and slot 0 (`s0`). This naming makes the interface names more predictable. In other words, if you had two old-style interfaces (say, `eth0` and `eth1`), there was no guarantee that a reboot or adding a new card wouldn't cause Linux to rename those interfaces.

For both `ifconfig` and `ip link`, you might be interested in the meaning of flags such as `LOWER_IP` or `MULTICAST`; these are documented in the netdevice man pages (*https://oreil.ly/OTB7R*).

Address Resolution Protocol

The Address Resolution Protocol (ARP) maps MAC addresses to IP addresses. In a sense, it bridges the link layer with the layer above it, the internet layer.

Let's see it in action:

```
$ arp ❶
Address                 HWtype  HWaddress           Flags Mask      Iface
mh9-imac.fritz.box      ether   00:25:4b:9b:64:49   C               wlp1s0
fritz.box               ether   3c:a6:2f:8e:66:b3   C               wlp1s0
```

❶ Use the `arp` command to show the cache of mapping MAC addresses to hostnames or IP addresses. Note that you can use `arp -n` to prevent hostname resolution and show IP addresses instead of DNS names.

Or, using a more modern approach with `ip`:

```
$ ip neigh ❶
192.168.178.34 dev wlp1s0 lladdr 00:25:4b:9b:64:49 STALE
192.168.178.1 dev wlp1s0 lladdr 3c:a6:2f:8e:66:b3 REACHABLE
```

❶ Use the `ip` command to show the cache of mapping MAC addresses to IP addresses.

To display, configure, and troubleshoot wireless devices, you want to use the `iw` command (*https://oreil.ly/fyR0y*). For example, I know that my wireless NIC is called `wlp1s0`, so I can query it:

```
$ iw dev wlp1s0 info ❶
Interface wlp1s0
        ifindex 2
        wdev 0x1
        addr 38:de:ad:37:32:0f
        ssid FRITZ!Box 7530 QJ ❷
        type managed
```

```
wiphy 0
    channel 5 (2432 MHz), width: 20 MHz, center1: 2432 MHz ❸
    txpower 20.00 dBm
```

❶ Show base information about wireless interface wlp1s0.

❷ The router the interface is connected to (see also the next example).

❸ The WiFi frequency band the interface is using.

Further, I can gather router- and traffic-related information like so:

```
$ iw dev wlp1s0 link ❶
Connected to 74:42:7f:67:ca:b5 (on wlp1s0)
        SSID: FRITZ!Box 7530 QJ
        freq: 2432
        RX: 28003606 bytes (45821 packets) ❷
        TX: 4993401 bytes (15605 packets)
        signal: -67 dBm
        tx bitrate: 65.0 MBit/s MCS 6 short GI

        bss flags:      short-preamble short-slot-time
        dtim period:    1
        beacon int:     100
```

❶ Show connection information about wireless interface wlp1s0.

❷ This and the next line send (TX stands for "transmit") and receive (RX) statistics—
   that is, bytes and packets sent and received via this interface.

Now that we have a good handle on what's going on in the lowest layer of the TCP/IP
stack, the (data) link layer, let's move up the stack.

The Internet Layer

The second-lowest layer of the TCP/IP stack, the internet layer, is concerned with
routing packets from one machine on the network to another. The design of the
internet layer assumes that the available network infrastructure is unreliable and that
the participants (such as nodes in the network or the connections between them)
change frequently.

The internet layer provides best-effort delivery (that is, no guarantees concerning
performance) and treats every packet as independent. As a consequence, higher layers, typically the transport layer, take care of addressing reliability issues, including
packet order, retries, or delivery guarantees.

How Routing Is Like Surface Mail

Think of an internet layer address as similar to your postal address. This postal address is made up of a number of parts, from the most coarse grained (the country) down to the street-level information, including house number.

That postal address is all I need to know to make sure that I can send, say, a postcard to you from anywhere in the world. Note also that I don't need to know the details of the transportation (such as when my postcard travels via ship or plane, or what exact path is taken). The contract between me and the post office is simple: if I put the correct address on it and pay the correct amount (via the right stamp), the post office promises to deliver it.

Likewise, your machine is identified by the internet layer via a logical address.

In this layer, the dominating protocol for logically identifying machines uniquely, worldwide, is the Internet Protocol (IP), which comes in two flavors, IP version 4 (IPv4) and IP version 6 (IPv6).

IPv4

IPv4 defines unique 32-bit numbers identifying a host or process acting as an endpoint in a TCP/IP communication.

One way to write IPv4 addresses is to split up the 32-bit into four 8-bit segments separated by a period, each segment in the 0 to 255 range, called an *octet* (hinting at that the segment covers 8 bits). Let's have a look at a concrete example:

❶ First octet in binary form: `00111111`

❷ Second octet in binary form: `00100000`

❸ Third octet in binary form: `01101010`

❹ Fourth octet in binary form: `10010101`

The IP header (Figure 7-3), as defined in RFC 791 (*https://oreil.ly/7u93r*) and related IETF specs, has a number of fields, but the following are the most important ones that you should be aware of:

Source address (32 bits)
    The IP address of the sender

Destination address (32 bits)
    The IP address of the receiver

Protocol (8 bits)
    The payload type (next-higher layer type), as per RFC 790 (*https://oreil.ly/Y8PPz*)
    —for example, TCP, UDP, or ICMP

Time to live, aka TTL (8 bits)
    The maximal time the packet is allowed to exist

Type of service (8 bits)
    Can be used for quality of service (QoS) purposes

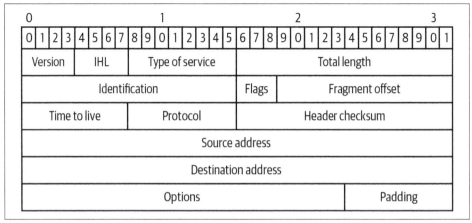

Figure 7-3. The IP header format as per RFC 791

Given that the internet is a network of networks, it seems natural to distinguish between networks and single machines (hosts) in the networks. IP address ranges are assigned to networks and within those networks to individual hosts.

Today, the Classless Inter-Domain Routing (CIDR) (*https://oreil.ly/VDVuy*) is the only relevant method for assigning IP addresses. The CIDR format consists of two parts:

- The first part represents the network address. This looks like a normal IP address —for example, `10.0.0.0`.

- The second part defines how many bits (and with that, IP addresses) fall within the address range—for example, `/24`.

So, a complete CIDR range example looks like the following:

```
10.0.0.0/24
```

In the preceding example, the first 24 bits (or three octets) represent the network, and the last 8 bits (32 bits overall minus the 24 bits for the network) are the IP addresses available for the 256 hosts (2^8). The first IP address in this CIDR range is `10.0.0.0`, and the last IP address is `10.0.0.255`. Strictly speaking, only the addresses `10.0.0.1` to `10.0.0.254` can be assigned to hosts since the `.0` and `.255` addresses are reserved for special purposes. In addition, we can say that the netmask is `255.255.255.0` since that's the first 24 bits representing the network.

In practice, you don't need to remember all the math here. If you're dealing with CIDR ranges on a daily basis, then you just know, and if you're a casual user, you may want to use some tooling. If you want to do CIDR range calculations, such as determining how many IPs are in a range, the following are available:

- Online tools such as those at *https://cidr.xyz* and *https://ipaddressguide.com/cidr*
- Command-line tools like mapcidr (*https://oreil.ly/2uTwU*) and cidrchk (by yours truly) (*https://oreil.ly/g88Yk*)

There are also some notable reserved IPv4 addresses (*https://oreil.ly/97Tp7*) you should know:

`127.0.0.0`
This subnet is reserved for local addresses, with the most prominent one being the loopback address `127.0.0.1`.

`169.254.0.0/16` (`169.254.0.0` *to* `169.254.255.255`)
These are link local addresses, meaning packets sent there should not be forwarded to other parts of the network. Some cloud providers such as Amazon Web Services use this for special services (metadata).

`224.0.0.0/24` (`224.0.0.0` *to* `239.255.255.255`)
This range is reserved for multicast.

RFC 1918 (*https://oreil.ly/2Ijxk*) defines private IP ranges. A private IP range means that the IP addresses in it are not routable on the public internet; hence, it is safe to assign them internally (for example, in the context of your company):

- `10.0.0.0` to `10.255.255.255` (the 10/8 prefix)
- `172.16.0.0` to `172.31.255.255` (172.16/12 prefix)
- `192.168.0.0` to `192.168.255.255` (192.168/16 prefix)

Another interesting IPv4 address is 0.0.0.0. It is a nonroutable address that has different use cases and different meanings depending on the context, but the most important one, from a server perspective, is that 0.0.0.0 refers to all IPv4 addresses present in the machine. That's a great way to say "listen on all available IP addresses" as a source until it turns into a known IP.

That was a lot of dry theory; let's see it in action. We'll start by querying the machine for IP-related things (output edited):

```
$ ip addr show ❶
1: lo: <LOOPBACK,UP,LOWER_UP> mtu 65536 qdisc noqueue
    state UNKNOWN group default qlen 1000
    link/loopback 00:00:00:00:00:00 brd 00:00:00:00:00:00
    inet 127.0.0.1/8 scope host lo ❷
       valid_lft forever preferred_lft forever
    inet6 ::1/128 scope host
       valid_lft forever preferred_lft forever
2: wlp1s0: <BROADCAST,MULTICAST,UP,LOWER_UP> mtu 1500 qdisc
    noqueue state UP group default qlen 1000
    link/ether 38:de:ad:37:32:0f brd ff:ff:ff:ff:ff:ff
    inet 192.168.178.40/24 brd 192.168.178.255 scope global dynamic ❸
    noprefixroute wlp1s0
       valid_lft 863625sec preferred_lft 863625sec
    inet6 fe80::be87:e600:7de7:e08f/64 scope link noprefixroute
       valid_lft forever preferred_lft forever
```

❶ List addresses of all interfaces.

❷ The IP address of the loopback interface (127.0.0.1, as expected).

❸ The (private) IP address of the wireless NIC. Note that this is the LAN-local IP address of the machine, which isn't publicly routable since it falls in the 192.168/16 range.

The IPv4 address space is already exhausted, and given that there are many more endpoints today than the internet designers thought there would be (for example, due to mobile devices and IoT), a sustainable solution is needed.

Luckily, with IPv6 there is a solution for the address-exhaustion issue. Unfortunately, at this time of writing, the ecosystem at large has still not made the move to IPv6, partly for infrastructure reasons but also due to a lack of tooling that supports IPv6. This means that for the time being you'll still have to deal with IPv4 and its limitations and workarounds (*https://oreil.ly/XSiTu*).

Let's have a look at the (hopefully not-to-distant) future: IPv6.

IPv6

Internet Protocol version 6 (IPv6) (*https://oreil.ly/T0ISm*) is a 128-bit number identifying an endpoint in a TCP/IP communication. This means that with IPv6 we can assign on the order of 10^{38} individual machines (devices). In contrast to IPv4, IPv6 uses a hexadecimal representation, eight groups of 16 bits each, separating the groups by a colon (:).

There are a few rules for shortening IPv6 addresses, such as removing leading zeros or compressing consecutive sections of zeros by replacing them with two colons (::). For example, the IPv6 loopback address (*https://oreil.ly/mGfiU*) can be written abbreviated as ::1 (the IPv4 variant would be 127.0.0.1).

Just like IPv4, IPv6 has a number of special and reserved addresses; see APNIC's listing of IPv6 address types (*https://oreil.ly/isoL1*) for examples.

It's important to note that IPv4 and IPv6 are not compatible. This means that IPv6 support needs to be built into each and every network participant, from edge devices (like your phone) to routers to server software. This IPv6 support has, at least in the context of Linux, already shown to be pretty wide. For example, the ip addr command we saw in the section "IPv4" on page 153 would already by default show us the IPv6 addresses.

Internet Control Message Protocol

The RFC 792 (*https://oreil.ly/6Nphe*) defines the Internet Control Message Protocol (ICMP), which is used for lower-level components to send error messages and operational information like availability.

Let's see ICMP in action by testing the reachability of a website with ping:

```
$ ping mhausenblas.info
PING mhausenblas.info (185.199.109.153): 56 data bytes
64 bytes from 185.199.109.153: icmp_seq=0 ttl=38 time=23.140 ms
64 bytes from 185.199.109.153: icmp_seq=1 ttl=38 time=23.237 ms
64 bytes from 185.199.109.153: icmp_seq=2 ttl=38 time=23.989 ms
64 bytes from 185.199.109.153: icmp_seq=3 ttl=38 time=24.028 ms
64 bytes from 185.199.109.153: icmp_seq=4 ttl=38 time=24.826 ms
64 bytes from 185.199.109.153: icmp_seq=5 ttl=38 time=23.579 ms
64 bytes from 185.199.109.153: icmp_seq=6 ttl=38 time=22.984 ms
^C
--- mhausenblas.info ping statistics ---
7 packets transmitted, 7 packets received, 0.0% packet loss
round-trip min/avg/max/stddev = 22.984/23.683/24.826/0.599 ms
```

Alternatively, you can use gping (*https://oreil.ly/1Y5qv*), which can ping multiple targets at the same time and plot a graph on the command line (see Figure 7-4).

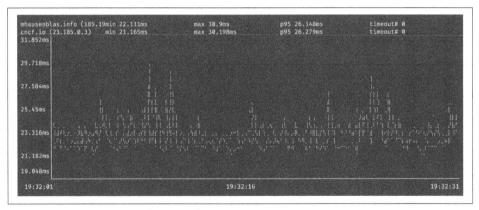

Figure 7-4. Pinging two websites with `gping`

Note that an equivalent tool is available for IPv6: the aptly named `ping6` (*https://oreil.ly/F6q6B*).

Routing

Part of the network stack in Linux is concerned with routing—that is, deciding on a per-packet basis where to send a packet. The destination could be a process on the same machine, or it could be an IP address on a different machine.

While the exact implementation details of routing are beyond the scope of this chapter, we'll provide a high-level overview: iptables (*https://oreil.ly/roRsv*), a widely used tool that allows you to manipulate the routing tables—for example, to reroute packets on certain conditions or implement a firewall—uses netfilter (*https://www.netfilter.org*) to intercept and manipulate packets.

What you should know is how to query and display routing information, as follows:

```
$ sudo route -n ❶
Kernel IP routing table
Destination     Gateway         Genmask         Flags Metric Ref    Use Iface
0.0.0.0         192.168.178.1   0.0.0.0         UG    600    0        0 wlp1s0
169.254.0.0     0.0.0.0         255.255.0.0     U     1000   0        0 wlp1s0
192.168.178.0   0.0.0.0         255.255.255.0   U     600    0        0 wlp1s0
```

❶ Use the `route` command with `-n`, forcing numerical IP addresses.

The detailed meaning of the tabular output in the previous `route` command is as follows:

Destination
: The IP address of the destination; `0.0.0.0` means it's unspecified or unknown, potentially sending it to the gateway.

Gateway
: For packets not on the same network, the gateway address.

Genmask
: The subnet mask used.

Flags
: UG means the network is up and is a gateway.

Iface
: The network interface the packet is going to use.

A modern way is using `ip` like so:

```
$ sudo ip route
default via 192.168.178.1 dev wlp1s0 proto dhcp metric 600
169.254.0.0/16 dev wlp1s0 scope link metric 1000
192.168.178.0/24 dev wlp1s0 proto kernel scope link src 192.168.178.40 metric 600
```

Is it down? We can check connectivity as follows:

```
$ traceroute mhausenblas.info
traceroute to mhausenblas.info (185.199.108.153), 30 hops max, 60 byte packets
 1  _gateway (192.168.5.2)  1.350 ms  1.306 ms  1.293 ms
```

Note that we will discuss a number of TCP/IP-related troubleshooting and performance tools in "Monitoring" on page 197.

To round things off, I'll also briefly mention the Border Gateway Protocol (BGP) (*https://oreil.ly/QMc1v*) as defined in RFC 4271 (*https://oreil.ly/iwRNE*) and other IETF specs. While it's unlikely that you'll interact directly with BGP (unless you work at a network provider or admin a network), it's crucial to be aware of its existence and understand at a high level what it does.

Facebook Disappears from the Internet

In late 2021, we saw the impact that BGP misconfiguration can have. Read the backstory and lessons learned in "Understanding How Facebook Disappeared from the Internet" (*https://oreil.ly/UTwSk*).

We said earlier on that the internet really is a network of networks. In BGP terminology, a network is called an *autonomous system* (AS). For IP routing to work, these ASs need to share their routing and reachability data, announcing routes to deliver packets across the internet.

Now that you know the fundamental workings of the internet layer—how addresses and routing work—let's move up the stack.

The Transport Layer

In this layer, it's all about the nature of the communication between endpoints. There are connection-oriented protocols and connection-less ones. Reliability, QoS, and in-order delivery may be a concern.

 There are attempts in modern protocol design—HTTP/3 (*https://oreil.ly/ecuPK*) is an example—to combine functionality, such as moving parts of TCP into higher-level protocols.

Ports

One core concept in this layer is that of ports. No matter which protocol is used in this layer, each requires ports. A *port* is a unique 16-bit number identifying a service available at an IP address. Think of it this way: a single (virtual) machine may have a number of services (see "Application Layer Networking" on page 173) running, and you need to be able to identify each in the context of the machine's IP.

We differentiate between the following:

Well-known ports (from 0 to 1023)
These are for daemons such as an SSH server or a web server. Using (binding to) one of them requires elevated privileges (`root` or `CAP_NET_BIND_SERVICE` capability, as discussed in "Capabilities" on page 87).

Registered ports (from 1024 to 49151)
These are managed by Internet Assigned Numbers Authority (IANA) through a publicly documented process.

Ephemeral ports (from 49152 to 65535)
These cannot be registered. They can be used for automatically allocating a temporary port (for example, if your app connects to a web server, it needs a port itself, as the other endpoint of the communication) as well as for private (say, company-internal) services.

You can see the ports and mapping in */etc/services*, and further, there is a comprehensive list of TCP and UDP port numbers (*https://oreil.ly/VBp7N*) you might want to consult if you're unsure.

If you want to see what's in use on your local machine (*do not* do this on someone else's machine/against a nonlocal IP):

```
$ nmap -A localhost ❶

Starting Nmap 7.60 ( https://nmap.org ) at 2021-09-19 14:53 IST
Nmap scan report for localhost (127.0.0.1)
Host is up (0.00025s latency).
Not shown: 999 closed ports
PORT    STATE SERVICE VERSION
631/tcp open  ipp     CUPS 2.2 ❷
| http-methods:
|_  Potentially risky methods: PUT
| http-robots.txt: 1 disallowed entry
|_/
|_http-server-header: CUPS/2.2 IPP/2.1
|_http-title: Home - CUPS 2.2.7

Service detection performed. Please report any incorrect results
at https://nmap.org/submit/ .
Nmap done: 1 IP address (1 host up) scanned in 6.93 seconds
```

❶ Scan ports on local machine.

❷ Found one open port, 631, which is the Internet Printing Protocol (IPP).

With the general idea of ports explained, let's now have a look how these ports are used in different transport layer protocols.

Transmission Control Protocol

The *Transmission Control Protocol* (TCP) is a connection-oriented transport layer protocol that is used by a number of higher-level protocols, including HTTP and SSH (see "Application Layer Networking" on page 173). It is a session-based protocol that guarantees delivery of the packets in order and supports retransmission in case of errors.

The TCP header (Figure 7-5), as defined in RFC 793 (*https://oreil.ly/4BY3T*) and related IETF specs, has these most important fields:

Source port (16 bits)
    The port used by the sender.

Destination port (16 bits)
    The port used by the receiver.

Sequence number (32 bits)
    Used to manage in-order delivery.

Acknowledgment number (32 bits)

> This number and the SYN and ACK flags are the core of the so-called *TCP/IP three-way handshake (https://oreil.ly/Icea3).*

Flags (9 bits)

> Most important, the SYN (synchronize) and the ACK (acknowledgement) bits.

Window (16 bits)

> The receive window size.

Checksum (16 bits)

> A checksum of the TCP-header, used for error checking.

Data

> The payload to transport.

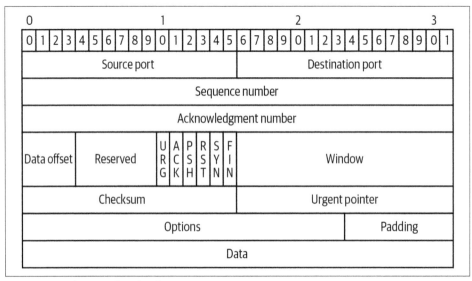

Figure 7-5. The TCP header format as per RFC 793

TCP tracks the state of the connection from establishment to termination, with both the sender and the receiver having to negotiate certain things, from how much data to send (TCP window size) to QoS.

From a security perspective, TCP is without any defense mechanisms. In other words, the payload is sent in plain text, and anyone between the sender and the receiver (and there are by design many hops) can inspect the packet; see "Wireshark and tshark" on page 183 for details on using Wireshark and tshark to inspect the payload. To enable encryption of the message, you need to use the Transport Layer Security (TLS) protocol, ideally in version 1.3 as per RFC 8446 (*https://oreil.ly/6dTwf*).

With that, let's move on to the most important stateless transport layer protocol: UDP.

User Datagram Protocol

User Datagram Protocol (UDP) is a connection-less transport layer protocol allowing you to send messages, called *datagrams* in UDP, without communication setups (such as TCP does with the handshake). It does, however, support datagram checksums to ensure integrity. There are a number of application-level protocols, such as NTP and DHCP (see "Application Layer Networking" on page 173) as well as DNS (see "DNS" on page 165), that use UDP.

The RFC 768 (*https://oreil.ly/dysc4*) defines the UDP header format as shown in Figure 7-6. Its most important fields are the following:

Source port (16 bits)
    The port used by the sender; optional, and if not, use 0

Destination port (16 bits)
    The port used by the receiver

Length (16 bits)
    The total length of the UDP header and data

Checksum (16 bits)
    Can optionally be used for error checking

Data
    The payload of the datagram

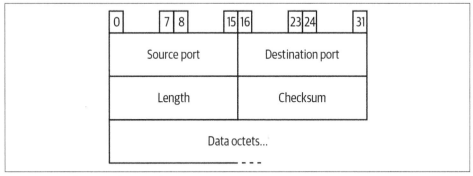

Figure 7-6. The UDP header format as per RFC 768

UDP is a very simple protocol and requires the higher-level protocol that works on top of it to take care of many of the things that TCP would handle itself. On the other hand, UDP has very little overhead and can achieve high throughput. It's very simple to use; see also the UDP manual page (*https://oreil.ly/NJiAQ*).

Sockets

A high-level communication interface that Linux provides are *sockets* (*https://oreil.ly/C7gQA*). Think of them as endpoints in a communication, with their distinct identity: a tuple made up of the TCP or UDP port and the IP address.

It's likely that you'll only use sockets if you want to develop network-related tooling or apps, but you should at least be aware of how to query them. For example, in the context of the Docker daemon (*https://oreil.ly/OUD5V*), you at least need to know about the required permissions for the socket.

Let's have a look at how to use the `ss` command (*https://oreil.ly/qtCkK*) to display socket-related information.

Let's assume we want to get an overview of the TCP sockets in use on the system:

```
$ ss -s ❶
Total: 913 (kernel 0)
TCP:   10 (estab 4, closed 1, orphaned 0, synrecv 0, timewait 1/0), ports 0 ❷

Transport Total    IP      IPv6 ❸
*         0        -       -
RAW       1        0       1
UDP       10       8       2
TCP       9        8       1
INET      20       16      4
FRAG      0        0       0
```

❶ Use the `ss` command to query ports (with `-s`, we ask for a summary).

❷ The summary for TCP; overall, 10 sockets in use.

❸ A more detailed overview, breaking down by type and IP version.

Now, what about UDP? Can we get this information, maybe with some more details, such as endpoint IP addresses? Turns out this is also possible with `ss` (output edited):

```
$ ss -ulp ❶
State   Recv-Q Send-Q    Local Address:Port      Peer Address:Port
UNCONN  0      0             0.0.0.0:60360        0.0.0.0:*
UNCONN  0      0      127.0.0.53%lo:domain        0.0.0.0:*
UNCONN  0      0             0.0.0.0:bootpc       0.0.0.0:*
UNCONN  0      0             0.0.0.0:ipp          0.0.0.0:*
UNCONN  0      0             0.0.0.0:mdns         0.0.0.0:*
UNCONN  0      0                [::]:mdns            [::]:*
UNCONN  0      0                [::]:38359          [::]:*
```

❶ Use `ss`: the `-u` parameter restricts to UDP sockets, `-l` is for selecting listening sockets, and `-p` also shows the process information (none in our case).

Another tool you might find handy in this context (sockets and processes) is `lsof` (*https://oreil.ly/YBhMB*). For example, let's see what UDP sockets Chrome uses on my machine (output edited):

```
$ lsof -c chrome -i udp | head -5 ❶
COMMAND   PID USER   FD   TYPE  DEVICE      NODE NAME
chrome   3131 mh9   cwd   DIR      0,5    265463 /proc/5321/fdinfo
chrome   3131 mh9   rtd   DIR      0,5    265463 /proc/5321/fdinfo
chrome   3131 mh9   txt   REG    253,0   3673554 /opt/google/chrome/chrome
chrome   3131 mh9   mem   REG    253,0   3673563 /opt/google/chrome/icudtl.dat
chrome   3131 mh9   mem   REG    253,0  12986737 /usr/lib/locale/locale-archive
```

❶ Use `lsof` with `-c` to specifically select a process by name as well as limit to UDP with `-i`. Note that the overall output would be many dozens of lines; that's why I cut it down to five with the `head -5` command in the pipe.

With that we've covered the three lower layers of the TCP/IP stack. Since the application layer has so much going on, I've dedicated two sections to it: first, we're looking into the global-scale naming system, and then we'll look into a number of application layer (or layer 7) protocols and applications, such as the web.

DNS

We learned that the internet layer of the TCP/IP stack defines so-called IP addresses whose main function it is to identify machines, virtual or physical alike. In the context of "Containers" on page 131, we go so far as to assign IP addresses to individual containers. There are two challenges with numerical IP addresses, no matter if IPv4 or IPv6:

- As humans, we generally remember names better than we do (long) numbers. For example, if you want to share a website with a friend, you can just say it's *ietf.org* they should check out rather than `4.31.198.44`.

- Due to the way the internet and its applications are built, IP addresses often change. You might get a new server with a new IP address in a more traditional setup. Or, in the context of containers, you may be rescheduled onto a different host, in which case the container automatically gets a new IP address assigned.

So, in a nutshell, IP addresses are hard to remember and can change, while a name (for a server or a service) remains the same. This challenge has existed since the beginning of the internet and since UNIX supported the TCP/IP stack.

The way to address this was to locally (in the context of a single machine) maintain a mapping between names and IP addresses via */etc/hosts*. The Network Information Center (NIC) would share a single file called *HOSTS.TXT* via FTP with all participating hosts.

Very soon it became clear that this centralized approach could not keep up with the growing internet, and in the early 1980s, a distributed system was designed. Paul Mockapetris was the lead architect.

The DNS is a worldwide, hierarchical naming system for hosts and services on the internet. While there are many related RFCs, the original one, RFC 1034 (*https://oreil.ly/rbQNY*), and its implementation guidance via RFC 1035 (*https://oreil.ly/c1eYB*) are still valid, and I strongly recommend you read them if you want to learn more about the motivation and design.

The DNS uses a number of terms, but the following are the main concepts:

Domain name space
> A tree structure with . as the root and each tree node and leaf containing information about a certain space. The labels (63 bytes maximum length) along the path from a leaf to the root is what we call a *fully qualified domain name* (FQDN). For example, *demo.mhausenblas.info.* is an FQDN with the so-called top-level domain *.info*. Note that the right-most dot, the root, is often left off.

Resource records
> The payload in the nodes or leaves of the domain name space (see "DNS Records" on page 168).

Name servers
> Server programs that hold information about the domain tree's structure. If a name server has the complete information about a space, it's called an *authoritative name server*. Authoritative information is organized into zones.

Resolvers
> Programs that extract information from name servers in response to client requests. They are machine local, and no explicit protocol is defined for the interaction between a resolver and a client. Often there are library calls supported for resolving the DNS.

Figure 7-7 shows a complete setup of a DNS system, including user program, resolver, and name server(s), as described in RFC 1035. In the query process, the resolver would iteratively query authoritative name servers (NS) starting from the root or, if supported, using a recursive query where an NS queries others on behalf of a resolver.

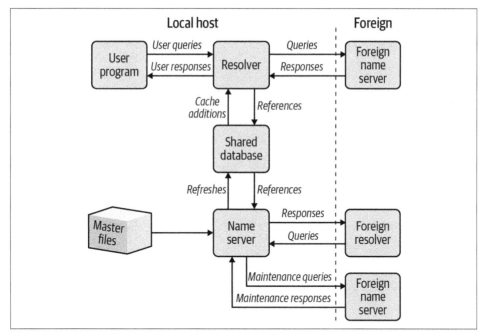

Figure 7-7. A complete DNS example setup

 Although they're still around, we usually don't use the DNS resolver configuration (*https://oreil.ly/2plq1*) in */etc/resolv.conf* in modern systems, especially when DHCP (see "Dynamic Host Configuration Protocol" on page 182) is deployed.

The DNS is a hierarchical naming system, and at its root sit 13 root servers (*https://oreil.ly/hNppq*) that manage the records for the top-level domains. Directly beneath the root are the top-level domains (TLD) (*https://oreil.ly/secgy*):

Infrastructure top-level domain
Managed by IANA on behalf of the IETF and including, for example, *example* and *localhost*

Generic top-level domains (gTLD)
Generic domains having three or more characters, such as *.org* or *.com*

Country-code top-level domains (ccTLD)
For countries or territories assigned two-letter ISO country codes (*https://oreil.ly/lBWjD*)

Sponsored top-level domains (sTLD)
> For private agencies or organizations that establish and enforce rules restricting the eligibility to use the TLD—for example, *.aero* and *.gov*

Let's have a closer look at some moving parts of the DNS and how to use it in practice.

DNS Records

A name server manages records that capture the type, the payload, and other fields, including things like the time to live (TTL), the time period after which the record is supposed to be discarded. You can think of the FQDN as the address of the node and the resource record (RR) as the payload, the data in the node.

DNS has a number of record types (*https://oreil.ly/5QTJ9*), including the following most important ones (in alphabetical order):

A *records (RFC 1035) and* AAAA *records (RFC 3596)*
> IPv4 and IPv6 address records, respectively; usually used to map hostnames to an IP address of the host.

CNAME *records (RFC 1035)*
> Canonical name records providing an alias of one name to another.

NS *records (RFC 1035)*
> Name server records delegating a DNS zone to use the authoritative name servers.

PTR *records (RFC 1035)*
> Pointer records used for performing reverse DNS lookups; the opposite of A records.

SRV *records (RFC 2782)*
> Service locator records. They are a generalized discovery mechanism, rather than hardcoded (as traditionally was the case with the MX record type for mail exchange).

TXT *records (RFC 1035)*
> Text records. These were originally meant for arbitrary human-readable text but over time found a new use case. Today, these records often have machine-readable data in the context of security-related DNS extensions.

There are also wildcard records (*https://oreil.ly/yL039*) starting with the asterisk label (*)—for example, **.mhausenblas.info*—as a catch-all to match requests for nonexistent names.

Let's see how these records look in practice. The DNS records are represented in a textual form in a zone file (*https://oreil.ly/4Ngai*) that a name server—such as bind (*https://oreil.ly/095v2*)—reads in and makes part of its database:

```
$ORIGIN example.com. ❶
$TTL 3600 ❷
@       SOA nse.example.com. nsmaster.example.com. (
                1234567890 ; serial number
                21600      ; refresh after 6 hours
                3600       ; retry after 1 hour
                604800     ; expire after 1 week
                3600 )     ; minimum TTL of 1 hour
example.com.  IN  NS    nse ❸
example.com.  IN  MX    10 mail.example.com. ❹
example.com.  IN  A     1.2.3.4 ❺
nse           IN  A     5.6.7.8 ❻
www           IN  CNAME example.com. ❼
mail          IN  A     9.0.0.9 ❽
```

❶ The start of this zone file in the namespace.

❷ Default expiration time in seconds of all RRs that don't define their own TTL.

❸ The nameserver for this domain.

❹ The mailserver for this domain.

❺ The IPv4 address for this domain.

❻ The IPv4 address for the nameserver.

❼ Make *www.example.com* an alias for this domain—that is, *example.com*.

❽ The IPv4 address for the mail server.

Putting all the concepts discussed together, we can now understand the example shown in Figure 7-8. This shows a part of the global domain name space and a concrete example FQDN, *demo.mhausenblas.info*:

.info
A generic TLD managed by a company called Afilias (*https://www.afilias.info*).

mhausenblas.info
A domain I bought. Within this zone I can assign subdomains as I please.

demo.mhausenblas.info
The subdomain I assigned for demo purposes.

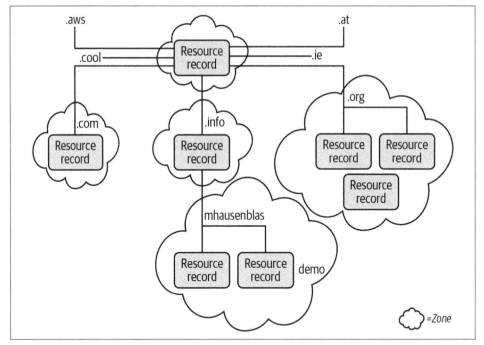

Figure 7-8. The domain name space and an example path (FQDN)

Consider how in the previous example each entity (Afilias or me) only looks after its part, and no coordination is required. For example, to create the *demo* subdomain, I only had to change my DNS settings for the zone, without asking anyone at Afilias for support or permissions. This seemingly simple fact is the core of the decentralized nature of DNS and is what makes it so scalable.

Now that we know how the domain name space is structured and the information in the nodes is represented, let's see how you can query them.

DNS Lookups

With all the infrastructure in place, mainly nameservers and resolvers, we now look at performing DNS queries. There is a lot of logic in the evaluation and construction of the resolution (mostly covered in RFC 1034 and 1035), but this is beyond the scope of the book. Let's have a look at how you can do the query without having to understand the internals.

You can use the host command to query local (and global) names to resolve them to IP addresses and the other way around:

```
$ host -a localhost ❶
Trying "localhost.fritz.box"
Trying "localhost"
```

```
;; ->>HEADER<<- opcode: QUERY, status: NOERROR, id: 49150
;; flags: qr rd ra; QUERY: 1, ANSWER: 2, AUTHORITY: 0, ADDITIONAL: 0

;; QUESTION SECTION:
;localhost.                      IN      ANY

;; ANSWER SECTION:
localhost.              0       IN      A       127.0.0.1
localhost.              0       IN      AAAA    ::1

Received 71 bytes from 127.0.0.53#53 in 0 ms

$ host mhausenblas.info ❷
mhausenblas.info has address 185.199.110.153
mhausenblas.info has address 185.199.109.153
mhausenblas.info has address 185.199.111.153
mhausenblas.info has address 185.199.108.153

$ host 185.199.110.153 ❸
153.110.199.185.in-addr.arpa domain name pointer cdn-185-199-110-153.github.com.
```

❶ Look up local IP addresses.

❷ Look up FQDN.

❸ Reverse lookup of IP address to find an FQDN; looks like the GitHub CDN.

A more powerful way to look up the DNS records is using the dig command:

```
$ dig mhausenblas.info ❶
; <<>> DiG 9.10.6 <<>> mhausenblas.info
;; global options: +cmd
;; Got answer:
;; ->>HEADER<<- opcode: QUERY, status: NOERROR, id: 43159
;; flags: qr rd ra; QUERY: 1, ANSWER: 4, AUTHORITY: 2, ADDITIONAL: 5

;; OPT PSEUDOSECTION:
; EDNS: version: 0, flags:; udp: 1232
;; QUESTION SECTION:
;mhausenblas.info.               IN      A

;; ANSWER SECTION: ❷
mhausenblas.info.       1799    IN      A       185.199.111.153
mhausenblas.info.       1799    IN      A       185.199.108.153
mhausenblas.info.       1799    IN      A       185.199.109.153
mhausenblas.info.       1799    IN      A       185.199.110.153

;; AUTHORITY SECTION: ❸
mhausenblas.info.       1800    IN      NS      dns1.registrar-servers.com.
mhausenblas.info.       1800    IN      NS      dns2.registrar-servers.com.
```

```
;; ADDITIONAL SECTION:
dns1.registrar-servers.com. 47950 IN    A       156.154.132.200
dns2.registrar-servers.com. 47950 IN    A       156.154.133.200
dns1.registrar-servers.com. 28066 IN    AAAA    2610:a1:1024::200
dns2.registrar-servers.com. 28066 IN    AAAA    2610:a1:1025::200

;; Query time: 58 msec
;; SERVER: 172.16.173.64#53(172.16.173.64)
;; WHEN: Wed Sep 15 19:22:26 IST 2021
;; MSG SIZE  rcvd: 256
```

❶ Using dig, look up the DNS records of the FQDN *mhausenblas.info*.

❷ The DNS A records.

❸ The authoritative nameserver.

There are alternatives to the dig command available, notably dog and nslookup; see Appendix B.

 One saying you will come across often is: "It's always DNS." But what does this mean? It's about troubleshooting and understanding that DNS is a distributed database with many moving parts. When debugging DNS-related issues, consider the TTL of records and that there are many caches, from local ones in your app to resolver, to anything between you and the nameservers.

In "DNS Records" on page 168, we mentioned the SRV record type and that it serves as a generic discovery mechanism. So, rather than defining a new record type for a new service in an RFC, the community came up with a generic way to address any upcoming service type. This mechanism, described in RFC 2782 (*https://oreil.ly/DIKbI*), explains how SRV records can be used to communicate the IP address and port of a service via DNS.

Let's see that in practice. Say we want to know what chat services—more specifically, Extensible Messaging and Presence Protocol (XMPP) (*https://oreil.ly/rDmcx*) services —if any, are available:

```
$ dig +short _xmpp-client._tcp.gmail.com. SRV ❶
20 0 5222 alt3.xmpp.l.google.com.
5 0 5222 xmpp.l.google.com. ❷
20 0 5222 alt4.xmpp.l.google.com.
20 0 5222 alt2.xmpp.l.google.com.
20 0 5222 alt1.xmpp.l.google.com.
```

❶ Use the `dig` command with the `+short` option to display only the relevant answer section. The `_xmpp-client._tcp` part is the format RFC 2782 prescribes, and the SRV at the end of this command specifies what record type we're interested in.

❷ Overall there are five answers. An example service instance is available at *xmpp.l.google.com:5222* with a TTL of 5 seconds. If you have an XMPP such as Jabber, you could use this address for configuration input.

With this, we've reached the end of the DNS section. Now we'll have a look at other application layer protocols and tooling.

Application Layer Networking

In this section, we focus on user space or application layer network protocols, tooling, and apps. As an end user, you'll likely spend most of your time here, using things such as web browsers or mail clients for your daily tasks.

The Web

The web, originally developed by Sir Tim Berners-Lee in the early 1990s, has three core components:

Uniform Resource Locators (URL)
As per RFC 1738 (*https://oreil.ly/EfgPm*) originally and a number of updates and related RFCs. A URL defines both the identity and the location of a resource on the web. A resource could be a static page or a process that generates content dynamically.

Hypertext Transfer Protocol (HTTP)
HTTP defines an application layer protocol and how to interact with content available via URLs. As per RFC 2616 (*https://oreil.ly/hGr3E*) for v1.1, but there are also more modern versions, such as HTTP/2, defined in RFC 7540 (*https://oreil.ly/1Z6pn*), and the HTTP/3 draft (*https://oreil.ly/XRkMf*) (which at the time of this writing was still in the works). Core HTTP concepts are:

HTTP methods (https://oreil.ly/FFWuP)
Including `GET` for read operations and, among others, `POST` for write operations, these define a CRUD-like interface.

Resource naming (https://oreil.ly/ttnOq)
This dictates how to form URLs.

HTTP status codes (https://oreil.ly/LppmX)
> With the 2xx range for success, 3xx for redirects, 4xx for client errors, and 5xx for server errors.

Hyper Text Markup Language (HTML)
> Initially a W3C specification, HTML is now a living standard available via WHATWG (*https://oreil.ly/lUcHo*). A hypertext markup allows you to define page elements such as headers or inputs.

W3C and standards

Technically neither IETF nor W3C (World Wide Web Consortium) do standards. They create specifications through formal processes that the community accepts as de facto standards. I strongly recommend that you read these specifications and try to understand what's going in there. For me, in 2006, after using and building web sites and applications for almost a decade, I started to take this seriously (when I got involved in W3C efforts), and the payoff was enormous.

Let's have a closer look at how URIs (the generic version of URLs) are constructed (as per RFC 3986) and how that maps to HTTP URLs:

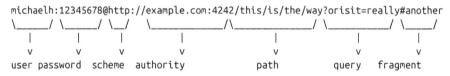

The components are as follows:

user *and* password *(both optional)*
> Initially used for basic authentication, these components should not be used anymore. Instead, for HTTP, you should be using a proper authentication mechanism (*https://oreil.ly/EHNfN*) together with HTTPS (*https://oreil.ly/Dvuh4*) for encryption on the wire.

scheme
> Refers to the URL scheme (*https://oreil.ly/R9QeW*), an IETF specification defining its meaning. For HTTP, that scheme is called http, which really is a family of HTTP specifications, such as RFC 2616.

authority
> The hierarchical naming part. For HTTP, this is:

> *Hostname*
> > Either as a DNS FQDN or an IP address.

Port

With a default of 80 (so *example.com:80* and *example.com* are the same).

path

A scheme-specific part for further resource details.

query *and* fragment *(both optional)*

The former appears after the ? for nonhierarchical data (for example, to express tags or form data), and the latter appears after the # for secondary resources (in the context of HTML, that could be a section).

Today, the web has advanced far beyond its humble 1990s roots, with a number of technologies such as JavaScript/ECMAScript (*https://oreil.ly/b8kFe*) and Cascading Style Sheets (CSS) (*https://oreil.ly/rSlYl*) considered core. Those additions, JavaScript for dynamic client-side content and CSS for styling, have eventually led to single-page web apps (*https://oreil.ly/E1SJu*). While this topic is beyond the scope of the book, it's important to remember that knowing the basics (URL, HTTP, and HTML) well goes a long way in terms of understanding how things work and troubleshooting issues you may have.

Let's now see web specifications in action by simulating the flow end to end, starting at the HTTP server end.

You can rather easily run a simple HTTP server that only serves the content of a directory in two ways: by using Python (*https://oreil.ly/clti0*) or by using netcat (nc) (*https://oreil.ly/AaCJG*).

With Python, to serve the content of a directory, you would do the following:

```
$ python3 -m http.server ❶
Serving HTTP on :: port 8000 (http://[::]:8000/) ... ❷
::ffff:127.0.0.1 - - [21/Sep/2021 08:53:53] "GET / HTTP/1.1" 200 - ❸
```

❶ Use the built-in Python module http.server to serve the content of the current directory (that is, the directory from which you launched this command).

❷ It confirms that it's ready to serve via port 8000. This means that you could enter *http://localhost:8000* into your browser and you would see the content of your directory there.

❸ This shows that an HTTP request against the root (/) has been issued and served successfully (the 200 HTTP response code).

If you want to do more advanced stuff, beyond serving a static directory, consider using a proper web server such as NGINX (*https://docs.nginx.com*). You could, for example, run NGINX using Docker (see "Docker" on page 138) with the following command:

```
$ docker run --name mywebserver \ ❶
              --rm -d \ ❷
              -v  "$PWD":/usr/share/nginx/html:ro \ ❸
              -p 8042:80 \ ❹
              nginx:1.21 ❺
```

❶ Call the running container `mywebserver`; you should see that when you issue a `docker ps` command to list running containers.

❷ The `--rm` removes the container on exit, and the `-d` turns it into a daemon (detach from terminal, run in background).

❸ Mounts the current directory (`$PWD`) into the container as the NGINX source content directory. Note that `$PWD` is a bash way to address the current directory. In Fish you would use (`pwd`) instead.

❹ Makes the container-internal port 80 available on the host via 8042. That means you would be able to access the web server via *http://localhost:8042* on your machine.

❺ The container image to use (`nginx:1.21`), and implicitly using Docker Hub since we didn't specify the registry part.

Now let's see how we can use `curl` (*https://curl.se*), a powerful and popular tool to interact with any kind of URLs, to get the content of the web server we launched in the previous example (make sure it's still running, or launch it again in a separate session if you terminated it already):

```
$ curl localhost:8000
<!DOCTYPE HTML PUBLIC "-//W3C//DTD HTML 4.01//EN"
                    "http://www.w3.org/TR/html4/strict.dtd">
<html>
<head>
<meta http-equiv="Content-Type" content="text/html; charset=utf-8">
<title>Directory listing for /</title>
</head>
<body>
<h1>Directory listing for /</h1>
<hr>
<ul>
<li><a href="app.yaml">app.yaml</a></li>
<li><a href="Dockerfile">Dockerfile</a></li>
```

```
<li><a href="example.json">example.json</a></li>
<li><a href="gh-user-info.sh">gh-user-info.sh</a></li>
<li><a href="main.go">main.go</a></li>
<li><a href="script.sh">script.sh</a></li>
<li><a href="test">test</a></li>
</ul>
<hr>
</body>
```

In Table 7-1 you see some common options for `curl` that you may find useful. The selection is based on my usage history for a range of tasks, from developing to system administration.

Table 7-1. Useful options for `curl`

Option	Long-form option	Description and use case
-v	--verbose	For verbose output, use for debugging.
-s	--silent	Silence `curl`: do not show the progress meter or error messages.
-L	--location	Follow page redirects (3XX HTTP response codes).
-o	--output	By default, the content goes to `stdout`; if you want to directly store it in a file, specify it via this option.
-m	--max-time	Maximum time (in seconds) you are willing to wait for the operation to take.
-I	--head	Fetch the headers only (careful: not every HTTP server supports the HEAD method for a path).
-k	--insecure	By default, HTTPS calls are verified. Use this option to ignore the errors for cases where that's not possible.

If `curl` is not available, you can fall back to `wget` (*https://oreil.ly/0jYJj*), which is more limited but sufficient for simple HTTP-related interactions.

Secure Shell

Secure Shell (SSH) (*https://oreil.ly/dNVgt*) is a cryptographic network protocol for securely offering network services on an unsecured network. For example, as a replacement for `telnet`, you can use `ssh` to log into a remote machine and also move data securely between (virtual) machines.

Let's see SSH in action. I've provisioned a virtual machine in the cloud with an IP address of `63.32.106.149`, and the user name provided by default is `ec2-user`. To log into the machine, I can do the following (note that the output is edited and assumes that you or someone else created credentials in *~/.ssh/lml.pem* beforehand):

```
$ ssh \ ❶
    -i ~/.ssh/lml.pem \ ❷
    ec2-user@63.32.106.149 ❸

...
```

```
https://aws.amazon.com/amazon-linux-2/
11 package(s) needed for security, out of 35 available
Run "sudo yum update" to apply all updates.
[ec2-user@ip-172-26-8-138 ~]$ ❹
```

❶ Use the ssh command to log into a remote machine.

❷ Use the identity file *~/.ssh/lml.pem* rather than a password. Explicitly providing that file is a good practice but in our case would strictly speaking not be necessary as it resides in the default location *~/.ssh*.

❸ The SSH target machine in the format username@host.

❹ Once the login process is completed, I can tell from the prompt that I'm on the target machine and can use it just as if it were local.

Some general SSH usage tips:

- If you run an SSH server, that is, allow others to ssh into your machine, then you absolutely should disable password authentication (*https://oreil.ly/Jz5tA*). This forces users to create a key pair and share the public key with you that you then add to *~/.ssh/authorized_keys* and allow to log in via this mechanism.
- Use ssh -tt to force pseudo-tty allocation.
- Do export TERM=xterm when you ssh into a machine, in case you are having display issues.
- Configure timeouts for ssh sessions in your client. On a per-user basis, this is usually via *~/.ssh/config*, where you can set ServerAliveInterval and Server AliveCountMax options to keep your connections alive.
- If you're having issues, and you've excluded local permission issues with the key(s), then you can try launching ssh with the -v option, giving you details about what's going on under the hood (also, try multiple instances of v, like -vvv for finer-grained debug info).

SSH is not only used directly by humans, but it is also used as a building block under the hood—for example, in file-transfer tooling.

File Transfer

One very common task involving the network is transferring files. You can do this from your local machine to a server in the cloud or from another machine in the local network.

To copy to and from remote systems, you can use one basic tool. scp (short for "secure copy") (*https://oreil.ly/RKbEu*) works on top of SSH. Given that scp defaults to `ssh`, we need to make sure that we have the password (or even better, key-based authentication) in place for it to work.

Let's assume we have a remote machine with the IPv4 address `63.32.106.149`, and we want to copy a file there from our local machine:

```
$ scp copyme \ ❶
        ec2-user@63.32.106.149:/home/ec2-user/ ❷
copyme                        100%   0      0.0KB/s   00:00
```

❶ Source is the file *copyme* in the current directory.

❷ Destination is the */home/ec2-user/* directory on machine `63.32.106.149`.

Synchronizing files with `rsync` (*https://oreil.ly/eC6Kz*) is much more convenient and faster than `scp`. Under the hood, `rsync` uses SSH by default.

Let's now see how we can use `rsync` to transfer files from the *~/data/* from the local machine to the host at `63.32.106.149`:

```
$ rsync -avz \ ❶
        ~/data/ \ ❷
        mh9@:63.32.106.149: ❸
building file list ... done
./
example.txt

sent 155 bytes  received 48 bytes  135.33 bytes/sec
total size is 10  speedup is 0.05

$ ssh ec2-user@63.32.106.149 -- ls ❹
example.txt
```

❶ Options meaning `-a` for archive (incremental, preserve), `-v` for verbose so that we see something, and `-z` for using compression.

❷ Source directories (since `-a` includes `-r` which is recursive).

❸ Destination in `user@host` format.

❹ Verify if the data has arrived by executing an `ls` on the remote machine. The next line shows that it indeed worked—the data arrived in good order.

If you're unsure what `rsync` will do, use the `--dry-run` option in addition to the other ones. It will essentially tell you what it will do without actually carrying out the operation, so it's safe.

`rsync` is also a great tool to perform directory backups because it can be set to copy only files that have been added or changed.

Don't forget the : after the host! Without it, rsync will happily go ahead and interpret the source or destination as a local directory. That is, the command will work fine, but rather than copying the files to the remote machine, it will end up on your local machine. For example, *user@example.com* as the destination would be a subdirectory of the current directory called *user@example.com/*.

Last but not least, one use case you often come across is when someone provides files in an Amazon S3 bucket. To download those files, you can use the AWS CLI (*https://oreil.ly/mqQcr*) with the s3 subcommand as follows. We're using a dataset from the Open Data registry (*https://oreil.ly/cbYMH*) in a public S3 bucket (output edited to fit):

```
$ aws s3 sync \ ❶
    s3://commoncrawl/contrib/c4corpus/CC-MAIN-2016-07/ \ ❷
    . \ ❸
    --no-sign-request ❹
download: s3://commoncrawl/contrib/c4corpus/CC-MAIN-2016-07/
Lic_by-nc-nd_Lang_af_NoBoilerplate_true_MinHtml_true-r-00009.seg-00000.warc.gz to
./Lic_by-nc-nd_Lang_af_NoBoilerplate_true_MinHtml_true-r-00009.seg-00000.warc.gz
download: s3://commoncrawl/contrib/c4corpus/CC-MAIN-2016-07/
Lic_by-nc-nd_Lang_bn_NoBoilerplate_true_MinHtml_true-r-00017.seg-00000.warc.gz to
./Lic_by-nc-nd_Lang_bn_NoBoilerplate_true_MinHtml_true-r-00017.seg-00000.warc.gz
download: s3://commoncrawl/contrib/c4corpus/CC-MAIN-2016-07/
Lic_by-nc-nd_Lang_da_NoBoilerplate_true_MinHtml_true-r-00004.seg-00000.warc.gz to
./Lic_by-nc-nd_Lang_da_NoBoilerplate_true_MinHtml_true-r-00004.seg-00000.warc.gz
...
```

❶ Use the AWS S3 command to synchronize files from a public bucket.

❷ This is the source bucket, *s3://commoncrawl*, and the exact path of the source we want to sync. Warning: there are more than 8 GB of data in that directory, so try this only if you don't mind the bandwidth.

❸ The destination is the current directory, signaled by a single period (.).

❹ Ignore/skip authentication since this is a publicly available bucket (and thus the data in it).

The File Transfer Protocol (FTP) as per RFC 959 (*https://oreil.ly/Okegf*) is still in use, but we don't recommend using it anymore. Not only are these insecure, but there are also many better alternatives, such as the ones we discussed in this section. So, there's no actual need for FTP anymore.

Network File System

A widely supported and used way to share files from a central location over the net-work is via network file system (NFS), originally developed by Sun Microsystems in the early 1980s. It saw multiple iterations as per RFC 7530 (*https://oreil.ly/Uy4CZ*) and other related IETF specs and is very stable.

You would usually have an NFS server maintained by a cloud provider or central IT in a professional setup. All you would need to do is install the client (usually through a package called `nfs-common`). Then, you can mount a source directory from the NFS server as follows:

```
$ sudo mount nfs.example.com:/source_dir /opt/target_mount_dir
```

Many cloud providers, such as AWS and Azure, now offer NFS as a service. It's a nice way to provide your storage-hungry application with a lot of space in a way that looks and feels almost like local attached storage. For media applications, however, a network-attached storage (NAS) setup (*https://oreil.ly/JrQ8m*) is likely the better choice.

Sharing with Windows

If you have Windows machines in your local network and want to share it, you can use the Server Message Block (SMB) (*https://oreil.ly/mTAMe*), a protocol initially developed at IBM in the 1980s, or its Microsoft-owned successor, Common Internet File System (CIFS) (*https://oreil.ly/qMEjj*).

You would typically use Samba (*https://www.samba.org*), the standard Windows interoperability suite of programs for Linux, to achieve the file sharing.

Advanced Network Topics

In this section, we discuss some advanced network protocols and tooling across the TCP/IP stack. Their usage is normally beyond the scope of a casual user. However, if you're a developer or sys admin, you probably will want to be at least aware of them.

whois

`whois` (*https://oreil.ly/3m97l*) is a client for the whois directory service that you can use to look up registration and user information. For example, if I want to find out who is behind the *ietf.org* domain (note that you can pay your domain registrar to keep that information private), I would do the following:

```
$ whois ietf.org ❶
% IANA WHOIS server
% for more information on IANA, visit http://www.iana.org
% This query returned 1 object

refer:        whois.pir.org

domain:       ORG

organisation: Public Interest Registry (PIR)
address:      11911 Freedom Drive 10th Floor,
address:      Suite 1000
address:      Reston, VA 20190
address:      United States

contact:      administrative
name:         Director of Operations, Compliance and Customer Support
organisation: Public Interest Registry (PIR)
address:      11911 Freedom Drive 10th Floor,
address:      Suite 1000
address:      Reston, VA 20190
address:      United States
phone:        +1 703 889 5778
fax-no:       +1 703 889 5779
e-mail:       ops@pir.org
...
```

❶ Use whois to look up registration information about domain.

Dynamic Host Configuration Protocol

The Dynamic Host Configuration Protocol (DHCP) (*https://oreil.ly/C8vOE*) is a net-work protocol that enables automatic assignment of an IP address to a host. It's a client/server setup that removes the need for manually configuring network devices.

Setting up and managing a DHCP server is outside our scope, but you can use dhcpdump (*https://oreil.ly/uPvGn*) to scan for DHCP packets. For this, a device in your local network needs to join, trying to acquire an IP address, so you may need to be a bit patient to see something here (output shortened):

```
$ sudo dhcpdump -i wlp1s0 ❶
  TIME: 2021-09-19 17:26:24.115
    IP: 0.0.0.0 (88:cb:87:c9:19:92) > 255.255.255.255 (ff:ff:ff:ff:ff:ff)
    OP: 1 (BOOTPREQUEST)
 HTYPE: 1 (Ethernet)
  HLEN: 6
  HOPS: 0
   XID: 7533fb70
   ...
OPTION:  57 (  2) Maximum DHCP message size 1500
OPTION:  61 (  7) Client-identifier        01:88:cb:87:c9:19:92
```

```
OPTION:  50 (  4) Request IP address       192.168.178.42
OPTION:  51 (  4) IP address leasetime     7776000 (12w6d)
OPTION:  12 ( 15) Host name                MichaelminiiPad
...
```

❶   Using dhcpdump, sniff DHCP packets on interface wlp1s0.

Network Time Protocol

The Network Time Protocol (NTP) (*http://www.ntp.org*) is for synchronizing clocks
of computers over a network. For example, using the ntpq command (*https://oreil.ly/
0JxbJ*), a standard NTP query program, you could make an explicit time server query
like so:

```
$ ntpq -p ❶
     remote           refid      st t when poll reach   delay   offset  jitter
==============================================================================
 0.ubuntu.pool.n .POOL.          16 p    -   64    0   0.000    0.000   0.000
 1.ubuntu.pool.n .POOL.          16 p    -   64    0   0.000    0.000   0.000
 2.ubuntu.pool.n .POOL.          16 p    -   64    0   0.000    0.000   0.000
 3.ubuntu.pool.n .POOL.          16 p    -   64    0   0.000    0.000   0.000
 ntp.ubuntu.com  .POOL.          16 p    -   64    0   0.000    0.000   0.000
 ...
 ntp17.kashra-se 90.187.148.77    2 u    7   64    1  27.482   -3.451   2.285
 golem.canonical 17.253.34.123    2 u   13   64    1  20.338    0.057   0.000
 chilipepper.can 17.253.34.123    2 u   12   64    1  19.117   -0.439   0.000
 alphyn.canonica 140.203.204.77   2 u   14   64    1  91.462   -0.356   0.000
 pugot.canonical 145.238.203.14   2 u   13   64    1  20.788    0.226   0.000
```

❶   With the -p option, show a list of peers known to the machine, including their
state.

Usually, NTP works in the background, managed by systemd and other daemons, so
you are unlikely to need to manually query it.

Wireshark and tshark

If you want to do low-level network traffic analysis—that is, you want to see exactly
the packets across the stack—you can use either the command-line tool tshark
(*https://oreil.ly/n7Urm*) or its GUI-based version, wireshark (*https://oreil.ly/YQrSa*).

For example, after finding out via ip link that I have a network interface called
wlp1s0, I capture traffic there (output edited to fit):

```
$ sudo tshark -i wlp1s0 tcp ❶
Running as user "root" and group "root". This could be dangerous.
Capturing on 'wlp1s0'
    1 0.000000000 192.168.178.40 → 34.196.251.55 TCP 66 47618 → 443
    [ACK] Seq=1 Ack=1 Win=501 Len=0 TSval=3796364053 TSecr=153122458
    2 0.111215098 34.196.251.55 → 192.168.178.40 TCP 66
```

```
[TCP ACKed unseen segment] 443 → 47618 [ACK] Seq=1 Ack=2 Win=283
Len=0 TSval=153167579 TSecr=3796227866
...
8 7.712741925 192.168.178.40 → 185.199.109.153 HTTP 146 GET / HTTP/1.1 ❷
9 7.776535946 185.199.109.153 → 192.168.178.40 TCP 66 80 → 42000 [ACK]
Seq=1 Ack=81 Win=144896 Len=0 TSval=2759410860 TSecr=4258870662
10 7.878721682 185.199.109.153 → 192.168.178.40 TCP 2946 HTTP/1.1 200 OK
[TCP segment of a reassembled PDU]
11 7.878722366 185.199.109.153 → 192.168.178.40 TCP 2946 80 → 42000
[PSH, ACK] Seq=2881 Ack=81 Win=144896 Len=2880 TSval=2759410966 \
TSecr=4258870662
[TCP segment of a reassembled PDU]
...
```

❶ Use tshark to capture network traffic on network interface wlp1s0 and only look at TCP traffic.

❷ In another session, I issued a curl command to trigger an HTTP session, in which application layer interaction starts. You could also use the less powerful but on the other hand more widely available tcpdump (*http://www.tcpdump.org*) for this task.

Other Advanced Tooling

There are a number of advanced network-related tools out there you may find useful, including but not limited to the following:

socat (*https://oreil.ly/R4Upv*)
Establishes two bidirectional byte streams and enables the transferring of data between the endpoint.

geoiplookup (*https://oreil.ly/huZpl*)
Allows you to map an IP to a geographic region.

Tunnels
An easy-to-use alternative to VPNs and other site-to-site networking solutions. Enabled by such tools as inlets (*https://docs.inlets.dev*).

BitTorrent
A peer-to-peer system that groups files into a package called a *torrent*. Check out some clients (*https://oreil.ly/Z4rak*) to decide if this is something for your toolbox.

Conclusion

In this chapter, we defined common network terms, from the hardware level, such as NICs, to the TCP/IP stack, to application-layer, user-facing components, such as HTTP.

Linux provides a powerful, standards-based implementation of the TCP/IP stack that you can use programmatically (for example, sockets) and in the context of setting up and querying (usually with the `ip` command).

We further discussed application-layer protocols and interfaces that make up most of the daily (network-related) flows. Your command-line friends here include `curl` for transfer and `dig` for DNS lookups.

If you want to dive deeper into networking topics, check out the following resources:

The TCP/IP stack
- *Understanding Linux Network Internals* by Christian Benvenuti (O'Reilly)
- "A Protocol for Packet Network Intercommunication" (*https://oreil.ly/wRxdI*)
- DHCP server setup webpage (*https://oreil.ly/S6ZFJ*)
- "Hello IPv6: A Minimal Tutorial for IPv4 Users" (*https://oreil.ly/DPgZc*)
- "Understanding IPv6—7 Part Series" (*https://oreil.ly/91jkO*)
- Collection of IPv6 articles by Johannes Weber (*https://oreil.ly/MUcxG*)
- Iljitsch van Beijnum's BGP Expert website (*https://oreil.ly/K47dS*)
- "Everything You Ever Wanted to Know About UDP Sockets but Were Afraid to Ask" (*https://oreil.ly/CCrfA*)

DNS
- "An Introduction to DNS Terminology, Components, and Concepts" (*https://oreil.ly/K31GM*)
- "How to Install and Configure DNS Server in Linux" (*https://oreil.ly/eKdtK*)
- "Anatomy of a Linux DNS Lookup" (*https://oreil.ly/KkVSf*)
- "TLDs—Putting the *.fun* in the Top of the DNS" (*https://oreil.ly/qwRTx*)

Application layer and advanced networking

- "SSH Tunneling Explained" (*https://oreil.ly/3yhlV*)

- *Everything curl* (*https://oreil.ly/OzB6P*)

- "What Is DHCP and How to Configure DHCP Server in Linux" (*https://oreil.ly/hrLpo*)

- "How to Install and Configure Linux NTP Server and Client" (*https://oreil.ly/kHZhw*)

- NFS wiki (*https://oreil.ly/IOS4b*)

- "Use Wireshark at the Linux Command Line with TShark" (*https://oreil.ly/1ttt0*)

- "Getting Started with socat" (*https://oreil.ly/LWXCj*)

- "Geomapping Network Traffic" (*https://oreil.ly/TAd0b*)

With that, we're ready to move on to the next topic in the book: using observability to avoid flying blind.

## CHAPTER 8

Observability

You need visibility into what's going on across the stack—from the kernel to user-facing parts. Often, you get that visibility by knowing the right tool for the task.

This chapter is all about gathering and using different signals that Linux and its applications generate so that you can make informed decisions. For example, you'll see how you can do the following:

- Figure out how much memory a process consumes
- Understand how soon you will run out of disk space
- Get an alert on custom events for security reasons

To establish a common vocabulary, we'll first review different signal types you might come across, such as system or application logs, metrics, and process traces. We'll also have a look at how to go about troubleshooting and measuring performance. Next, we'll focus on logs specifically, reviewing different options and semantics. Then, we'll cover monitoring for different resource types, such as CPU cycles, memory, or I/O traffic. We'll review different tools that you can use and show certain end-to-end setup you may wish to adopt.

You'll learn that observability is often reactionary. That is, something crashes or runs slowly, and you start looking at processes and their CPU or memory usage, or dig into the logs. But there are also times when observability has more of an investigative nature—for example, when you want to figure out how long certain algorithms take. Last but not least, you can use predictive (rather than reactive) observability. For example, you can be alerted on a condition in the future, extrapolating the current behavior (disk usage for a predictable load is a good example where that might work well).

Likely the best visual overview on observability comes from performance maestro Brendan Gregg. Figure 8-1, taken from his Linux Performance site (*https://oreil.ly/KlzQP*), gives you a feeling for the wealth of moving parts and tooling available.

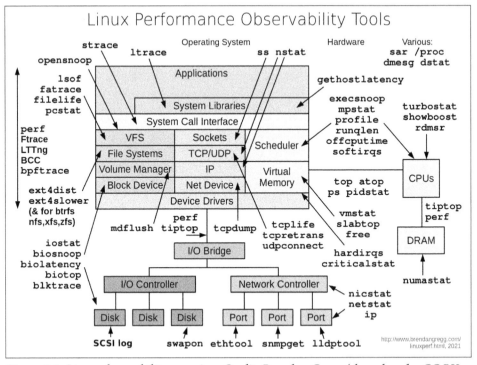

Figure 8-1. Linux observability overview. Credit: Brendan Gregg (shared under CC BY-SA 4.0 license)

Observability is an exciting topic with many use cases and lots of (open source) tooling available, so let's first establish a strategy and look at some common terms used.

Basics

Before we get into the observability terminology, let's step back a bit and look at how you turn the information provided into actionable insights and use it to fix an issue or optimize an app in a structured manner.

Observability Strategy

One widely established strategy in the observability context is the OODA loop (observe–orient–decide–act) (*https://oreil.ly/zLLET*). It offers a structured way to test a hypothesis based on observed data and act upon it—that is, a way to get actionable insights from signals.

For example, let's say an application is slow. Let's further assume there are multiple possible reasons for this (not enough memory, too few CPU cycles, network I/O insufficient, etc.). First, you want to be able to measure each resource consumption. Then you would change each resource allocation individually (keeping the others unchanged) and measure the outcome.

Does the performance improve after you provided more RAM to the app? If so, you may have found the reason. If not, you continue with a different resource, always measuring the consumption and trying to relate to the observed impact on the situation.

Terminology

There are a range of terms in the observability space,[1] and not all have formal definitions. In addition, the meanings might slightly differ if you're looking at a single machine or are in a networked (distributed) setup:

Observability
Assessing the internal state of a system (such as Linux) by measuring external information, usually with the goal of acting upon it. For example, if you notice that your system reacts sluggishly, and measure how much main memory is available, you might find that a particular app hogs all the memory, and you may decide to terminate it to remedy the situation.

Signal types
Different ways to represent and emit information about the state of a system, either via symbolic means (payload is text, such as the case with logs) or numerical values (as with metrics) or combinations thereof. See also "Signal Types" on page 190.

Source
Generates signals, potentially of different types. Sources can be the Linux operating system or an application.

Destination
Where you consume, store, and further process signals. We call a destination that exposes a user interface (GUI, TUI, or CLI) a *frontend*. For example, a log viewer or a dashboard plotting time series is a frontend, whereas an S3 bucket is not (but can still act as a destination for, say, logs).

---

1 *Observability* is also sometimes referred to with the numeronym *o11y*, as there are 11 letters between the *o* and the *y*.

Telemetry

> The process of extracting signals from sources and transporting (or routing, shipping) the signals to destinations, often employing agents that collect and/or preprocess signals (for example, filter or downsample).

Signal Types

Signals are how we communicate the state of a system for further processing or interpretation. By and large we distinguish between text payload (which is most suited for a human to search and interpret) and numerical payload (good for both machines and, in processed form, for humans). The three basic and common signal types relevant to our discussion in this chapter are: logs, metrics, and traces.

Logs

Logs are a fundamental signal type that every system, to some extent, generates. Logs are discrete events with a textual payload, meant for human consumption. Typically, these events are timestamped. Ideally, the logs are structured so that there is a clear meaning defined for each part of the log message. This meaning is potentially expressed through a formal schema so that validation can be automatically performed.

Interestingly, while every log has some structure (even if it's not well defined and parsing is hard, potentially due to delimiter or edge cases), you will often hear the term *structured logging*. When people say that, they actually mean that the log is structured using JSON.

While automating log content is hard (given its textual nature), logs are still very useful for humans, and thus they will likely stay the dominating signal type for some time. We'll dig deeper into handling logs in "Logging" on page 191. Logs are the most important signal type (for our considerations), and that's why we'll spend most of the time in this chapter dealing with them.

Metrics

Metrics are (usually regularly) sampled numerical data points, forming a time series. The individual data points can have additional context in the form of dimensions or identifying metadata. Normally, you don't directly consume the raw metrics; instead, you use some sort of aggregation or graphical representation, or you get notified if a certain condition is met. Metrics can be useful both for operational tasks and for troubleshooting to answer questions like how many transactions an app completed or how long a certain operation took (in the past X minutes).

We distinguish between different types of metrics:

Counter

> The value of a counter can only ever go up (besides resetting a counter to zero). An example of a counter metric is the total number of requests handled by a service or the bytes sent via an interface over a time period.

Gauges

> A gauge value can go up or down. For example, you gauge the currently available overall main memory or the number of processes running.

Histograms

> A sophisticated way to build a distribution of values. Using buckets, histograms allow you to assess how the data overall is structured. They also enable you to make flexible statements (such as 50% or 90% of the values fall into a certain range).

In "Monitoring" on page 197, we have a look at a range of tools that you can use for simple use cases, and in "Prometheus and Grafana" on page 207, you see an advanced example setup for metrics.

Traces

Traces are a dynamic collection of runtime information (for example, information about what syscalls a process uses, or the sequence of events in the kernel, for a given cause). Traces are often used not only for debugging but also for performance assessments. We have a look at this advanced topic in "Tracing and Profiling" on page 205.

Logging

As mentioned before, logs are (a collection of) discrete events with a textual payload, optimized for human consumption. Let's decompose this statement to understand it better:

Discrete events

> Think of a discrete event in the context of the codebase. You want to share information about what is going on in the code using an (atomic) log item. For example, you emit a log line that a database connection has been established successfully. Another log item might be to flag an error because a file is missing. Keep the scope of the log message small and specific, so it's easier for someone consuming the message to find the respective location in the code.

Textual payload

> The payload of a log message is of textual nature. The default consumers are humans. In other words, no matter if you're using a log viewer on the command line, or a fancy log-processing system with visual UI, a human reads and interprets the content of the log message and decides on an action based on it.

From a structural perspective, overall, a log comprises the following:

A collection of log items, messages, or lines
> Captures information about a discrete event.

Metadata or context
> Can be present on a per-message basis as well as on a global scope (the entire log file, for example).

A format for how an individual log message is to be interpreted
> Defines the log's parts and meanings. Examples are line-oriented, space-separated messages or a JSON schema.

In Table 8-1, you can see some common log formats. There are many (more-specific, narrower-scoped) formats and frameworks—for example, for database or programming languages.

Table 8-1. Common log formats

Format	Note
Common event format (*https://oreil.ly/rHBWs*)	Developed by ArcSight; used for devices, security use cases
Common log format (*https://oreil.ly/Da7uC*)	For web servers; see also extended log format
Graylog extended log format (*https://oreil.ly/6MBHm*)	Developed by Graylog; improves Syslog
Syslog	For operating systems, apps, devices; see "Syslog" on page 194
Embedded metric format (*https://oreil.ly/LeXhe*)	Developed by Amazon (both logs and metrics)

As a good practice, you want to avoid overhead with logs (enabling fast lookups and a small footprint—that is, not taking up too much disk space). In this context, log rotation, for example, via `logrotate` (*https://oreil.ly/jX6Jy*), is used. An advanced concept called *data temperature* may also be useful, moving older log files to cheaper and slower storage (attached disk, S3 bucket, Glacier).

> There's one case where you need to be careful about logging information, especially in production environments. Whenever you decide to emit a log line in your app, ask yourself if you could potentially leak sensitive information. This sensitive information could be a password, an API key, or even simply user-identifying information (email, account ID).
>
> The problem is that the logs are usually stored in a persistent form (say, on local disk or even in an S3 bucket). This means that even long after the process has terminated, someone could get access to the sensitive information and use it for an attack.

To signal the importance or intended target consumer of a log item, logs often define levels (for example DEBUG for development, INFO for normal status, or ERROR for unexpected situations that may require human intervention).

Now it's time to get our hands dirty: let's start with something simple and, as an overview, have a look at Linux's central log directory (output shortened for readability):

```
$ ls -al /var/log
drwxrwxr-x   8 root     syslog              4096 Jul 13 06:16 .
drwxr-xr-x  13 root     root                4096 Jun  3 07:52 ..
drwxr-xr-x   2 root     root                4096 Jul 12 11:38 apt/ ❶
-rw-r-----   1 syslog   adm                 7319 Jul 13 07:17 auth.log ❷
-rw-rw----   1 root     utmp                1536 Sep 21 14:07 btmp ❸
drwxr-xr-x   2 root     root                4096 Sep 26 08:35 cups/ ❹
-rw-r--r--   1 root     root               28896 Sep 21 16:59 dpkg.log ❺
-rw-r-----   1 root     adm                51166 Jul 13 06:16 dmesg ❻
drwxrwxr-x   2 root     root                4096 Jan 24  2021 installer/ ❼
drwxr-sr-x+  3 root     systemd-journal     4096 Jan 24  2021 journal/ ❽
-rw-r-----   1 syslog   adm                 4437 Sep 26 13:30 kern.log ❾
-rw-rw-r--   1 root     utmp              292584 Sep 21 15:01 lastlog ❿
drwxr-xr-x   2 ntp      ntp                 4096 Aug 18  2020 ntpstats/ ⓫
-rw-r-----   1 syslog   adm               549081 Jul 13 07:57 syslog ⓬
```

❶ Logs of the apt package manager

❷ Logs of all login attempts (successful and failed) and authentication processes

❸ Failed login attempts

❹ Printing related logs

❺ Logs of the dpkg package manager

❻ Device driver logs; use dmesg to inspect

❼ System install logs (when the Linux distro was originally installed)

❽ The journalctl location; see "journalctl" on page 196 for details

❾ The kernel logs

❿ All last logins of all users; use lastlog to inspect

⓫ NTP-related logs (see also "Network Time Protocol" on page 183)

⓬ The syslogd location; see "Syslog" on page 194 for details

One common pattern for consuming logs live (that is, as it happens) is to *follow logs*; that is, you watch the end of the log as new log lines are added (edited to fit):

```
$ tail -f /var/log/syslog ❶
Sep 26 15:06:41 starlite nm-applet[31555]: ... 'GTK_IS_WIDGET (widget)' failed
Sep 26 15:06:41 starlite nm-dispatcher: ... new request (3 scripts)
Sep 26 15:06:41 starlite systemd[1]: Starting PackageKit Daemon...
Sep 26 15:06:41 starlite nm-dispatcher: ... start running ordered scripts...
Sep 26 15:06:42 starlite PackageKit: daemon start ❷
^C
```

❶ Follow the logs of the `syslogd` process with the `-f` option.

❷ An example log line; see "Syslog" on page 194 for the format.

> If you want to see the log output of a process and at the same time store it in a file, you can use the `tee` command (*https://oreil.ly/X1Gqo*):
>
> ```
> $ someprocess | tee -a some.log
> ```
>
> Now you'd see the output of `someprocess` in your terminal, and the output would at the same time be stored in *some.log*. Note that we're using the `-a` option to append to the log file, otherwise it would be truncated.

Let's now have a look at the two most commonly used Linux logging systems.

Syslog

Syslog is a logging standard for a range of sources, from the kernel to daemons to user space. It has its roots in networked environments, and today the protocol comprises a textual format defined in RFC 5424 (*https://oreil.ly/1Qqng*), along with deployment scenarios and security considerations. Figure 8-2 shows the high-level format of Syslog, but be aware that there are many seldom-used optional fields.

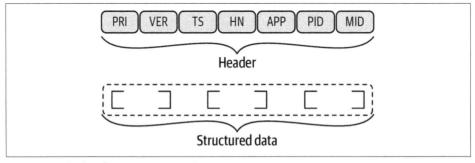

Figure 8-2. Syslog format as per RFC 5424

The Syslog format as defined in RFC 5424 has the following header fields (with TS and HN the most often used):

PRI
> The message facility/severity

VER
> The Syslog protocol number (usually left out since it can only be 1)

TS
> Contains the time when the message was generated using ISO 8601 format

HN
> Identifies the machine that sent the message

APP
> Identifies the application (or a device) that sent the message

PID
> Identifies the process that sent the message

MID
> An optional message ID

The format also includes *structured data*, which is the payload in a structured (key/value-based) list where each element is bounded by [ ].

Usually, one would use the syslogd binary (*https://oreil.ly/su6IX*) to take care of the log management. Over time, other options have become available that you should be aware of:

syslog-ng (*https://oreil.ly/qETe9*)
> An enhanced log daemon that you can use as a drop-in replacement for syslogd and that in addition supports TLS, content-based filtering, and logging into databases such as PostgreSQL and MongoDB. Available since late 1990.

rsyslog (*https://oreil.ly/QDPmv*)
> Extends the Syslog protocol and can also be used with systemd. Available since 2004.

Despite its age, the Syslog family of protocols and tools is still around and widely available. With systemd becoming the de facto standard of init systems, used in every major Linux distro, there is, however, a new way to go about logging: meet the systemd journal.

journalctl

In "systemd" on page 119, we briefly touched upon a component that is part of the systemd ecosystem, responsible for log management: journalctl (*https://oreil.ly/ M4sbo*). In contrast to Syslog and the other systems we've used so far, journalctl uses a binary format to store the log items. This allows faster access and better storage footprints.

The binary storage format did attract some criticism when it was introduced since people are not able to continue to use the familiar tail, cat, and grep commands to view and search logs. Having said that, while one has to learn a new way to interact with logs when using journalctl, the learning curve is not too bad.

Let's have a look at some common tasks. If you launch journalctl without parameters, it will present itself as an interactive pager (you can use the arrow keys or space bar to scroll through it and exit with q) for all the logs.

To restrict the time range, you can, for example, use the following:

```
$ journalctl --since "3 hours ago" ❶
```

```
$ journalctl --since "2021-09-26 15:30:00" --until "2021-09-26 18:30:00" ❷
```

❶ Restrict the time range to what happened in the past three hours.

❷ Another way to restrict the time range, with explicit start and stop times.

You can limit the output to specific systemd units like so (assuming there is a service called abc.service):

```
$ journalctl -u abc.service
```

 The journalctl tool has a powerful way to format the output of the log items. Using the --output (or -o for short) parameter, you can optimize the output for a certain use case. Important values are the following:

cat
> Short form, without time stamp or source

short
> The default, emulating Syslog output

json
> One JSON-formatted entry per line (for automation)

You can have the same experience to follow the logs as you'd have with `tail -f` using the following:

```
$ journalctl -f
```

Let's put all the preceding information together into a concrete example. Assume you want to relaunch a security component of the Linux distro, managed by `systemd`: AppArmor (*https://www.apparmor.net*). That is, in one terminal we restart the service using `systemctl restart apparmor`, and in another we execute the following command (output edited; the actual output is one log item per line):

```
$ journalctl -f -u apparmor.service ❶
-- Logs begin at Sun 2021-01-24 14:36:30 GMT. --
Sep 26 17:10:02 starlite apparmor[13883]: All profile caches have been cleared,
                                          but no profiles have been unloaded.
Sep 26 17:10:02 starlite apparmor[13883]: Unloading profiles will leave already
                                          running processes permanently
...
Sep 26 17:10:02 starlite systemd[1]: Stopped AppArmor initialization.
Sep 26 17:10:02 starlite systemd[1]: Starting AppArmor initialization... ❷
Sep 26 17:10:02 starlite apparmor[13904]:  * Starting AppArmor profiles
Sep 26 17:10:03 starlite apparmor[13904]: Skipping profile in
                                /etc/apparmor.d/disable: usr.sbin.rsyslogd
Sep 26 17:10:09 starlite apparmor[13904]:    ...done.
Sep 26 17:10:09 starlite systemd[1]: Started AppArmor initialization.
```

❶ Follow the logs of the AppArmor service.

❷ After `systemd` has stopped the service, here it comes back up again.

With that we are at the end of the logging section and move on to numerical values with metrics and the wider topic of monitoring.

Monitoring

Monitoring is the capturing of system and application metrics for a variety of reasons. For example, you may be interested in how long something takes or how many resources a process consumes (performance monitoring), or you may be trouble-shooting an unhealthy system. The two types of activities you'll carry out most often in the context of monitoring are as follows:

- Tracking one or more metrics (over time)
- Alerting on a condition

In this section, we first focus on some foundations and tools you should be aware of, and as we move further into the section, we get into more advanced techniques that may be relevant only in certain situations.

Let's look at a simple example that displays some basic metrics, such as how long a system is running, memory usage, and more, using the `uptime` command (*https://oreil.ly/smiz6*):

```
$ uptime ❶
08:48:29 up 21 days, 20:59,  1 user,  load average: 0.76, 0.20, 0.09 ❷
```

❶ Use the `uptime` command to display some basic system metrics.

❷ Separated by commas, the output tells us how long the system is running, the number of users logged in, and then (in the `load average` section) three gauges: the 1-minute, 5-minute, and 15-minute average. These averages are the number of jobs in the run queue or waiting for disk I/O; the numbers are normalized and indicate how busy the CPUs are. For example, here the load average for the past 5 minutes was 0.2 (which in isolation doesn't tell you much, so you have to compare it with the other values and track it over time).

Next, let's monitor some basic memory utilization, using the `free` command (output compressed to fit):

```
$ free -h ❶
              total   used   free  shared  buff/cache   available
Mem:           7.6G   1.3G   355M    395M        6.0G        5.6G ❷
Swap:          975M   1.2M   974M ❸
```

❶ Show memory usage using a human-friendly output.

❷ The memory stats: total/used/free/shared memory, memory used in buffers and used for caching (use `-w` if you don't want the combined value), and the available memory.

❸ The total/used/free amount of swap space—that is, physical memory moved out to a swap disk space.

A more sophisticated way to look at memory usage is using the `vmstat` (short for virtual memory stats) command (*https://oreil.ly/x8wrI*). The following example uses `vmstat` in a self-updating manner (output edited to fit):

```
$ vmstat 1 ❶
procs -----------memory--------- ---swap-- ----io---- -system- -----cpu-----
 r  b   swpd   free   buff  cache   si   so   bi    bo   in   cs us sy id wa st ❷
 4  0   1184 482116 682388 5447048    0    0   12   105   28  191  6  3 91  0  0
 0  0   1184 483444 682388 5446600    0    0    0     0  369  522  1  0 99  0  0
 0  0   1184 483696 682392 5446600    0    0    0   104  278  374  1  1 99  0  0
^C
```

❶ Show memory stats. The argument 1 means to print a new summary line every second.

❷ Some important column headers: r is for the number of processes running or waiting for CPU (should be less than or equal to the number of CPUs you have), free is the free main memory in KB, in is the number of interrupts per second, cs is the number of context switches per second, and us to st are percentages of total CPU time across user space, kernel, idle, and the like.

To see how long a certain operation takes, you can use the time command:

```
$ time (ls -R /etc 2&> /dev/null) ❶

real    0m0.022s ❷
user    0m0.012s ❸
sys     0m0.007s ❹
```

❶ Measure how long recursively listing all */etc* subdirectories takes (we throw away all output, including errors, with 2&> /dev/null).

❷ The total (wall clock) time it took (not really useful other than for performance).

❸ How long ls itself spent on-CPU (user space).

❹ How long ls was waiting for Linux to do something (kernel space).

In the previous example, if you're interested in how long an operation took, taking the sum of user and sys is a good approximation, and the ratio of the two gives you a good idea where it spends most of the execution time.

Now we focus on some more specific topics: network interfaces and block devices.

Device I/O and Network Interfaces

With iostat (*https://oreil.ly/L4Pbu*) you can monitor I/O devices (output edited):

```
$ iostat -z --human ❶
Linux 5.4.0-81-generic (starlite)    09/26/21    _x86_64_    (4 CPU)

avg-cpu:  %user  %nice %system %iowait  %steal   %idle
           5.8%   0.0%    2.7%    0.1%    0.0%   91.4%

Device           tps    kB_read/s    kB_wrtn/s    kB_read    kB_wrtn
loop0           0.00        0.0k        0.0k      343.0k       0.0k
loop1           0.00        0.0k        0.0k        2.8M       0.0k
...
sda             0.38        1.4k       12.4k        2.5G      22.5G ❷
dm-0            0.72        1.3k       12.5k        2.4G      22.7G
...
loop12          0.00        0.0k        0.0k        1.5M       0.0k
```

❶ Use iostat to show I/O device metrics. With -z, we tell it to show only devices where there was some activity, and the --human makes the output nicer (units are in human-readable form).

❷ Example row: tps is the number of transfers (I/O requests) per second for that device, read is data volume, and wrtn is written data.

Next up: network interfaces with the ss command (*https://oreil.ly/BAIiv*) that can dump socket statistics (see also "Sockets" on page 164). The following command lists both TCP and UDP sockets along with process IDs (output edited to fit):

```
$ ss -atup ❶
Netid State   Recv-Q Send-Q  Local Address:Port        Peer Address:Port
udp   UNCONN  0      0           0.0.0.0:60360             0.0.0.0:*
...
udp   UNCONN  0      0           0.0.0.0:ipp               0.0.0.0:*
udp   UNCONN  0      0           0.0.0.0:789               0.0.0.0:*
udp   UNCONN  0      0         224.0.0.251:mdns            0.0.0.0:*
udp   UNCONN  0      0           0.0.0.0:mdns              0.0.0.0:*
udp   ESTAB   0      0      192.168.178.40:51008     74.125.193.113:443
...
tcp   LISTEN  0      128         0.0.0.0:sunrpc            0.0.0.0:*
tcp   LISTEN  0      128   127.0.0.53%lo:domain            0.0.0.0:*
tcp   LISTEN  0      5         127.0.0.1:ipp               0.0.0.0:*
tcp   LISTEN  0      4096      127.0.0.1:45313             0.0.0.0:*
tcp   ESTAB   0      0      192.168.178.40:57628     74.125.193.188:5228 ❷
tcp   LISTEN  0      128            [::]:sunrpc               [::]:*
tcp   LISTEN  0      5             [::1]:ipp                  [::]:*
```

❶ Use ss with the following options: with -a, we select all (that is, both listening and nonlistening sockets); the -t and -u select TCP and UDP, respectively; and -p shows the processes using the sockets.

❷ An example socket in use. It's an established TCP connection between local IPv4 address 192.168.178.40 and remote 74.125.193.188 that seems idle: both data queued for receive (Recv-Q) and transmit (Send-Q) report zero.

> An outdated way to gather and display interface stats is using netstat (*https://oreil.ly/UBqge*). For example, if you want to have a continuously updated view on TCP and UDP, including process ID and using IP addresses rather than FQDNs, you could use netstat -ctulpn.

lsof (*https://oreil.ly/qDT67*) stands for "list open files" and is a versatile tool with many use cases. The following example shows lsof used in the context of network connections (output edited to fit):

```
$ sudo lsof -i TCP:1-1024 ❶
COMMAND        PID          USER   FD   TYPE DEVICE SIZE/OFF NODE NAME
...
rpcbind     26901          root    8u  IPv4 615970     0t0  TCP *:sunrpc (LISTEN)
rpcbind     26901          root   11u  IPv6 615973     0t0  TCP *:sunrpc (LISTEN)
```

❶ List privileged TCP ports (needs `root` privileges).

Another usage example for `lsof` is a process-centric view: if you know the PID of a process (here, Chrome), you can use `lsof` to track file descriptors, I/O, etc. (output edited to fit):

```
$ lsof -p 5299
COMMAND  PID USER   FD TYPE  DEVICE  SIZE/OFF     NODE NAME
chrome  5299  mh9  cwd  DIR   253,0      4096  6291458 /home/mh9
chrome  5299  mh9  rtd  DIR   253,0      4096        2 /
chrome  5299  mh9  txt  REG   253,0 179093936  3673554 /opt/google/chrome/chrome
...
```

There are many more tools for (performance) monitoring available—for example, `sar` (*https://oreil.ly/dYWwR*) (covering a range of counters, nice for scripts) and `perf` (*https://oreil.ly/TJ4gP*)—some of which we will discuss in "Advanced Observability" on page 205.

Now that you have a handle on individual tools, let's move on to integrated tools that allow you to interactively monitor Linux.

Integrated Performance Monitors

Using the tooling we discussed in the previous section, such as `lsof` or `vmstat`, is a good starting point and also useful in scripts. For more convenient monitoring, you may prefer integrated solutions. These typically come with a textual user interface (TUI), sometimes in color, and offer the following features:

- Support for multiple resource types (CPU, RAM, I/O)
- Interactive sorting and filtering (by process, user, resource)
- Live updates and drill-down into details such as a process group or even cgroups and namespaces

For example, the widely available `top` (*https://oreil.ly/NqKO2*) provides an overview in the header—akin to what we saw in the `uptime` output—and then a tabular rendering of CPU and memory details, followed by a list of processes you can track (output edited):

```
top - 12:52:54 up 22 days,  1:04,  1 user,  load average: 0.23, 0.26, 0.23 ❶
Tasks: 263 total,   1 running, 205 sleeping,   0 stopped,   0 zombie ❷
%Cpu(s):  0.2 us,  0.4 sy,  0.0 ni, 99.3 id,  0.0 wa,  0.0 hi,  0.0 si, \
   0.0 st% ❸
```

```
KiB Mem :  7975928 total,    363608 free,   1360348 used,   6251972 buff/cache
KiB Swap:   999420 total,    998236 free,      1184 used.   5914992 avail Mem

 PID USER      PR  NI    VIRT    RES    SHR S  %CPU %MEM     TIME+ COMMAND
   1 root      20   0  225776   9580   6712 S   0.0  0.1   0:25.84 systemd
 ...
 433 root      20   0  105908   1928   1700 S   0.0  0.0   0:00.05  `- lvmetad
 ...
 775 root      20   0   36552   4240   3880 S   0.0  0.1   0:00.16  `- bluetoothd
 789 syslog    20   0  263040   4384   3616 S   0.0  0.1   0:01.98  `- rsyslogd
```

❶ Summary of system (compare with uptime output)

❷ Task statistics

❸ CPU usage statistics (user, kernel, etc.; similar to vmstat output)

❹ The dynamic process list, including details on a per-process level; comparable to ps aux output

The following are the most important keys to remember in top:

?

To list the help (including key mappings)

V

To toggle to and from process tree view

m

To sort by memory usage

P

To sort by CPU consumption

k

To send a signal (like to kill)

q

To quit

While top is available in virtually any environment, there are a number of alternatives available, including the following:

htop (*https://oreil.ly/P9elE*) (*Figure 8-3*)

An incremental top improvement that is faster than top and has a nicer user interface.

`atop` *(https://oreil.ly/luRoU) (Figure 8-4)*

A powerful alternative to `top`. In addition to CPU and memory, it covers resources such as I/O and network stats in great detail.

`below` *(https://oreil.ly/XdOHB)*

A relatively new tool that is notable especially because it is cgroups v2–aware (see "Linux cgroups" on page 135). Other tools do not understand cgroups and hence provide only a global resource view.

Figure 8-3. A screenshot of the `htop` tool

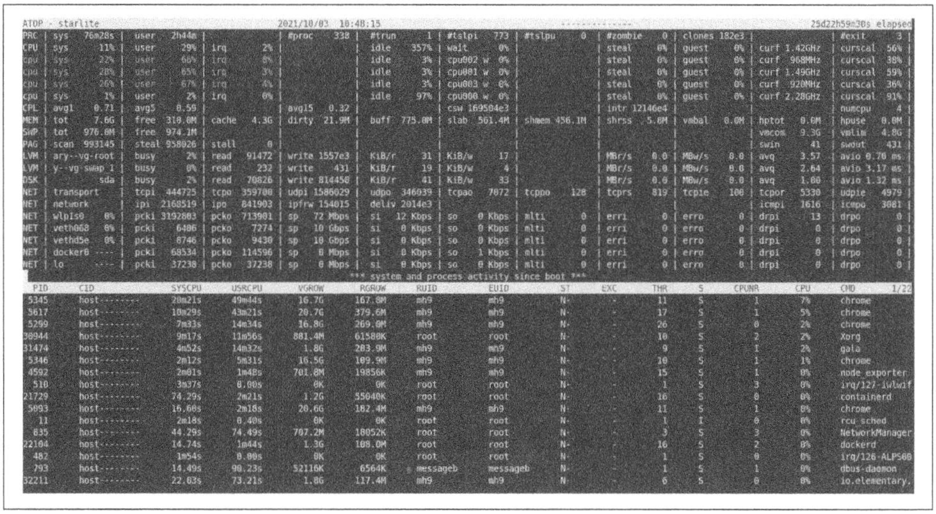

Figure 8-4. A screenshot of the `atop` tool

There are a number of other integrated monitoring tools available that go beyond the basic sources or that specialize in certain use cases. These include but are not limited to the following:

glances (https://oreil.ly/zOC9e)
> A powerful hybrid that covers devices in addition to the usual resources

guider (https://oreil.ly/uqBH1)
> An integrated performance analyzer that allows you to display and graph a range of metrics

neoss (https://oreil.ly/O4BHS)
> For network traffic monitoring; an `ss` replacement that offers a nice TUI

mtr (https://oreil.ly/uL38A)
> For network traffic monitoring; a more powerful alternative to `traceroute` (see "Routing" on page 158 for details on `traceroute`)

Now that you have a broad understanding of the tooling to consume system metrics, let's see how you can expose those from your own code.

Instrumentation

So far we've focused on signals coming from the kernel or existing applications (that is, code that you don't own). Now we move to the topic of how you can, similar to logs, equip your code to emit metrics.

The process of inserting code to emit signals, especially metrics, is mainly relevant if you're developing software. This process is usually referred to as *instrumentation*, and there are two common instrumentation strategies: *autoinstrumentation* (no additional effort for you as a developer) and *custom instrumentation*, where you manually insert code snippets to, for example, emit a metric at a certain point in your code base.

You can use StatsD (*https://oreil.ly/XOYFE*), with client-side libraries available for a number of programming languages, such as Ruby (*https://oreil.ly/VfE4D*), Node.js (*https://oreil.ly/G9Jt3*), Python (*https://oreil.ly/hQBMf*), and Go (*https://oreil.ly/whpZV*). StatsD is nice, but it has a few limitations, especially in dynamic environments such as Kubernetes or IoT. In those environments, a different approach—sometimes called *pull-based* or *scraping*—is usually a better choice. With scraping, applications expose metrics (usually via an HTTP endpoint), and an agent then calls this endpoint to retrieve metrics, rather than configuring the app with where to send the metrics to. We'll return to this topic in "Prometheus and Grafana" on page 207.

Advanced Observability

Now that you know the basics of Linux observability, let's have a look at some more advanced topics in this space.

Tracing and Profiling

The term *tracing* is overloaded: in the context of Linux, on a single machine, tracing means capturing the process execution (function calls in user space, syscalls, etc.) over time.

> In a distributed setup like containerized microservices in Kubernetes or a bunch of Lambda functions that are part of a serverless app, we sometimes shorten *distributed tracing* (*https://oreil.ly/tTjY9*) (for example, with OpenTelemetry and Jaeger) to *tracing*. This type of tracing is out of scope for this book.

There are a number of data sources in the context of a single Linux machine. You can use the following as sources for tracing:

The Linux kernel
Traces can come from functions in the kernel or be triggered by syscalls. Examples include kernel probes (*https://oreil.ly/lAolL*) (kprobes) or kernel tracepoints (*https://oreil.ly/wZcXE*).

User space
Application function calls, for example via user space probes (uprobes) (*https://oreil.ly/I8ICY*), can act as a source for traces.

Use cases for tracing include the following:

- Debugging a program using, for example, the `strace` (*https://strace.io*) tracing tool
- Performance analysis with a frontend, using `perf` (*https://oreil.ly/izMpR*)

> You may be tempted to use `strace` everywhere; however, you should be aware of the overhead it causes. This is particularly relevant for production environments. Read "strace Wow Much Syscall" (*https://oreil.ly/eSLOT*) by Brendan Gregg to understand the background.

See Figure 8-5 for an example output of `sudo perf top`, which generates a summary by process.

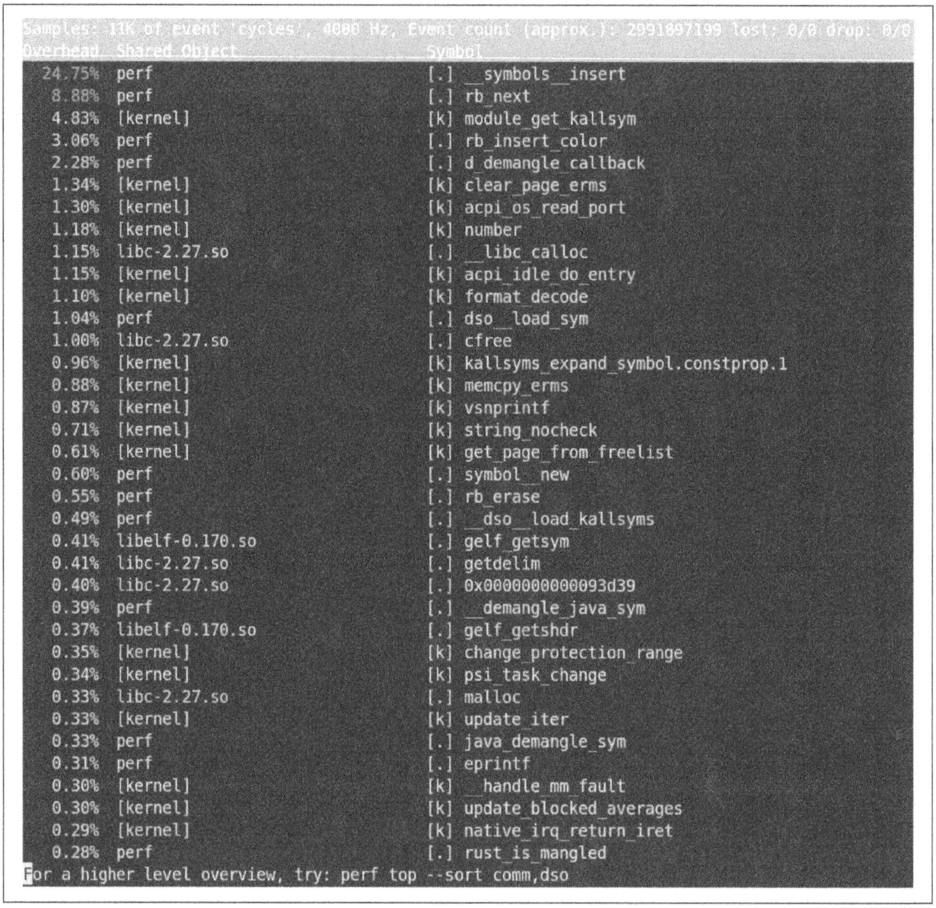

```
Samples: 11K of event 'cycles', 4000 Hz, Event count (approx.): 2991897199 lost: 0/0 drop: 0/0
Overhead  Shared Object       Symbol
  24.75%  perf                [.] __symbols__insert
   8.88%  perf                [.] rb_next
   4.83%  [kernel]            [k] module_get_kallsym
   3.06%  perf                [.] rb_insert_color
   2.28%  perf                [.] d_demangle_callback
   1.34%  [kernel]            [k] clear_page_erms
   1.30%  [kernel]            [k] acpi_os_read_port
   1.18%  [kernel]            [k] number
   1.15%  libc-2.27.so        [.] __libc_calloc
   1.15%  [kernel]            [k] acpi_idle_do_entry
   1.10%  [kernel]            [k] format_decode
   1.04%  perf                [.] dso__load_sym
   1.00%  libc-2.27.so        [.] cfree
   0.96%  [kernel]            [k] kallsyms_expand_symbol.constprop.1
   0.88%  [kernel]            [k] memcpy_erms
   0.87%  [kernel]            [k] vsnprintf
   0.71%  [kernel]            [k] string_nocheck
   0.61%  [kernel]            [k] get_page_from_freelist
   0.60%  perf                [.] symbol__new
   0.55%  perf                [.] rb_erase
   0.49%  perf                [.] __dso__load_kallsyms
   0.41%  libelf-0.170.so     [.] gelf_getsym
   0.41%  libc-2.27.so        [.] getdelim
   0.40%  libc-2.27.so        [.] 0x0000000000093d39
   0.39%  perf                [.] __demangle_java_sym
   0.37%  libelf-0.170.so     [.] gelf_getshdr
   0.35%  [kernel]            [k] change_protection_range
   0.34%  [kernel]            [k] psi_task_change
   0.33%  libc-2.27.so        [.] malloc
   0.33%  [kernel]            [k] update_iter
   0.33%  perf                [.] java_demangle_sym
   0.31%  perf                [.] eprintf
   0.30%  [kernel]            [k] __handle_mm_fault
   0.30%  [kernel]            [k] update_blocked_averages
   0.29%  [kernel]            [k] native_irq_return_iret
   0.28%  perf                [.] rust_is_mangled
For a higher level overview, try: perf top --sort comm,dso
```

Figure 8-5. A screenshot of the perf tracing tool

Going forward, it seems that eBPF (see "A Modern Way to Extend the Kernel: eBPF" on page 27) will become the de facto standard to implement tracing, especially for custom cases. It has a rich ecosystem and growing vendor support, so if you're looking for a future-proof tracing method, make sure it's using eBPF.

One particular use case for tracing is *profiling*—that is, to identify frequently called code sections. Some relevant low-level tooling for profiling include pprof (*https://oreil.ly/tETfk*), Valgrind (*https://oreil.ly/p9HQJ*), and flame graph visualizations (*https://oreil.ly/bCgbJ*).

There are many options to consume perf output interactively and visualize traces; for example, see Mark Hansen's blog post "Linux perf Profiler UIs" (*https://oreil.ly/dGH1S*).

Continuous profiling is an advanced variant of profiling, which captures traces (kernel and user space) over time. Once these timestamped traces are collected, you can plot and compare them and drill down into interesting segments. One very promising example is the eBPF-based open source project parca (*https://www.parca.dev*), shown in Figure 8-6.

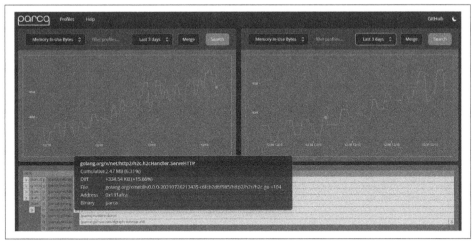

Figure 8-6. A screenshot of parca, a continuous profiling tool

Prometheus and Grafana

If you're dealing with metrics over time (time series data), using the Prometheus (*https://prometheus.io*) and Grafana (*https://grafana.com*) combo is something you may want to consider for advanced observability.

I'll show you a simple, single-machine setup that you can use to dashboard and even alert on things going on in your Linux machine.

We'll use the node exporter (*https://oreil.ly/0L4KJ*) to expose a range of system metrics, from CPU to memory and network. We'll then use Prometheus to scrape the node exporter. Scraping means that Prometheus calls an HTTP endpoint that the node exporter offers via the URL path */metrics*, returning the metrics in OpenMetrics format (*https://openmetrics.io*). For that to happen, we need to configure Prometheus with the URL of the node exporter's HTTP endpoint. The final step in our setup is using Prometheus as a datasource in Grafana, where you can see the time series data (metrics over time) in dashboards and can even alert on certain conditions, such as low disk space or CPUs overloading.

So, as a first step, download and untar the node exporter, and have it run the binary with ./node_exporter & in the background. You can check if it's running properly with the following (output edited):

```
$ curl localhost:9100/metrics
...
# TYPE go_gc_duration_seconds summary
go_gc_duration_seconds{quantile="0"} 7.2575e-05
go_gc_duration_seconds{quantile="0.25"} 0.00011246
go_gc_duration_seconds{quantile="0.5"} 0.000227351
go_gc_duration_seconds{quantile="0.75"} 0.000336613
go_gc_duration_seconds{quantile="1"} 0.002659194
go_gc_duration_seconds_sum 0.126529838
go_gc_duration_seconds_count 390
...
```

Now that we have the signal data source set up, we run both Prometheus and Grafana as containers. For the following, you'll need Docker (see "Docker" on page 138) installed and configured.

Create a Prometheus configuration file called *prometheus.yml* with the following content:

```
global:
  scrape_interval: 15s
  evaluation_interval: 15s
  external_labels:
      monitor: 'mymachine'
scrape_configs:
  - job_name: 'prometheus'  ❶
    static_configs:
    - targets: ['localhost:9090']
  - job_name: 'machine'  ❷
    static_configs:
    - targets: ['172.17.0.1:9100']
```

❶ Prometheus itself exposes metrics, so we include this (self-monitoring).

❷ That's our node exporter. Since we're running Prometheus in Docker, we can't use localhost but rather use the IP address Docker uses by default.

We use the Prometheus configuration file we created in the previous step and mount it into the container via a volume, like so:

```
$ docker run --name prometheus \
        --rm -d -p 9090:9090 \  ❶
        -v /home/mh9/lml/o11y/prometheus.yml:/etc/prometheus/prometheus.yml \  ❷
        prom/prometheus:main
```

❶ The parameters here make Docker remove the container on exit (--rm), run as a daemon (-d), and expose the port 9090 (-p) so we can use it from our machine.

❷ Mapping our config file as a volume into the container. Note that here you will have to replace */home/mh9/lml/o11y/* with the path where you stored it. Also, this has to be an absolute path. So, if you want to keep this flexible, you could use $PWD in bash or (pwd) in Fish rather than the hardcoded path.

After you've executed the previous command, open *localhost:9000* in your browser, then click Targets in the Status dropdown menu at the top. You should, after a few seconds, see something like the screen shown in Figure 8-7, confirming that Prometheus has successfully scraped metrics from itself and the node exporter.

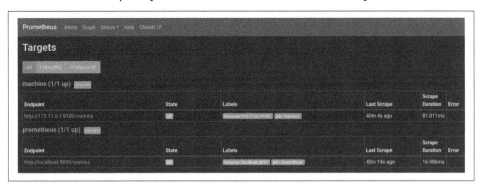

Figure 8-7. A screenshot of Prometheus targets in the Web UI

Next, we launch Grafana:

```
$ docker run --name grafana \
        --rm -d -p 3000:3000 \
        grafana/grafana:8.0.3
```

After you've executed the preceding command, open *localhost:3000* in your browser and use admin for both the username and password. Next, we need to do two things:

1. Add Prometheus as a datasource (*https://oreil.ly/9Efhy*) in Grafana, using 172.17.0.1:9100 as the URL

2. Import the Node Exporter Full dashboard (*https://oreil.ly/RpCDe*)

Once you've done this, you should see something akin to Figure 8-8.

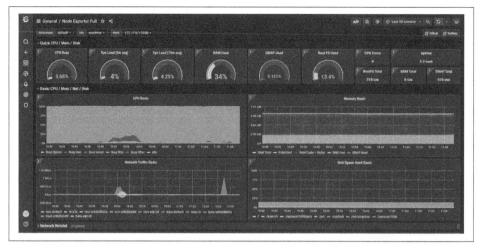

Figure 8-8. A screenshot of the Grafana UI with the Node Exporter Full dashboard

That was some exciting advanced observability for Linux, using modern tooling. Given that the Prometheus/Grafana setup is more elaborate and has a number of moving parts, you'll likely not use it for a trivial task. In other words, the Linux native tooling we discussed in this section should go a long way; however, there are more advanced use cases—for example, home automation or a media server—where you want to have a more complete solution, in which case Prometheus/Grafana makes a lot of sense.

Conclusion

In this chapter, we looked at making sure you're not flying blind when you're running into issues with your Linux system. The main signal types you'd typically use for diagnostics are logs (textual) and metrics (numerical). For advanced cases, you can apply profiling techniques, rendering resource usage of processes along with the execution context (source file and lines of the source code that is being executed).

If you want to learn more and dive deeper into this topic, have a look at these resources:

Basics
- *Systems Performance: Enterprise and the Cloud*, second edition (*https://oreil.ly/sxtPd*), by Brendan Gregg (Addison-Wesley)
- "Linux Performance Analysis in 60,000 Milliseconds" (*https://oreil.ly/YVxJt*)

Logging
- "Linux Logging Complete Guide" (*https://oreil.ly/fMNT7*)
- "Unix/Linux—System Logging" (*https://oreil.ly/hnMGz*)
- "syslog-ng" on ArchWiki (*https://oreil.ly/wzRqG*)
- fluentd website (*https://oreil.ly/hJ3nr*)

Monitoring
- "80+ Linux Monitoring Tools for SysAdmins" (*https://oreil.ly/C4ZJX*)
- "Monitoring StatsD: Metric Types, Format and Code Examples" (*https://oreil.ly/JaUEK*)

Advanced
- "Linux Performance" (*https://oreil.ly/EIPYd*)
- "Linux Tracing Systems & How They Fit Together" (*https://oreil.ly/SuGPM*)
- "Profilerpedia: A Map of the Software Profiling Ecosystem" (*https://oreil.ly/Sk0zL*)
- "On the State of Continuous Profiling" (*https://oreil.ly/wHLqr*)
- eBPF website (*https://oreil.ly/DFYMN*)
- "Monitoring Linux Host Metrics with the Node Exporter" (*https://oreil.ly/5fA6z*)

Having completed this chapter and those that preceded it, you now know the basics of Linux, from kernel to shell to filesystems and networking. The last chapter of this book is a collection of advanced topics that didn't quite fit in other chapters. You may find them interesting and useful, depending on your goals, but for most day-to-day tasks, you now know everything you need to get by.

## CHAPTER 9

Advanced Topics

This final chapter is a bit of a mixed bag. We cover a range of topics, from virtual machines to security to new ways to use Linux. What the topics in this chapter have in common is that most of them are relevant for you only if you have a specific use case in mind, or if you require them in a professional setup.

We start off the chapter with how processes on a single machine can communicate and share data. There is a wealth of interprocess communication (IPC) mechanisms available, and here we focus on well-established and -used features: signals, named pipes, and Unix domain sockets.

Then, we look at virtual machines (VMs). In contrast to the containers we discussed in "Containers" on page 131 (which are good for application-level dependency management), VMs provide strong isolation for your workloads. You come across VMs most often in the context of the public cloud and in the general case in data centers. Having said that, using VMs locally can also be useful, such as for testing or to simulate distributed systems.

The next section in this chapter focuses on modern Linux distributions, which are usually container-centric and assume immutability. You'll often find said distros in the context of distributed systems such as Kubernetes.

We then move on to selected security topics, covering Kerberos, a widely used authentication suite, and pluggable authentication modules (PAM), an extension mechanism Linux provides for authentication.

In the last part of this chapter, we review Linux solutions and use cases that, at the time of writing, are not yet mainstream. But they could be relevant to you and are worth exploring.

Interprocess Communication

In Linux there is a long list of interprocess communication (IPC) (*https://oreil.ly/tWp40*) options available, ranging from pipes to sockets to shared memory. IPC enables processes to communicate, synchronize activities, and share data. For example, the Docker daemon (*https://oreil.ly/aZur8*) uses configurable sockets to manage containers. In this section, we review some popular IPC options and their use cases.

Signals

Signals (*https://oreil.ly/0y6ru*) were originally developed as a way for the kernel to notify user space processes about a certain event. Think of signals as an asynchronous notification sent to a process. There are many signals available (use the `man 7 signal` command to learn more), and most of them come with a default action, such as stop or terminate the process.

With most signals, you define a custom handler, rather than letting Linux carry on with the default action. This is useful when you want to, for example, do some cleanup work or simply ignore certain signals. Table 9-1 shows the most common signals that you should be familiar with.

Table 9-1. Common signals

Signal	Meaning	Default action	Handle option	Key combination
SIGHUP	Tell a daemon process to reread its config file	Terminate process	nohup or custom handler	N/A
SIGINT	User interruption from keyboard	Terminate process	Custom handler	Ctrl+C
SIGQUIT	User quit from keyboard	core dump (*https://oreil.ly/jeuEo*) and terminate process	Custom handler	Ctrl+\
SIGKILL	Kill signal	Terminate process	Cannot be handled	N/A
SIGSTOP	Stop process	Stop process	Cannot be handled	N/A
SIGTSTP	User caused stop from keyboard	Stop process	Custom handler	Ctrl+Z
SIGTERM	Graceful termination	Terminate process	Custom handler	N/A

There are also signals that don't have defined meanings (SIGUSR1 and SIGUSR2) that processes can use to communicate with each other, sending asynchronous notification, if both parties agree on the semantics of the signal.

One typical way to send a signal to a process is the somewhat strangely named `kill` command (due to its default behavior to cause processes to terminate):

```
$ while true ; do sleep 1 ; done & ❶
[1] 17030 ❷
```

```
$ ps ❸
  PID TTY          TIME CMD
16939 pts/2    00:00:00 bash
17030 pts/2    00:00:00 bash ❹
17041 pts/2    00:00:00 sleep
17045 pts/2    00:00:00 ps

$ kill 17030 ❺
[1]+  Terminated              while true; do
    sleep 1;
done
```

❶ We set up a very simple program here that simply sleeps. With &, we put it into the background.

❷ The shell job control confirms that our program runs as a job with ID 1 in the background and reports its PID (17030).

❸ Using ps, we check if the program is still running.

❹ Here is our program (compare PID).

❺ By default, kill sends the SIGTERM to the process, and the default action is to terminate the process gracefully. We provide kill with the PID of our process (17030), and since we didn't register a custom handler, it is terminated.

Now we'll look at how to handle a signal with trap (*https://oreil.ly/pp6O4*). This allows us to define a custom handler in a shell environment (command line or script):

```
$ trap "echo kthxbye" SIGINT ; while true ; do sleep 1 ; done ❶
^Ckthxbye ❷
```

❶ With trap "echo kthxbye" SIGINT, we register a handler, telling Linux that when the user presses Ctrl+C (causing a SIGINT signal to be sent to our process), Linux should execute echo kthxbye before the default action (terminate).

❷ We see the user interruption (^C is the same as Ctrl+C) and then our custom handler getting executed, printing kthxbye, as expected.

Signals are a simple yet powerful IPC mechanism, and now you know the basics of how to send and handle signals in Linux. Next up, we discuss two more elaborate and powerful IPC mechanisms—named pipes and UNIX domain sockets.

Named Pipes

In "Streams" on page 34, we talked about pipes (|) that you can use to pass data from one process to another by connecting the stdout of one process with stdin of another process. We call these pipes *unnamed*. Taking this idea a step further, named pipes (*https://oreil.ly/iHMrK*) are pipes to which you can assign custom names.

Just like unnamed pipes, named pipes work with normal file I/O (open, write, etc.) and provide first in, first out (FIFO) delivery. Unlike unnamed pipes, the lifetime of a named pipe is not limited to the processes it's used with. Technically, named pipes are a wrapper around pipes, using the pipefs pseudo filesystem (see "Pseudo Filesystems" on page 104).

Let's see a named pipe in action to better appreciate what you can do with them. We create a named pipe called examplepipe in the following, along with one publisher and one consumer process:

```
$ mkfifo examplepipe ❶

$ ls -l examplepipe
prw-rw-r-- 1 mh9 mh9 0 Oct  2 14:04 examplepipe ❷

$ while true ; do echo "x" > examplepipe ; sleep 5 ; done & ❸
[1] 19628

$ while true ; do cat < examplepipe ; sleep 5 ; done & ❹
[2] 19636
x ❺
x
...
```

❶ We create a named pipe called examplepipe.

❷ Looking at the pipe with ls reveals its type: the first letter is a p, indicating it's a named pipe we're looking at.

❸ Using a loop, we publish the character x into our pipe. Note that unless some other process reads from examplepipe, the pipe is blocked. No further writing into it is possible.

❹ We launch a second process that reads from the pipe in a loop.

❺ As a result of our setup we see x appearing on the terminal, roughly every five seconds. In other words, it appears every time the process with PID 19636 is able to read from the named pipe with cat.

Named pipes are easy to use. Thanks to their design, they look and feel like normal files. But they're also limited, since they support only one direction and one consumer. The next IPC mechanism we look at addresses these limitations.

UNIX Domain Sockets

We've already talked about sockets in the context of networking. There are also other kinds of sockets that work exclusively in the context of a single machine, and one such kind is called UNIX domain sockets (*https://oreil.ly/nCd6r*): these are bidirectional, multiway communication endpoints. This means you can have multiple consumers.

Domain sockets come in three flavors (*https://oreil.ly/AlVUf*): stream-oriented (`SOCK_STREAM`), datagram-oriented (`SOCK_DGRAM`), and sequenced-packet (`SOCK_SEQ PACKET`). The addressing works based on filesystem pathnames. Rather than having IP addresses and ports, a simple file path is sufficient.

Usually, you would be using domain sockets programmatically (*https://oreil.ly/o8Ikj*). However, you might find yourself in a situation where you need to troubleshoot a system and want to use, for example, the `socat` tool (*https://oreil.ly/lWjrs*) from the command line to interact manually with a socket.

Virtual Machines

This section is about an established technique that allows us to emulate multiple VMs using a physical machine such as your laptop or a server in a data center. This yields a more flexible and powerful way to run different workloads, potentially from different tenants in a strongly isolated manner. We focus on hardware-assisted virtualization for x86 architectures.

In Figure 9-1, you see the virtualization architecture on a conceptual level, comprising the following (starting from the bottom):

The CPU
Must support hardware virtualization.

The kernel-based virtual machine
Found in the Linux kernel; discussed in "Kernel-Based Virtual Machine" on page 218.

Components in the user space
Components in the user space include the following:

A Virtual Machine Monitor (VMM)
Manages VMs and emulates virtual devices, such as QEMU (*https://www.qemu.org*) and Firecracker (see "Firecracker" on page 219). There is

also libvirt (*https://libvirt.org*), a library that exposes a generic API aiming to standardize VMM, which you can use programmatically (not explicitly shown in the figure; consider it part of the VMM block).

The guest kernel
Typically also a Linux kernel but could also be Windows.

The guest processes
Running on the guest kernel.

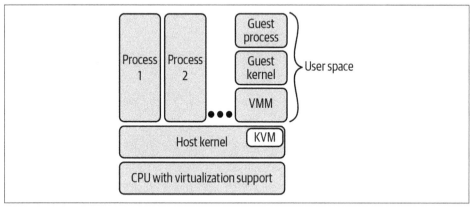

Figure 9-1. Virtualization architecture

The processes that run natively on the host kernel (in Figure 9-1, process 1 and process 2) are isolated from the guest processes. This means that in general the physical CPU and memory of the host are not affected by guest activities. For example, if there's an attack going on in the VM, the host kernel and processes are unaffected (as long as the VM is not given special access to the host system). Note that there may be exceptions to this in practice, such as rowhammer (*https://oreil.ly/L7qH9*) or Meltdown and Spectre (*https://oreil.ly/ZlgRE*).

Kernel-Based Virtual Machine

The Kernel-based Virtual Machine (KVM) (*https://oreil.ly/vTINW*) is a Linux-native virtualization solution for x86 hardware that supports virtualization extensions, such as the case with AMD-V (*https://oreil.ly/XXAM8*) or Intel VT (*https://oreil.ly/SAbNc*).

There are two parts to the KVM kernel modules: the core module (kvm.ko) and CPU architecture-specific modules (kvm-intel.ko/kvm-amd.ko). With KVM, the Linux kernel is the hypervisor, taking care of most of the heavy lifting. In addition, there are drivers such as the integrated Virtio (*https://oreil.ly/g37Qe*) that allow for I/O virtualization.

Today, hardware usually supports virtualization and KVM is already available, but in order to see if your system is capable of using KVM, you can do the following check (output edited):

```
$ grep 'svm\|vmx' /proc/cpuinfo ❶
flags          : fpu vme de pse tsc msr pae mce cx8 apic sep mtrr pge mca cmov
pat pse36 clflush dts acpi mmx fxsr sse sse2 ss ht tm pbe syscall nx pdpe1gb
rdtscp lm constant_tsc art arch_perfmon pebs bts rep_good nopl xtopology
tsc_reliable nonstop_tsc cpuid aperfmperf tsc_known_freq pni pclmulqdq dtes64
ds_cpl vmx tm2 ssse3 sdbg cx16 xtpr pdcm sse4_1 sse4_2 x2apic movbe popcnt ❷
tsc_deadline_timer aes xsave rdrand lahf_lm 3dnowprefetch cpuid_fault cat_l2
ibrs ibpb stibp tpr_shadow vnmi flexpriority ept vpid ept_ad fsgsbase tsc_adjust
smep erms mpx rdt_a rdseed smap clflushopt intel_pt sha_ni xsaveopt xsavec
xgetbv1 xsaves dtherm ida arat pln pts md_clear arch_capabilities
...

$ lsmod | grep kvm ❸

kvm_intel             253952  0 ❹
kvm                   659456  1 kvm_intel
```

❶ Search for svm or vmx in the CPU information (note that it reports on a per-CPU basis, so if you have eight cores, you would see this flags block repeated eight times).

❷ We see vmx is listed, so we're good concerning hardware-assisted virtualization.

❸ Here we check if the KVM kernel modules are available.

❹ This tells us that we have the kvm_intel kernel module loaded, so we're all set concerning KVM usage.

One modern way to manage KVMs is with Firecracker.

Firecracker

Firecracker (*https://oreil.ly/UpNPK*) is a VMM that can manage KVM instances. It is written in Rust and was developed at Amazon Web Services primarily for serverless offerings, such as AWS Lambda and AWS Fargate.

Firecracker is designed (*https://oreil.ly/6D8Wk*) to safely run multitenant workloads on the same physical machine. The Firecracker VMM manages so-called *microVMs* that expose an HTTP API to the host, allowing you to launch, query, and stop the microVMs. It emulates network interfaces by using TUN/TAP devices (*https://oreil.ly/ojWvm*) on the host, and block devices are backed by files on the host, supporting Virtio devices.

From a security perspective, in addition to the virtualization discussed so far, Firecracker by default uses seccomp filters (see "seccomp Profiles" on page 89) to limit the host system calls it can use. cgroups can also be used. From an observability point of view, you can gather logs and metrics from Firecracker, via named pipes.

With that we move on to modern Linux distributions that focus on immutability and leverage containers.

Modern Linux Distros

The most prominent traditional Linux distributions include the following:

- The Red Hat family (RHEL, Fedora, and CentOS/Rocky)
- The Debian-based family (Ubuntu, Mint, Kali, Parrot OS, elementary OS, etc.)
- The SUSE family (openSUSE and Enterprise)
- Gentoo
- Arch Linux

These are all perfectly fine distros. Depending on your needs and preferences, you can choose from being fully in control and taking care of everything yourself (from installation to patching) to having a fully managed offering where the distro takes care of most of the tasks.

With the rise of containers, as discussed in "Containers" on page 131, the role of the host operating system has changed. In the context of containers, traditional package managers (see "Packages and Package Managers" on page 126) play a different role: most base container images tend to be built from particular Linux distros, and dependencies are met within the containers with *.deb* or *.rpm* packages, while the container images package up all the application-level dependencies on top of them.

Further, making incremental changes to a system turns out to be a big challenge. This is especially true when you need to do it at scale, such as when you need to administrate a fleet of machines. Hence, for modern distros, the focus is increasingly on immutability. The idea is that any change in the configuration or code (think: a patch that fixes a security issue or a new feature) causes the creation of a new artifact, such as a container image that gets launched (in contrast to changing the running system).

When I say "modern Linux distros," I mean distros that are container-centric, with immutability and auto-upgrading (pioneered by Chrome) front and center. Let's have a look at some examples of modern distros.

Red Hat Enterprise Linux CoreOS

In 2013, a young start-up called CoreOS made CoreOS Linux (later renamed Container Linux) (*https://oreil.ly/XjqPV*) available. Its main features included a dual-partition scheme for system updates and the lack of a package manager. In other words, all apps would run as containers natively. In the ecosystem, a number of tools were developed that are still in use (such as `etcd`; think: a distributed version of the */etc* directory for configuration tasks).

After Red Hat acquired CoreOS (the company), it announced the intention to merge the CoreOS Linux with Red Hat's own Project Atomic (that had similar goals). This merger led to Red Hat Enterprise Linux CoreOS (RHCOS) (*https://oreil.ly/38kzX*), which is not meant to be used on its own but in the context of the Red Hat Kubernetes distribution called OpenShift Container Platform.

Flatcar Container Linux

A little bit after Red Hat announced its plans around Container Linux, a German startup called Kinvolk GmbH (now part of Microsoft) announced that it would fork and continue to develop Container Linux under the new brand name Flatcar Container Linux (*https://oreil.ly/rNJrt*).

Flatcar describes itself as a container-native, lightweight operating system with use cases in container orchestrators such as Kubernetes and IoT/edge computing. It continues the CoreOS tradition of auto-upgrades (optional with its own update manager, Nebraska (*https://oreil.ly/Qepv6*)) and has a powerful yet simple-to-use provisioning utility called Ignition (*https://oreil.ly/4vEQv*) that enables you to have fine-grained control over boot devices (also used by RHCOS for that purpose). Further, there is no package manager; everything is running in containers. You can manage the life cycle of the containerized apps with `systemctl` on a single machine or more typically with Kubernetes.

Bottlerocket

Bottlerocket (*https://oreil.ly/fIKrQ*) is a Linux-based operating system developed by AWS and meant for hosting containers (*https://oreil.ly/5Eaxd*). Written in Rust, it is used in a number of their offerings, such as Amazon EKS and Amazon ECS.

Akin to Flatcar and CoreOS, instead of a package manager, Bottlerocket uses an OCI image-based model for app upgrades and rollbacks. Bottlerocket uses a (by and large) read-only, integrity-checked filesystem based on dm-verity (*https://oreil.ly/xicaW*). To gain access (via SSH, although discouraged) and control Bottlerocket, it runs a so-called control container (*https://oreil.ly/KB6eX*), in a separate `containerd` instance.

RancherOS

RancherOS (*https://oreil.ly/73UxM*) is a Linux distro where everything is a container managed by Docker. Sponsored by Rancher (now SUSE), it is optimized for container workloads as in their Kubernetes distro. It runs two Docker instances: the system Docker, which runs as the first process, and the user Docker, which is used to create application containers. RancherOS has a small footprint, which makes it really great to use in the context of embedded systems and edge computing.

Selected Security Topics

In Chapter 4, we discussed a number of access control mechanisms. We discussed *authentication* (*authn*, for short), which verifies the identity of a user and is a precondition for any sort of *authorization* (*authz*, for short). In this section, we briefly discuss two widely used authn tools that you should be aware of.

Kerberos

Kerberos (*https://kerberos.org*) is an authn suite developed by the Massachusetts Institute of Technology in the 1980s. Today, it's formally specified in RFC 4120 (*https://oreil.ly/7woDK*) and related IETF documents. The core idea of Kerberos is that we're usually dealing with insecure networks, but we want a secure way for clients and services to prove their identity to one another.

Conceptually, the Kerberos authn process, shown in Figure 9-2, works as follows:

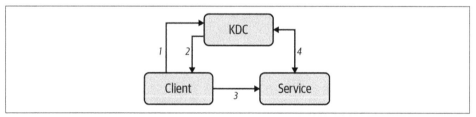

Figure 9-2. Kerberos protocol concept

1. A client (for example, a program on your laptop) sends a request to a Kerberos component called the Key Distribution Center (KDC), asking for credentials for a given service, such as printing or a directory.
2. The KDC responds with the requested credentials—that is, a ticket for the service and a temporary encryption key (session key).

3. The client transmits the ticket (which contains the client's identity and a copy of the session key) to the service.

4. The session key, shared by the client and service, is used to authenticate the client and may optionally be used to authenticate the service.

There are also challenges with Kerberos, such as the central role that the KDC plays (a single point of failure) and its strict time requirements (it requires clock synchronization between the client and the server via NTP). Overall, while not simple to operate and administrate, Kerberos is widely used and supported in the enterprise and cloud providers.

Pluggable Authentication Modules

Historically, a program would manage the user authentication process itself. With pluggable authentication modules (PAM) (*http://www.linux-pam.org*), a flexible way to develop programs that are independent of a concrete authentication scheme has arrived in Linux (PAM has been around since the end of the 1990s in the wider UNIX ecosystem). PAM uses a modular architecture, providing developers a powerful library to interface with it. It also allows system administrators to plug in different modules, such as the following:

pam_localuser *(https://oreil.ly/NCs0A)*
  Requires that a user is listed in */etc/passwd*

pam_keyinit *(https://oreil.ly/PkGt9)*
  For session keyrings

pam_krb5 *(https://oreil.ly/YinOv)*
  For Kerberos 5 password-based checks

With that, we've reached the end of the advanced security topics and now turn to more aspirational topics.

Other Modern and Future Offerings

In this section, we look at exciting Linux offerings, including new ways to set up Linux and ways to work with Linux in new environments. In the server world (be it an on-premises data center or the public cloud), Linux is already the de facto standard, and Linux is under the hood in many mobile devices.

What the topics here in this section have in common is that at the time of writing, they have not yet entered the mainstream. However, if you're curious about what future developments might look like or where there's still high growth potential for Linux, read on.

NixOS

NixOS (*https://nixos.org*) is a source-based Linux distro, taking a functional approach to package management and system configuration as well as rollbacks for upgrades. I call this a "functional approach" because the artifacts are based on immutability.

The Nix package manager (*https://oreil.ly/Km84W*) builds the entire operating system, from the kernel to system packages and apps. Nix offers multiuser package management and even allows you to install and use multiple versions of the same package.

Unlike most other Linux distros, NixOS does not follow the Linux Standard Base filesystem layout as discussed in "Common Filesystem Layouts" on page 103 (with system programs located in */usr/bin*, */usr/lib*, and so on, and the configuration usually located in */etc*).

There are a number of interesting ideas in NixOS and its ecosystem, making it especially relevant for CI pipelines. Even if you don't want to go all in, you can, for example, use the Nix package manager standalone (outside of NixOS).

Linux on the Desktop

While the viability of Linux on the desktop (*https://oreil.ly/eBPYT*) is subject to ongoing discussions, there is without doubt plenty of choice concerning desktop-friendly distros and with them a selection of window managers (*https://oreil.ly/qylKC*).

In good UNIX tradition, the Graphical User Interface (GUI) part is separated from the rest of the operating system. Usually, an X window manager (*https://oreil.ly/bTcHy*) takes care of the GUI responsibilities (from window management to styling and rendering) with the help of a display manager (*https://oreil.ly/hl5gv*).

On top of the window manager, implementing a desktop experience (such as icons, widgets, and toolbars), sit the desktop environments (*https://oreil.ly/y1VIr*), such as KDE or MATE.

There are many beginner-friendly desktop Linux distros available nowadays, making it easy to switch from Windows or macOS. The same is true for a range of open source applications, from office apps (writing docs or working with spreadsheets, such as LibreOffice) to drawing and image editing (Gimp), to all major web browsers, games, media players, and utilities, to development environments.

The catalyst for Linux on the desktop might in fact come from a rather unexpected direction: with Windows 11 allowing you to run graphical Linux apps (*https://oreil.ly/ tGgaf*) out of the box, this might change the incentives and uptake for good. Time will tell.

Linux on Embedded Systems

Linux on embedded systems (*https://oreil.ly/mFKVR*) is a wide field, with implementations ranging from cars to networking equipment (such as routers), to smart home devices (for example fridges) and media devices/smart TVs.

One particularly interesting generic platform you can acquire for little money is a Raspberry Pi (RPI) (*https://www.raspberrypi.org*). It comes with its own Linux distro called Raspberry Pi OS (a Debian-based system) and lets you install this and other Linux distros simply via a microSD card. The RPI has a number of General Purpose Input/Outputs (GPIOs), making it straightforward to use external sensors and circuits via a breadboard. You can experiment with, and learn electronics and program the hardware with, for example, Python.

Linux in Cloud IDE

In recent years, the viability of cloud-based development environments has made enormous progress to a point where now (commercial) offerings exist that combine an IDE (usually Visual Studio Code), Git, and a range of programming languages in a Linux environment. All you as a developer need is a web browser and network access, and you can edit, test, and run code "in the cloud."

Two notable examples of Cloud IDEs, at the time of writing, are Gitpod (*https:// www.gitpod.io*), which is available either as a managed offering or as an open source to host yourself, and Codespaces (*https://oreil.ly/bWNDT*), which is deeply integrated into GitHub.

Conclusion

This chapter covered advanced topics and refined your knowledge of basic techniques and tooling. If you want to enable IPC, you can use signals and named pipes. For isolating workloads, you can use VMs, especially modern variants such as Firecracker. We also discussed modern Linux distributions: if you plan to run containers (Docker), you may want to consider these container-centric distros that enforce immutability. We then moved on to selected security topics, specially Kerberos and PAM for flexible and/or large-scale authentication. Finally, we reviewed not-yet-mainstream Linux solutions such as Linux on the desktop and how you can get started with Linux on embedded systems, such as the Raspberry Pi, for local experimentation or development.

Some further reading for this chapter:

IPC
- "An Introduction to Linux IPC" (*https://oreil.ly/C2iwX*)
- "Inter-process Communication in Linux: Using Pipes and Message Queues" (*https://oreil.ly/cbi1Z*)
- "The Linux Kernel Implementation of Pipes and FIFOs" (*https://oreil.ly/FUvoo*)
- "Socat Cheatsheet" (*https://oreil.ly/IwiyP*)

VMs
- "What Is a Virtual Machine?" (VMware) (*https://oreil.ly/vJ9Uf*)
- "What Is a Virtual Machine (VM)?" (Red Hat/IBM) (*https://oreil.ly/wJEG1*)
- "How to Create and Manage KVM Virtual Machines from CLI" (*https://oreil.ly/cTH8b*)
- "KVM" via Debian Wiki (*https://oreil.ly/XLVwj*)
- QEMU machine emulator and virtualizer website (*https://oreil.ly/wDCrH*)
- Firecracker website (*https://oreil.ly/yIOxz*)

Modern distros
- "Containers and Clustering" (*https://oreil.ly/Z8ZNC*)
- "Immutability & Loose Coupling: A Match Made in Heaven" (*https://oreil.ly/T89ed*)
- "Tutorial: Install Flatcar Container Linux on Remote Bare Metal Servers" (*https://oreil.ly/hZN1b*)
- List of image-based Linux distributions and associated tooling (*https://oreil.ly/gTav0*)
- "Security Features of Bottlerocket, an Open Source Linux-Based Operating System" (*https://oreil.ly/Bfj7l*)
- "RancherOS: A Simpler Linux for Docker Lovers" (*https://oreil.ly/61t6G*)

Selected security
- "Kerberos: The Network Authentication Protocol" (*https://oreil.ly/rSPKm*)
- "PAM Tutorial" (*https://oreil.ly/Pn9fL*)

Other modern and future offerings
- "How X Window Managers Work, and How to Write One" (*https://oreil.ly/LryXW*)
- "Purely Functional Linux with NixOS" (*https://oreil.ly/qY62s*)
- "NixOS: Purely Functional System Configuration Management" (*https://oreil.ly/8YALG*)
- "What Is a Raspberry Pi?" (*https://oreil.ly/wnHxa*)
- "Kubernetes on Raspberry Pi 4b with 64-bit OS from Scratch" (*https://oreil.ly/cnAsx*)

We've reached the end of the book. I hope this is the start of your own Linux journey. Thanks for staying with me, and if you have feedback, I'm always interested to hear from you, either via Twitter or via good old email: *modern-linux@pm.me*.

Helpful Recipes

In this appendix, I've compiled a list of recipes for common tasks. This is just a selection of recipes that I've gathered over time, tasks that I often carry out and like to have handy as a reference. By no means is this a complete or deep coverage of Linux usage and admin tasks. For a comprehensive collection of recipes, I strongly recommend you check out Carla Schroder's *Linux Cookbook* (O'Reilly), covering a range of recipes in great detail.

Gathering System Information

To learn about the Linux version, kernel, and other related information, use any of the following commands:

```
cat /etc/*-release
cat /proc/version
uname -a
```

To learn about basic hardware equipment (CPU, RAM, disks), do:

```
cat /proc/cpuinfo
cat /proc/meminfo
cat /proc/diskstats
```

To learn more about the hardware of your system, such as about the BIOS, use:

```
sudo dmidecode -t bios
```

Note for the previous command: other interesting options for -t include system and memory.

To query overall main memory and swap usage, do:

```
free -ht
```

To query how many file descriptors a process can have, use:

```
ulimit -n
```

Working with Users and Processes

You can list logged-in users with either who or w (more detailed output).

To show system metrics (CPU, memory, etc.) on a per-process basis for a specific user, SOMEUSER, use the following command:

```
top -U SOMEUSER
```

List all processes (for all users) in tree format with details by using:

```
ps faux
```

Find a specific process (python here):

```
ps -e | grep python
```

To terminate a process, use its PID if you know it (and add -9 as a parameter if the process ignores this signal):

```
kill PID
```

Alternatively, you can terminate a process by name using killall.

Gathering File Information

To query file details (including filesystem information such as inodes):

```
stat somefile
```

To learn about a command, how the shell interprets it, and where the executable file is located, use:

```
type somecommand
which somebinary
```

Working with Files and Directories

To display the content of a text file called afile:

```
cat afile
```

To list the contents of a directory, use ls, and you may wish to further use the output. For example, to count the number of files in a directory, use:

```
ls -l /etc | wc -l
```

Finding files and file content:

```
find /etc -name "*.conf" ❶
find . -type f -exec grep -H FINDME {} \; ❷
```

❶ Find files ending in *.conf* in directory */etc*.

❷ Find "FINDME" in current directory by executing `grep`.

To show the differences in files, use:

```
diff -u somefile anotherfile
```

To replace characters, use `tr` like so:

```
echo 'Com_Acme_Library' | tr '_A-Z' '.a-z'
```

Another way to replace parts of a string is with `sed` (note that the delimiter doesn't have to be /, which is handy for cases where you replace content in a path or URL):

```
cat 'foo bar baz' | sed -e 's/foo/quux/'
```

To create a file of a specific size (for testing), you can use the `dd` command, as shown here:

```
dd if=/dev/zero of=output.dat bs=1024 count=1000 ❶
```

❶ This creates a 1 MB file (1,000 times 1 KB blocks) called *output.dat* that is filled with zeros.

Working with Redirection and Pipes

In "Streams" on page 34, we discussed file descriptors and streams. Here are a few recipes around this topic.

File I/O redirection:

```
command 1> file ❶
command 2> file ❷
command &> file ❸
command >file 2>&1 ❹
command > /dev/null ❺
command < file ❻
```

❶ Redirect `stdout` of *command* into *file*.

❷ Redirect `stderr` of *command* into *file*.

❸ Redirect both `stdout` and `stderr` of *command* into *file*.

❹ An alternative way to redirect `stdout` and `stderr` of *command* into *file*.

❺   Discard output of *command* (by redirecting it to */dev/null*).

❻   Redirect `stdin` (inputs *file* to *command*).

To connect `stdout` of one process to `stdin` of another process, use a pipe (`|`):

```
cmd1 | cmd2 | cmd3
```

To show the exit codes of each command in a pipe:

```
echo ${PIPESTATUS[@]}
```

Working with Time and Dates

To query time-related information, such as local and UTC time as well as synchronization status, use:

```
timedatectl status
```

Working with dates, you usually want to either get a date or timestamp for the current time or convert existing timestamps from one format to another.

To get the date in the format `YYYY-MM-DD`—for example, `2021-10-09`—use the following:

```
date +"%Y-%m-%d"
```

To generate a Unix epoch timestamp (such as `1633787676`), do:

```
date +%s
```

To create an ISO 8601 timestamp for UTC (something like `2021-10-09T13:55:47Z`), you can use:

```
date -u +"%Y-%m-%dT%H:%M:%SZ"
```

Same ISO 8601 timestamp format but for local time:

```
date +%FT%TZ
```

Working with Git

To clone a Git repo—that is, to make a local copy on your Linux system—use the following:

```
git clone https://github.com/exampleorg/examplerepo.git
```

After the previous `git clone` command is completed, the Git repo will be in the directory *examplerepo*, and you should execute the rest of the following commands in this directory.

To view local changes in color and show where lines have been added and removed side by side, use:

```
git diff --color-moved
```

To see what has changed locally (files edited, new files, removed files), do:

```
git status
```

To add all local changes and commit them:

```
git add --all && git commit -m "adds a super cool feature"
```

To find out the commit ID of the current commit, use:

```
git rev-parse HEAD
```

To tag a commit with ID HASH using the tag ATAG, do:

```
git tag ATAG HASH
```

To push the local changes to a remote (upstream) repo with a tag ATAG:

```
git push origin ATAG
```

To see the commit history use git log; specifically, to get a summary, do:

```
git log (git describe --tags --abbrev=0)..HEAD --oneline
```

System Performance

Sometimes you need to see how fast a device is or how your Linux system performs under load. Here some ways to generate system load.

Simulate memory load (and also burn some CPU cycles) with the following command:

```
yes | tr \\n x | head -c 450m | grep z
```

In the preceding pipe, yes generates an endless supply of y characters, each on its own line, and then the tr command converts it into a continuous stream of yx that the head command chops off at 450 million bytes (ca. 450 MB). Last but not least, we let grep consume the resulting yx block for something that doesn't exist (z), and hence we see no output, but it is still generating load.

More detailed disk usage for a directory:

```
du -h /home
```

Listing free disk space (globally, in this case):

```
df -h
```

Load test a disk and measure I/O throughput with:

```
dd if=/dev/zero of=/home/some/file bs=1G count=1 oflag=direct
```

Modern Linux Tools

In this appendix, we focus on modern Linux tools and commands. Some of the commands are drop-in replacements of existing commands; others are new ones. Most of the tools listed here improve on the user experience (UX), including simpler usage and making use of colored output, resulting in a more efficient flow.

I've compiled a list of relevant tools in Table B-1, showing features and potential replacement scenarios.

Table B-1. Modern Linux tools and commands

Command	License	Features	Can replace or enhance:
bat (*https://oreil.ly/zg9xE*)	MIT License and Apache License 2.0	Display, page, syntax highlighting	cat
envsubst (*https://oreil.ly/4i1gz*)	MIT License	Template-based env variables	N/A
exa (*https://oreil.ly/F3dRV*)	MIT License	Meaningful colored output, sane defaults	ls
dog (*https://oreil.ly/tHgYT*)	European Union Public Licence v1.2	Simple, powerful DNS lookups	dig
fx (*https://oreil.ly/oCQ20*)	MIT License	JSON processing tool	jq
fzf (*https://oreil.ly/0l0Va*)	MIT License	Command-line fuzzy finder	ls + find + grep
gping (*https://oreil.ly/psKX3*)	MIT License	Multitarget, graphing	ping
httpie (*https://oreil.ly/pu9f2*)	BSD 3-Clause "New" or "Revised" License	Simple UX	curl (also note there is curlie)
jo (*https://oreil.ly/VhLXG*)	GPL	Generate JSON	N/A
jq (*https://oreil.ly/tL5fR*)	MIT License	Native JSON processor	sed, awk

Command	License	Features	Can replace or enhance:
`rg` (*https://oreil.ly/n9Jmj*)	MIT License	Fast, sane defaults	`find`, `grep`
`sysz` (*https://oreil.ly/aYGlL*)	The Unlicense	`fzf` user interface for `systemctl`	`systemctl`
`tldr` (*https://oreil.ly/wDQwB*)	CC-BY (content) and MIT License (scripts)	Focus on usage examples of commands	`man`
`zoxide` (*https://oreil.ly/Fx2kl*)	MIT License	Quickly change directories	`cd`

To learn more about the background and usage of many of the tools listed in this appendix, you can make use of the following resources:

- Check out the podcast episode on modern UNIX tools (*https://oreil.ly/9sfmW*) from *The Changelog: Software Development, Open Source.*

- There is an active list of modern tools available via the GitHub repo Modern UNIX (*https://oreil.ly/LdtI2*).

Index

About the Author

Michael Hausenblas is a solution engineering lead on the Amazon Web Services (AWS) open source observability service team. His background is in data engineering and container orchestration, from Mesos to Kubernetes. Michael is experienced in advocacy and standardization at W3C and IETF and writes code these days mainly in Go. Before Amazon, he worked at Red Hat, Mesosphere (now D2iQ), and MapR (now part of HPE) and spent a decade in applied research.

Colophon

The stately animal on the cover of *Learning Modern Linux* is an emperor penguin (*Aptenodytes forsteri*), the largest and arguably most iconic of the penguin species.

These large, flightless birds are uniquely adapted to thrive in a harsh Antarctic habitat. Their streamlined bodies make them highly efficient swimmers, and solid bones enable them to withstand intense barometric pressures as they dive to depths of more than 1,750 feet while hunting for fish, squid, and krill. They may spend up to 20 minutes underwater before resurfacing for air.

Emperor penguins are highly social, relying on cooperative nesting and foraging behaviors to survive. Gathering in large colonies, they huddle together for warmth amid temperatures that can drop below -50°F. When returning to the colony after a lengthy sojourn at sea, emperors employ distinct vocalizations to locate their mate among many thousands of penguins, despite their not maintaining fixed nesting sites.

During the winter breeding season, the female emperor penguin lays a single egg, which is then incubated by the male. The male penguin protects the egg by balancing it on his feet and draping it with a flap of skin called a *brood pouch*. For this two-month incubation period, the vigilant male penguin eats nothing and may lose significant body mass.

The emperor penguin is currently considered *near threatened*. Scientific models predict steep population reductions as sea ice continues to decline due to climate change. Like all of the animals featured on O'Reilly covers, whether endangered or not, emperor penguins are vitally important to our world.

The cover illustration is by Karen Montgomery, based on an antique line engraving from *Meyers Kleines Lexicon*. The cover fonts are Gilroy Semibold and Guardian Sans. The text font is Adobe Minion Pro; the heading font is Adobe Myriad Condensed; and the code font is Dalton Maag's Ubuntu Mono.

CPSIA information can be obtained
at www.ICGtesting.com
Printed in the USA
LVHW071910130522
718732LV00030B/2160